Bernard and Regula Verdet-Fierz

Willow Basketry

Bernard and Regula Verdet-Fierz

Willow Basketry

Interweave Press • Loveland, Colorado

Originally published in 1993 as *Anleitung zum Flechten mit Weiden*
©1993, Paul Haupt

Translation ©1993 Interweave Press
All rights reserved

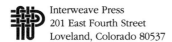 Interweave Press
201 East Fourth Street
Loveland, Colorado 80537

Editor: Deborah Cannarella
Technical editor: Linda Lugenbill
Translator: W. Smith
Assistants to translator: Kay Johnson, Ken Stott

Illustrator: Regula Verdet-Fierz

Cover design: Susan Strawn
Production: Colorado Typographics

First printing: 2:94 BC 10,000
Printed in the United States of America

Library of Congress Cataloging-in-Publication Data
Verdet, Bernard, 1952-
        Willow basketry / Bernard Verdet and Regula Verdet-Fierz.
                p.   cm.
        Translated from the German.
        Includes bibliographical references and index.
        ISBN 0-934026-88-2 : $21.95
        1. Basket making. 2. Osiers. I. Verdet-Fierz, Regula, 1952- II. Title.
TT879.B3V47   1993
746.41'2—dc20   93-28133
                                                                                    CIP

Foreword
to the English edition

There has long been a need in the basketmaking world for texts detailing the techniques of willow basketry. Routinely, the traditions of European willow basketmaking have been passed on through study at the few trade schools in Europe and through hands-on learning. Basketmakers have spent their time making baskets. The documentation has existed within the objects, not in printed records.

This book provides a rare and valuable presentation of traditional European willow basketry. The Swiss authors have mastered their subject through years of training and experience. Based on this, they have written a handbook to provide both aspiring and experienced basketmakers with access to the traditional forms and techniques. Through them, one becomes aware of the respect and patience that the traditional basketmaker has for willow.

This book is a reference tool, rather than a complete primer. There's a wealth of information in the authors' unique approach that can be integrated into your work processes and finished basket forms. Historically, and around the world, basketmaking methods and materials have been richly varied. The continual development of techniques and styles specific to local needs and materials has contributed to the craft's vitality and diversity.

How to use the book
The best way to use this book is to read the opening chapters on materials and techniques, and then work through the projects presented, which build on that information. For the most part, specialized terms have been clarified and defined where they first occur in the text, and there is a more extensive

I

glossary at the back of the book for easy reference. The glossary includes some alternate terms for tools or techniques that American or British basketmakers may be more familiar with.

In the translation from German to English and in the editing, attempts were continually made to keep the concepts and viewpoint of the authors as originally intended, while making the English text useful to a wide range of readers. Metric quantities and measurements were retained.

An extensive listing of sources and references is also included at the back of the book for those seeking additional information. The authors have asked to be listed also, and, with the hope of making the community of willow basketmakers a stronger one, invite you to write to them for further information or support.

The Editors

Preface

Writing this book was an interesting and rewarding experience, but not an easy one. We have been learning the techniques of willow basketry for more than twenty years. It was difficult to decide which techniques to include.

The basketry industry was not significantly changed by mechanization. As a result, weaving baskets became less and less viable as a way to earn a living, and very few people today are professional basketmakers. Today's makers, however, are preserving their traditional techniques, as well as revitalizing the craft by creating new designs and unique objects. They are also active in presenting their craft to the public. They teach courses, participate in educational demonstrations, set up exhibitions, and publish books such as this one.

The throw-away mentality of our age seems to have robbed all objects of their worth. Here, however, is a stimulating craft, whose basic material, willow, can be easily found in woods and meadows.

When weaving baskets, I am in my element. It is an invigorating craft, but not one that you can plunge into without first learning the basics. When people pick up the willow rods for the first time, they may feel a little awkward. The willow rod is an organic whole, made up of bark, wood, veins, and pith. To learn how to work with it you need to know it, respect it, and have a lot of patience. The point of this book is to make your first steps in this learning process enjoyable.

Bernard Verdet

Introduction

Most specialized books about basketmaking presume their readers have already acquired some knowledge of basic weaving techniques. This book, however, is both an introduction to the basics of weaving and a guide to the range of design possibilities.

This book was written for people who enjoy working with their hands, teachers of industrial arts, those involved in occupational therapy, apprentice basketmakers, and hobby enthusiasts. We have also included information of interest to specialists in museums or experts in the fields of folklore, history, and archeology.

Our goals were to present the subject in a clearly organized manner and to provide simply worded instructions in an easy-to-use reference work. The table of contents, the headings in the margins, the drawings, and the index make it possible to find any particular step quickly and easily. The first section outlines the sequence of tasks required to cultivate your own willows. The second section presents the process of making individual baskets, from the very first step, and the projects are presented in order of difficulty.

We preferred drawings to photographs because they are more helpful in illustrating the steps in the basketmaking process. Generally, the drawings with the dark backgrounds illustrate how something is done; those with light backgrounds illustrate the results. The illustrations are not meant as models to be copied, but rather to help readers develop their own ideas. The tools and precision involved in making these linocuts make the process a close relative to weaving. I'd like to express my thanks to my advisor and drawing critic, the woodcutter and painter Karl Landolt.

At the beginning of this century, machines were developed for preparing and finishing willows, but they were suitable only for large-scale production. Basketmaking is today still a hand craft. For those just beginning to learn, the first important contact with the material is when processing it for use, with the help of a few simple tools.

The materials suitable for basketmaking are so numerous it would be impossible to mention them all in this book. The queen of weaving material, in our latitudes, is the willow, and it will be our companion throughout the entire book. As a plant, willow is so interesting that we have also set aside some space to examine its botany. Much information was provided to us by Mrs. Gertrud Oberli, with the help of her salicetum and its many species of willow. We also received help from Mr. Markus Fierz and the Institute for Systematic Botany at the University of Zurich. We would like to thank them as well as the German and French technical schools of basketmaking (see p. 350), and all those who provided us with useful information.

We also thank Mrs. Annemarie Streit at the Paul Haupt publishing house for her great patience and for copy editing the manuscript for the German edition.

Regula Verdet-Fierz

Contents

5

Stilts from the copperplate print "The Dream" 1497–98 by Albrecht Dürer (Berlin, Kupferstichkabinett SMPK). The foot support has been woven.

6▶

Left: Willow bark basket. The unwoven little basket is made from the bark of a thick, freshly cut willow branch. Folded across its width, two corners are connected with a handle. Such baskets are good for immediate use, for example, when you are picking berries. Their size is limited.

Right: The need for a larger container led to the 'idea of connecting several strips of bark together and thus of using the thinner branches as well. The weavers in this case must be trimmed at the end of each round and be reinserted. The secret is the even number of vertical, or warp, rods.

The Origins of Weaving

6

People may have started weaving elements together inspired by what they saw in nature. Organic weave structures are all around us, in the networks of plants, animals, and minerals.

Organic Weave Structures

Among plants and animals

Examine your immediate surroundings with a basketmaker's eye. You might envision the espalier on the house wall or the hedge surrounding the garden as weavings.

7

Looking beyond the garden, you might see ivy that has grown up the trunk of a fir tree at the edge of the woods. If the ivy is older, it may have nearly covered the bark at the base of its host with a thick, woven mat of runners. Then there are the wild brambleberries whose new shoots and old shoots interlace to form the light framework of an open dome. On the ground there is the pretty whitish green weave that looks like a very delicately woven filigree.

The search may lead you farther into the woods. Consider the smallest weeds. Aren't their roots interwoven? Can't you see weave structures in their tissues? If you look farther still, you may suddenly perceive that the whole

8

forest seems to be one enormous woven pattern made of many different types of weavings: delicate, heavy, thin, loose, thick, tender, or thorny.

Aren't there also woven patterns in the animal world? At first these seem more difficult to find, but consider the antlers of the stag, the criss-crossing tendons or arteries of an animal, the rigid labyrinth hidden inside bone marrow.

Such observations can enrich your work and inspire you with many new ideas.

Mineral weave structures

The rounded stones that can be found on the bed of a stream are often covered with a network of arteries. In mineral exhibitions, you can admire the weavelike patterns of penetrating crystals, as shown in the drawing of barite below. The short, woven bundles were formed into their present shape millions of years ago by the pressures exerted by natural forces.

9

Constructed Weave Structures

The first constructed weavings that come to mind are bird nests. Their form, structure, and material make them very similar to round baskets. Birds use various materials, which differ according to species and location. The nest material might be soft or rigid and brittle. A bird's nest includes blades of grass, twigs, hair, moss, synthetic twine, wire, and whatever else is lying about.

10

Many species of tropical birds weave hanging, bag-shaped nests out of the materials available to them, such as long vines or palm leaves. The egg-shaped nest is constructed like a basket. After building a framework, the talented bird can stick a weaver into one opening and pull it out of the next. The structure is so solidly built that it can stand up to the weather for years.

Even some species of fish weave. The stickleback makes its spawning nest out of water plants and roots.

The spider knows how to build a nest with its threads of webbing. The cylindrical nest and egg sacks also resemble woven objects. There are other species of animals that also have an instinctive drive to weave. The dwarf mouse, for example, collects grass and weaves it carefully together in its hole, wrapping each blade around the next until it has created a ball-shaped nest. When the nest is done, the mouse lines the interior completely with soft material for its babies.

Gorillas weave large nests for themselves of twigs and leaves. Orangutans and chimpanzees build their nests skillfully in trees.

Made by primitive man

We know with some certainty that during the Paleolithic Age (circa 7000 B.C.), people made a variety of types of weavings. But for what primary purpose? Perhaps to fasten a stone axe to its handle? This might have been done with animal tendons, strips of skin, inner bark fibers, or tough grasses.

It's easy to imagine that, prior to the manufacture of woven containers and protective surfaces for floors, the creation of walls and roofs was a more pressing need. Primitive man certainly could not find ideal, natural housing everywhere, so he invented building materials that were easy to use. The stakes were simply vertical posts and the weavers were vines or small branches. To keep out the wind and weather, the woven structures were smeared with clay, resin, or blood.

11

12

The drawing at left shows the weave structure of the wall of a hut found on the shore of Lake Zurich in Switzerland.

Numerous lake or pile dwellings dating from circa 3000 B.C. have been discovered around the Swiss lakes in southern Germany and northern Italy, all of which bear evidence of woven material in their construction.

An interesting underwater find was made in 1979-80 in the lagoon at Zurich—a large surface made of a fenced weave from the late Bronze Age (circa 1100 B.C.). Judging from the rods and the kind of weave used it was presumably made of osier. A similar find (dating from circa 850 B.C.) was dug out of the Warft Eliesenhof in Eiderstedt, a town in the northern German state of Schleswig-Holstein.

13

The Bronze Age provides the first evidence of containerlike radial weaving. The technique is very similar to the one used today for willow and round-reed basketry.

The drawing at left shows a basket that has been pressed flat, with an easily recognizable base and sides. It was found in the old Alpenquai area of Zurich. The only earlier known basketmaking was done with softer materials, such as raffia, clematis, honeysuckle, fir roots, flax, and grasses. The techniques that were used are the same as those used today.

The Basics of Weaving

In general, weave structures are fixed structures whose shapes do not easily change. They have a permanence about them, but they may be hard or soft, flexible or rigid, depending on the specific qualities of the materials.

Light and Shadow

How the material has been processed, colored, and woven together determines the intensity of its pattern of light and shadow. These patterns lend vitality, depth, and decoration to a woven surface.

Enclosed spaces   The interplay of light and shadow also vitalizes the space around the woven object. Containers with small openings hide an especially interesting, secretive interior. This effect is intensified by the physical structure of the basket. The intensity of the light entering the basket is significant. Looking from the inside out we would be able to perceive the openings created by the weave

14

structure, as patterns of bright, scattering light. In dark areas, the material and the effect disappear.

If you consider baskets this way, the weave structure becomes less important than the effects of light it creates. You can observe this in chests, laundry baskets, fisherman's baskets, and other types of covered baskets. The effect created by lamp shades, where the light is projected outwards, is the exact opposite.

Made by Hand

A basket is made by hand. Handmade objects can be recognized by their small irregularities, which may not always be readily noticeable.

Even in our age, baskets are being made by hand all over the globe. The only exceptions are those baskets or bags made from woven mats sold by the meter and sewn together.

Willows and many other natural weaving materials are stubbornly resistant to being processed by machine due to their limited length and their organic substance.

Characteristics

15

In this age of the machine, woven goods for trade and industry are no longer as widely used as they were in the past. Modernization in business and farming has meant the disappearance of most of the industrially used basketry items. Over the centuries, these items had come to reflect the basic qualities of the countryside where they were created and the people who used them. For example, the widely separated stakes of the panniers (large carrying baskets) in certain regions of Tessin, Germany, reveal not only the natural vegetation, but also the simple, energetic, easy-going qualities of the people there who often work on the steep slopes. The material's wide surface area gives the object a bright and open appearance.

A squat basket with a severely compressed weave whose lines are emphatically horizontal seems by contrast especially heavy and lethargic.

The Range of Uses

We'd like to see the activity of weaving flourish. Basketmaking has a place in today's world, especially for people who have left their work behind and are seeking diversion. Modern basketmakers can save their knowledge from vanishing by producing household and interior decorative items, as well as objects for gardens, museums, the theater, and the building trades. This handicraft tradition goes back thousands of years, and encompasses more than miniature, cheaply woven baskets, stuffed with dried flowers for decoration.

The essential, characteristic qualities of woven baskets can be determined in advance by the choice of material, shape, weaving technique, and density of weave structure. Depending on the use of the object, the weave structure may absorb shocks (such as for hot-air-balloon baskets), act as a spring (beds), conceal a view (paravent), support loads (wood-carrying baskets), let air and light through (fruit baskets or lamp shades), keep water out (shepherd's bottles or old fire-brigade buckets), keep sound out (ceilings), be lightweight (panniers), or be massive (shop-window decorations or theatrical stage sets).

Willow baskets are resistant to scratches and soiling because of the willow's cambium surface. Like any plant material, however, the rods will disintegrate if exposed continuously to moisture.

The magic of woven objects results from the warmth of the material, the vitality of the weave strucures, and their wide variety of uses.

Decoration   Weave structures have had ornamental and symbolic uses in many places through the ages. A fencelike weave is frequently found on much of the decorative Engadine scratchwork made in plaster.

Many of the marble reliefs in the churches of the early Middle Ages include flat, two-dimensional bands of woven patterns, as shown below. They are Byzantine in origin and can be found throughout Italy and southern Germany. Metalwork with reliefs of woven patterns dating from the eighth century are known in Ireland. Finland is the home of carved woven motifs and Osman knots, mounted in churches as wood reliefs from the Middle Ages to the nineteenth century as symbols of armed strength.

Then there are all the woven and braided breads and pastries. Do they have only a decorative value? We should also include the hair styles of the women who, in many places, used plaits to identify themselves, their background, civil status, or religion.

16

The Willow Plant

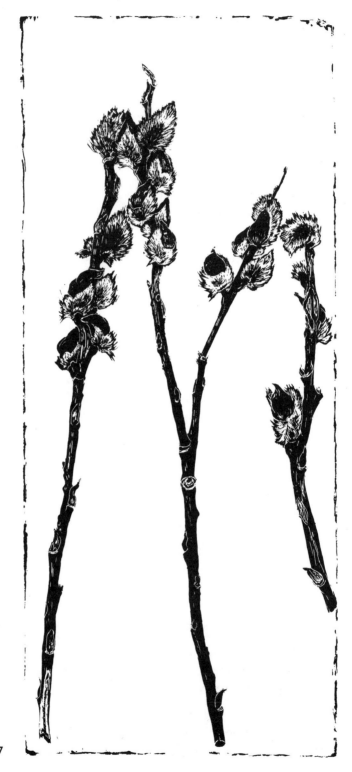

17

The genus *Salix*, meaning willow, belongs to the *Salicaceae* family, together with the poplars *(Populus)* and *Chosenia*, another genus found only in East Asia.

The table below should help make these terms easier to understand:

Genus	Species	Subspecies or Hybrid
Salix	alba	ssp. vitellina (Golden Willow)

The Species

There are some 300 to 500 species of *Salix* plants, depending on whether hybrids, subspecies, etc., are included. Some 40 of these can be found in mountainous regions. In Switzerland there are on the whole about an equal number of mountain and lowland species.

Distribution
Willows are found from the arctic to the temperate zones. They flourish from the seacoasts to the mountain highlands. The willow is a simple, ordinary plant that is pliant and, at the same time, mysterious. Its characteristics vary from species to species.

If you wish to master use of the willow, you must first understand its characteristics and qualities.

Characteristics

Habit
Willows occur naturally in a wide variety of shapes. The White Willow and the Crack Willow grow into very tall trees (25 m). Most willow species, however, range in size from dwarf shrubs to small trees. Most creeping willows are native to the mountains. Their branches are only a few centimeters long, feature small, generally rounded leaves, and develop tiny blossoms. In the summer, many willows develop long shoots that are generally very pliant yet tough. These year-old, woody rods are used for weaving. The buds for the subsequent growth period are located in the leaf axils. On these branches the buds from the previous year open in spring and unexpectedly bring forth catkins, which are usually grey. As they grow longer, often turning yellow, they are the first blossoms to attract the bees in spring, which visit them for the pollen on the male flowers and for the nectar produced by both male and female flowers.

18

Male and female plants

Willows are dioecious, which means there are separate male and female plants. The sexes can be distinguished solely by the blossoms appearing on the catkins.

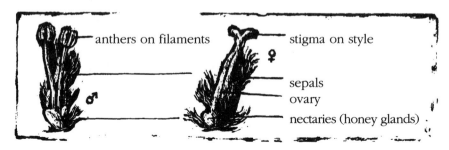

anthers on filaments — stigma on style

♂ ♀

sepals
ovary
nectaries (honey glands)

19

20

Almost all the willows are pioneer plants, which means they can grow in barren environments. They also often grow on stony, compact soil (after earth slides, near construction work or avalanche cones) and on wet soil where broken-off branches take root (in gravel pits or marshes and river banks). Most willows don't need extra watering or fertilizing, but the plant loves damp soil and sunny locations. The light hairy seeds from the fruit capsule are carried far off by the wind and, if they land where enough dampness and sunlight are available, they can sprout (they don't spread easily). Thanks to their quick growth, they are effective against soil erosion and prepare the way for more demanding vegetation.

Species identification There is no characteristic that is entirely typical of one species; individuals of the same species can even vary in shape. For that reason a species can hardly be identified with certainty by a single leaf or catkin, particularly in the winter. The whole plant has to be studied; its form, mature bark, yearly branches, summer leaves, and catkins (male and female).

Planting and Pruning Willow

As already mentioned, willows can grow into shrubs or trees, but some people have trained them to grow into other shapes.

The pollard willow Pollard willow, also sometimes called head willow, is a shape into which the willow is pruned and not a particular species, as is sometimes thought. Once pollard willow could be found along many streams and river banks. Today, however, it's less common because it's used less. The best pollard willows are primarily White Willow, Common Osier, Crack Willow, and Almond Willow. The trunk is formed as follows: in the second year after planting, when winter is over, all the shoots except the strongest one are pruned; this strongest shoot is cut, leaving a 30 cm stalk; the following winter this shoot will be about 70 cm long. The new shoots are trimmed back every winter or at least every three years to the height of the trunk. Over the years, this results in the top part of the trunk taking on the rounded shape of a head.

Pollard willows are the so-called farmer's willows, because in the past farmers used these to weave baskets for many uses.

In the autumn mist, details are blurred and the gnarled figures of the pollard willows, with their long, upward stretching arms, seem to come to life like ghosts. Stories, superstitious tales, and poetry fed on this image before the advent of modern media. Especially in the winter months, the pollard willows stand out because their rods are warmly colored. Their orange, yellow, ocher, and wine red inspired the Impressionist painters.

21

Willow fields Willows have been cultivated since Roman times. The need was substantial as many utility goods were woven.

The basketmaker who wants to harvest his or her own material plants a willow field. Cultivating willows in fields means cutting them so that they grow as single shoots emerging out of the soil. So, in fact, they are shrubs without branches arranged in straight rows. To discourage pests, a field should be planted with several species. In summer, the fields look like a lush, green sea of leaves. In winter, when the leaves have fallen, the stark, multicolored rods come into view. They grow so thickly that from a distance they resemble an enormous, soft fur thrown over the landscape.

22

The Uses of Willow

Medicinal use

As well as being used for basketmaking, willows, particularly their bark and leaves, are used for pharmaceutical purposes. They contain flavone compounds and phenolic glucosides, tannin, salicin, and relaxants. Infusions of bark and leaves have traditionally been used to make teas to ease fevers, headaches, and rheumatism.

The willow is one of the most mentioned plants in traditional medicine. You also find willow substances in cosmetic products.

Beekeeping

Beekeepers really appreciate willows. Bees collect pollen from the yellow catkins. At the same time they harvest the nectar located in the nectaries (honey glands) at the base of each blossom.

By visiting both the male and female blossoms, the bees also pollinate the female stigmas. Willows that are cut every year do not bear any flowers (see p. 23).

23

Natural building materials Instead of relying only on concrete, engineers are increasingly using woven fresh willow for hillside and shoreline retaining walls. The suitable species (Silver Willow, *Salix alba*; Grey Sallow, *Salix cinerea*; Common Osier *Salix viminalis*) root quickly and hold soil. When planted by flowing water, they reduce the speed of flow, provide hiding places for fish, and promote sedimentation.

Ornamentals	Here in Switzerland the winter-hardy hybrids of Weeping Willow are common in parks and along the shores of lakes, ponds, and other calm bodies of water. In private gardens, shrubs and small trees are planted—for example, Violet Willow (*Salix daphnoides*) and Halberd-Leaved Willow (*Salix hastata*, a compact shiny-branched shrub)—some featuring richly colored bark.
Carpentry wood	When they are fully grown trees with impressively large trunks, the largest domestic willows, the White Willows and the winter-hardy hybrids of Weeping Willow, are harvested for low-quality carpenter's wood. The wood is similar to poplar: light and finely pored with evenly structured grain. Because of its quick growth, it is not very durable, but it is easy to work. Willow wood is used for veneer, matchsticks, excelsior (wood shavings used as packing material), boxes, spoons, and the like. Goat, or Florist's, Willow (*Salix caprea*) is also used as a carpenter's wood. (The branches are the very popular pussy willows.)
Pulp wood	In 1950, a company in Zurich, Switzerland, publicized a sensationally successful willow for paper pulp. The willow was planted under contract in the royal forest of the Principality of Lichtenstein (although this venture collapsed for financial reasons after several years).
	This very fast growing species of willow, which has a high yield (an artificial multiplication hybrid involving *Salix caprea* and *Salix viminalis,* among others), is now in the living willow collection of G. Oberli-Debrunner (see p. 351). In Hannover-Münden, Germany, the research institute specializing in rapidly growing tree species has been looking into the cultivation of these willows for the purposes of producing biomass and forestry breeding. Studies have been conducted at the school of basketry and willow cultivation in Fayl-Billot, France, and in cooperation with the technical wood center. Even though yields of up to 20 to 30 tons per hectare (about 100 acres) each year have been achieved using hybrids, there have still been no successful practical results.
Wood for weaving	In Switzerland and other countries with similar climates, the willow is the most important source of basketmaking material. The favorite species and varieties are those with long, flexible shoots and little pith. The greater the wood content, the more durable the resulting object will be.
	The drawing on p. 30 shows the cross section of a summer shoot with its woody tissue, the kind harvested for weaving. The bark is frequently removed, and the smooth surface beneath is highly resistant to soiling.

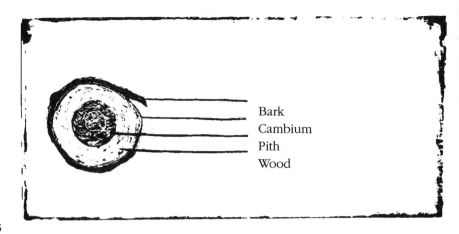

Bark
Cambium
Pith
Wood

25

The firmness and the weaving qualities of the rods depend on the wood, which differs from species to species, as does the spongy pith, which regulates the water content of the growing shoot.

In addition to the willow species discussed in the next chapter, the following are also suitable for weaving: Violet Willow, *Salix daphnoides*; Grey or Ash Willow, *Salix cinerea*; Silver or White Willow, *Salix alba.*

Osiers

The willow plants, or osiers, described in this chapter are ideal for weaving. Also included are numerous subspecies and hybrids that have either occurred by accident or have been bred specifically for the purpose of weaving. The characteristics of each species and subspecies vary depending on soil, climate, and geographical location. They also have regional variations in color, leaf shape, and rod length.

Common Osier, *Salix viminalis*

Basket Willow, Osier. The Latin designation *vimen* means rod and *viminis* means wickerwork.

Native
environment

Common Osier is found along river and pond shores, in meadows along rivers with fertile soils, on sandy islands, and in light, clay soils. It does not grow in swamps.

Growth

If it is not harvested, osier grows into a shrub about 10 m tall. The trunk and the thin, straight branches are smooth and grey-brown to grey-green. The old bark is rough and splits along its length. The rods are greenish yellow to reddish brown, are smooth, and break off where they branch. The young shoots are greenish to brownish with lightly colored, short hairs.

Catkins

The catkins are packed tightly with blossoms and grow to a length of 4 cm and have a 1 cm long, heavily haired stalk with small leaves. The male and female catkins, both about 1 cm thick, are cylindrical and vertical.

Flowers

The flowers form the catkins. The scaly bract at the base of each flower is lightly colored underneath and has a black tip with bright little hairs. The filaments (the two slender stalks of the male flowers) are white, smooth, and oblong, and bear yellow anthers. The stemless ovary, which has no female flower, is squat and has little white hairs. The style is long, thin, and yellowish and bears a split, yellowish green stigma at its tip. The flowers feature only one nectary, which resembles a little white worm on the male (see the drawing on p. 32).

The leaves are approximately one-half their actual size. The winter branch has been slightly scaled down. The catkins are approximately actual size. The flowers have been enlarged 3x.

26

Blossoming time	March/April, shortly before the leaves appear.
Leaves	The first leaves are silky haired and widen slightly at the apex. The summer leaves grow alternately on short twigs from the branches. They are the longest willow leaves (about 15 cm long and 1.5 cm wide) and are lanceolate with curled edges. The dark green dorsal sides are shiny. The veins are recessed. The underside is silky haired (with short hairs, parallel to the side veins) and features a raised center vein. Leaf glands (little nodules at the base of the leaf) are not always present.
Subspecies and hybrids	Quite a few hybrids and subspecies of Common Osier are planted for basket-making. In the living willow collection of the French basketry school, we counted 18 varieties. In Germany a large number are also well known. The Common Osier of the Regal variety *(Salix viminalis* var. *regalis)*, Shoreline Common Osier *(Salix viminalis var. riparia)*, and the Silesian Common Osier *(Salix viminalis var. silesiaca)* are suitable for green work and barrel hoops.
Weaving rods	The rapidly growing, green and yellow-green rods are from 1.4 m to 2.8 m long depending on the variety. In general, *Salix viminalis* produces longer rods than other species. The wood is white and covered with fissures. Common Osier is cultivated all over Europe for basketmaking.
Use	The Common Osier, along with the American Willow, is the most commonly used of the osiers. It is ideal for items made with the bark still on the rods, but because of its white wood, it is often peeled. While drying, the wood shrinks quite a bit, and cracks and fissures appear. Common Osier is also good for cultivating two- to three-year-old willow sticks, which are used for corners, handles, and hoops for white coopery.

27

Almond Willow, *Salix triandra*

This species has three stamens in each flower. The prefix *tri* in Greek and Latin means three and *triade* means three in number. The related French word *triandre* signifies three individual stamens.

Native environment

Almond Willow is found along rivers, ponds, and ditches on the plains, but also in hilly countryside and in the mountains. It likes sandy and silty soils and can tolerate wet soil.

Growth

In the wild, it grows as a shrub, more rarely as a tree of up to 5 m. A reliable identifying characteristic is the bark, which sheds from older trunks, exposing a bright, orange-brown layer. The smooth branches are greenish yellow to reddish and break easily at their base. They have a delicate structure.

Catkins

The thin, light, and slightly bent catkins grow out of dark, reddish brown, smallish buds and begin blossoming at their base. They grow upright on 2 cm long stalks, to a length of 4 to 5 cm.

Flowers

The bract is light green, thin, wavy, and smooth. The female capsule is hairless, light green, and extremely long with stigmas at the tip. The male blossoms feature one narrow and one broad nectary (shown in drawing 28 as a dark, heart-shaped surface).

Blossoming time

The catkins with their easily visible, light green fuzzy spikes appear with the first leaves from the late April to mid-May.

Leaves

The first smooth-edged leaves have hairy undersides. The grey-blue to shiny, dark green summer foliage is lanceolate with toothed edges that taper sharply toward their stems. They are elongated and pointed at their apexes. The leaf is about 13 cm long, and its almost parallel edges are about 2.5 cm wide. The shiny dorsal surface is complemented by a glaucous ventral side. Both sides and the 1 cm long stem are hairless. The wide, wavy, 1 cm long auxiliary leaves almost cover the rod. They are frequently only present on shoots that do not blossom.

Crossbreeds and subspecies

A very popular subspecies of Almond Willow is the "little grey willow." It is so thin and pliant that people like to use it for smaller pieces of work. In France 25 different Almond Willows are commonly planted for weaving— for example, the subspecies whose leaves have a white ventral side, *Salix triandra ssp. discolor. Salix triandra ssp. concolor* has leaves with green undersides.

Weaving rods

The green, grey, or greyish white, marble-patterned rods are 0.8 to 1.6 m long. They are very thin relative to their length and especially pliant. They can be pricked up without breaking.

Use

Almond Willow is unfortunately very susceptible to insect damage and has been replaced by the American, or Universal, Willow for commercial cultivation in Germany. Almond Willow tends to produce lots of branches and twigs, but yields a large harvest.

The Almond Willow is ideal for open work and braided weave structures. Many people like to use them peeled.

The leaves are one-third actual size. The winter branch is almost actual size. The catkins are actual size. The flowers are enlarged 7x.

28

Purple Osier, *Salix purpurea*

Stone Willow, Red Haired Willow, Red Band Willow. The Latin term *purpur* refers to red and violet coloring.

Native environment

Purple Osier can be found on shorelines, along paths, or on the edges of forests, in hedgerows, and in thick patches of pine trees. They are rarely found more than 1200 m above sea level. Above this altitude, the subspecies *angustior* (whose leaves are very thin) is found. In sandy, dry soil, Purple Osier grows as a small shrub with thin leaves. It is resistant to dryness and prefers calcium-rich, kaolinitic, stony, and sandy soils.

Growth

The dense shrub grows up to 6 m tall. Its thin branches point upward and are tough and pliant. They are covered with smooth, yellowish brown or purple bark. The emerging shoots are initially purplish and sometimes thinly haired.

Catkins

The catkins are stalkless and they feature two longish bracts at the base. They have a narrow and bent shape. Before blossoming, they are purple-green in color.

The male catkins grow 3 to 5 cm long. The female catkins are about 1 cm shorter.

Flowers

The bracts are clearly two-colored, light below, with a black tip that features a long beardlike fringe of hairs. There are two single filaments, which are fused into a four-part, reddish yellow anther. The female ovary is ash-colored, stalkless, squat, and egg-shaped and it is covered with white hair. The style is so short that it merges directly with the greenish yellow, double-branched stigma. Both flowers feature only one, small, cylindrical nectary.

Blossoming time

In March and April, the flowers emerge along with the leaves.

Leaves

The first leaves are hairy at their base and smoother toward their tips. The lanceolate summer leaves grow to a length of 12 cm on long rods, 4 to 7 cm on shorter shoots. The widest point is in the upper third of the leaf, which is flat and egg-shaped. Near the stalk (1/2 cm long), the edges are parallel (an important identifying feature); then they gradually expand. The tip of the leaf is toothed. The color is blue green to bright green, dull, and smooth. The underside is lighter. The raised vein is whitish yellow. Unlike other willows, the leaves are usually opposite.

Subspecies and hybrids

This species has numerous well-known relatives. The Ural Willow *(Salix purpurea var. uralensis)* and the green Purple Osier *(Salix purpurea var. helix)* are common in German basketry. The rods are used for brown-willow weaving and for binding. The Imperial Willow *(Salix x helix or Salix purpurea x viminalis)* is easy to peel.

Weaving rods

Use

The reddish brown, one-year-old rods grow to a length of 1.2 to 1.6 m. The rods are almost the same width along their entire lengths, but they are difficult to peel. Many people grow them as borders around their fields because their high levels of salicin make them unpalatable to animals. Purple Osier that has grown for longer periods does not yield suitable rods for weaving.

The light-colored Purple Osiers contain less pith and are therefore more valued than the darker colored. The very tough, thin rods are ideal for fine work and are also suitable for tying up vines.

The leaves are about half actual size. The winter branch is actual size. The catkins are one-half actual size. The flowers are enlarged 5x.

29

Crack Willow, *Salix fragilis*

The Latin word *fragilis* means easy to break and is related to the English word *fragile*.

Native environment

Crack willow is found in riverside marshes, hill country, and more rarely in the mountains. It doesn't tolerate long periods of flooding. In Switzerland, the hybrids are more common than the pure species, particularly *Salix × rubens*, the cross with *Salix alba*.

Physical features

This tree does best near water. It grows as tall as 15 m. The mature bark is rough and sinewy; the young sprouts are shiny and smooth. The branches almost form right angles and make a snapping sound when broken off, which they are easily by snow and wind.

Catkins

The long, thin, twisting catkins are on a 1 cm long stem, which has yellowish green, tender leaves. The male catkins grow to 6 cm long. They are at first compact with a silver-grey sheen. When the stamens appear, they turn bright yellow. The female catkin grows to 7 cm long, is initially bright green, and has flowers at its base.

Flowers

The bract is a single color with either yellowish or greenish hairs. The two stamens are $\frac{1}{2}$ cm long, with a thick cover of yellow anthers. There are two male nectaries, one larger than the other. The ovary of the female flower is in the catkin axil. It is smooth, lance-shaped, and grass green, and it ends in split, yellow scales on both sides. The broad female nectary usually appears singly. The second, if there is one, is like a little bud.

Blossoming time

The long, thick, egg-shaped buds are covered by yellow or reddish brown bracts, and appear with the leaves in March and April.

Leaves

The first leaves are a tender green. Later foliage is alternate on stems at least 1 cm long. The leaf grows to 14 cm (four to six times longer than wide). The long, lance-shaped form has toothed edges and a waxy, smooth, dark green dorsal side. The underside, also smooth, is somewhat brighter and more bluish. The veins are raised on the dorsal side. At the tips of the rods are kidney-shaped, large-toothed stipules. The purebreds have leaf glands in indentations between the teeth (an important feature).

Subspecies and hybrids

The hybrid *Salix × rubens* or *Salix alba × fragilis* is frequently cultivated for basketry, as is true of numerous related varieties.

Weaving rods

The length of the rods varies from 1.2 to 1.8 m. The color of the bark can be shades of yellow, brownish grey, or olive green.

Use

The rods are used for general basketry (shopping baskets, laundry baskets, and other medium-sized items). Slender rods are used for tying vines.

The leaves are about one-third actual size. The winter rod and the catkins are one-half actual size. The flowers have been enlarged 6x.

30

American Willow, *Salix americana*

Universal Willow. Presumably the same as *Salix cordata, Salix eriocephala,* and *Salix regida, Salix americana* is not a botanically defined species. The Latin word *americana* simply means coming from America.

    As the story goes, fresh rods were smuggled to Europe from North America at the turn of the century as a small woven suitcase. A German basketmaker took the weave apart and made cuttings that he was then able to cultivate. Only the male plant is found in Europe.

Native environment

The shrub is especially sensitive to frost and cannot be found in higher altitudes. It cannot tolerate extremely wet conditions or flooding. The water table must be at least 70 cm deep. It thrives in rich, soft soil.

Growth

The American Willow is found in the wild as a short shrub that spreads by means of runners. Its branches hang down somewhat and are lightly haired near their tips. Typically, the tips of new shoots are red and hanging. The American Willow requires fertile soil and care. The leaves and wood are favorite targets for pests.

Catkins

The generally loosely packed catkins, on the end of a 1 cm long stalk, are rounded at the tip and partially bent. On the stalk itself is a pair of pointed leaves.

Blossoms

The white filaments are basally fused and are topped by a dark yellow anther. The stamen, which is half as long, is thickly haired.

Blossoming time

The quite small, reddish yellow buds burst open in April before the leaves appear.

Leaves

The lanceolate leaves appear opposite on the shoot, grow to a length of 14 cm, and are pointed at the tip. The smooth, deep-green surface is divided by a lightly haired center vein; the edge features large, glandular teeth. The ventral side is smooth and bluish green with a raised center vein. The felt-textured leaf stalk is slightly reddish and features two very wide, serrated, heart-shaped basal stipules.

Subspecies

Subspecies and hybrids are unknown.

Weaving rods

The American Willow yields less and has a shorter life span than the Common Osier. Its wood is firm and white.

The rods are extremely tough, thin, pliant, and resistant to kinking. The bark is brownish green and changes to red toward the tips of the rods. The length varies from 1.5 to 2.8 m. Today American Willow is the most frequently used osier. In Spain it is cultivated commercially on a wide scale for export.

As its other name, Universal Willow, suggests, American Willow is excellent both as weaving rods and stakes. It provides the best white willow, and even finely woven items can be made with it.

Use

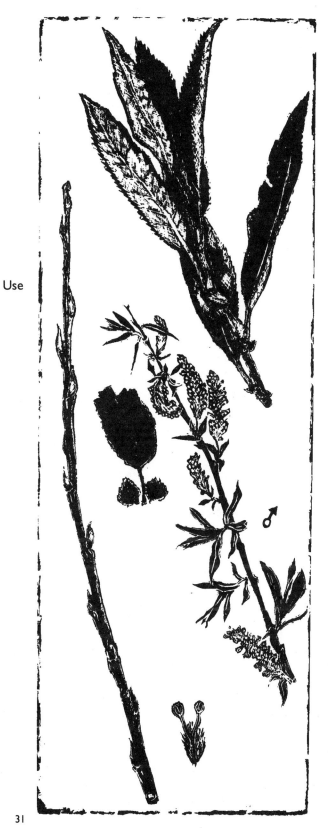

31

The leaves are almost half actual size. The winter branches are actual size. The catkins are two-thirds actual size. The flowers are enlarged 7x.

Cultivation

Large willow farms are rarely found in western Europe because they are not commercially viable.

Easy planting If you want to have a few willows in your garden, they are easy to plant and generally take root, as discussed on p. 43.

Large-scale willow farms A healthy willow field can last anywhere from 15 to 20 years. To grow willow commercially, you need substantial background knowledge and a thorough education in the subject. The technical schools of basketry in Germany and France (see p. 347) have the necessary facilities and experience to provide this kind of training. In this chapter we'll present a few details that are useful to know.

Soil and Climate

Humus and water are the main active ingredients in soil composition. Suitable soils include those with deep water tables, slightly peaty soils, somehat sandy and kaolinitic soils, but also those rich in clay.

To a certain degree, the dampness of the soil affects the pith portion of the rod: when the soil is drier there is less pith in the rods, and the work woven with them will have a longer life.

In general, however, willows suitable for weaving can be planted in most soils as long as the soils are damp, but not swampy. Most willow cannot survive stagnant water for any length of time. Yet swampy land can be made cultivable with drainage ditches. Drainage pipes are not advisable, however, because after a few years' time, they will become clogged with willow roots.

Locations Those patches of land otherwise unsuitable for farming, such as embankments, depressions, and steep slopes, can be used for growing willows. Because harvesting is done by machine on large farms in Romania, Poland, Spain, and a few in France, the willow can only be planted in large, fallow fields.

Climate and yield In humid climates, with a lot of precipitation and where the top soil is deep and damp, yields are especially high—up to 100 kg per hectare. Depending on the site, you can expect long rods up to an altitude of 1000 m. Willows need at least 700 mm of precipitation per year. A rule of thumb is that osiers can be planted wherever the soil is frost-free from March to the end of October.

Cuttings

The easiest way to obtain new willows is by vegetative reproduction, using cuttings from a mature plant. The cuttings are stuck into the ground and, if the soil is damp enough, they will take root and begin to grow shoots. (Not all species are suitable for this kind of reproduction, however.) It's important that the rods that are used for cuttings not be infested with insects or larvae. You should also carefully inspect them for any sort of fungus or other diseases.

If you are thinking of getting your cuttings from willows in the wild, refer to the previous chapter for guidelines as to where to look. You need to locate them in the spring or summer. The cuttings are made in the winter before the shoots appear. You should only use strong rods. Cuttings made from mature shoots at the base of the plant have larger quantities of stored-up anabolic material than those in the upper portion of the rod.

You can speed up the process of root formation by letting the cuttings stand in water for two days before planting.

One-year- or two-year-old rods should be cut in 20 to 25 cm lengths. Cut off the tip of a 2 m long rod, and you can make about five cuttings with the remainder. While you are cutting, you must arrange all the lengths in the same direction. To avoid confusing the rooting and the growing ends, dip the rooting ends of the cuttings into a solution of chalk or dye and water, or mark them in some other way. It's important which end is stuck into the ground. If the growing end is planted, long shoots may develop, but they'll soon die, and the young plant will wither.

If the cuttings cannot be put into soil immediately, store them in a cool, damp location protected from wind—perhaps in a bed of damp sand.

To protect them from drying out, you can dip both ends in warm paraffin. You can expect to get 15 to 20 cuttings per square meter, which would be about 1500 per hectare.

32

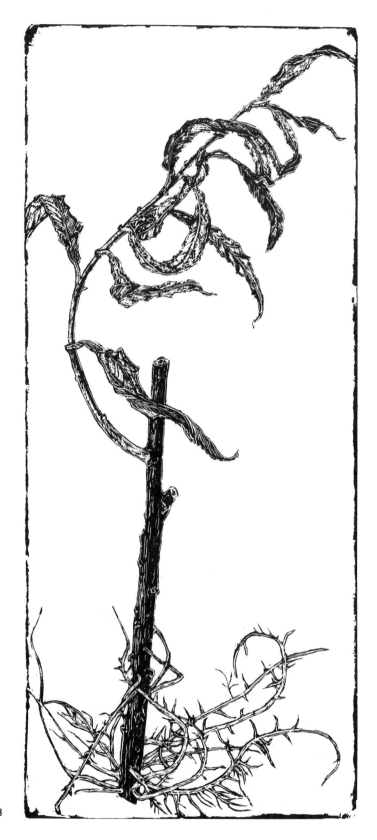

33

34   **Offshoots**   As with other kinds of plants, it is possible to root willow rods by partially burying them while they are still on the mother plant. Once the rod has taken root, it can then be separated from the mother plant.

Planting   Depending on the kind of growth expected, the willow field is divided into rows of 60 to 100 cm. The cuttings are put into the ground in a row and are spaced 10 to 20 cm from each other—smaller growing species somewhat closer, larger growing species somewhat farther apart. Be sure to stick in the marked end first and insert the cuttings so deep into the ground that little or nothing is visible; throw away any pinched or damaged cuttings. We recommend cultivating several species side by side on one plot so that the plants are less susceptible to pests.

The kind and quantity of soil nutrients needed for cultivating willow are determined by the type of soil you are working with. If the willows are not being planted for commercial reasons, there is really no need for additional fertilizer (use bone meal at most). Large-scale willow growers should have soil tests made.

Care in Summer

The newly planted willows require close supervision. During the warm weather, weeds have to be removed frequently. The weeds can be left lying on the ground to protect the bare topsoil and strengthen the tender shoots. As soon as the leaves appear, they must be checked regularly. These newcomers are facing their first dangers.

Weather damage   *Hail:* The rods are bruised by hail, and the wood is weakened so that you often can no longer use them for weaving.

Frost: Sometimes the shoots that have just appeared are attacked by a spring frost. They turn black and wither. The cuttings will sprout new shoots, but they will be a few weeks late.

35

Pests   *Deer:* In sparsely settled areas and near forests, deer feed on the young shoots and chew off the juicy bark in winter. Fences are necessary.

Insects: One of the most feared is a long-snouted weevil. These black and white weevils feed on the bark and lay their eggs in the exposed areas. The white larvae chew long tunnels through the wood. Wood dust betrays the presence of these pests.

In addition, there are several species of willow-leaf beetles that chew holes in the leaves. The beetles hibernate in or under the willow stools and the larvae emerge in spring.

Formerly, willow growers would keep fowl to check the spread of insects. Calcium, chalk, and similar substances were also used. Today the willow grower can choose from a large number of pesticides, some good and some that cannot be recommended.

Aphids, wireworms, white grubs, the bell moth, and mice can also damage your plants.

36   37

Damage from plants

Weeds: Bindweed is the most insidious. These weeds entwine the new shoots, leaving a spiral-shaped scar behind them. Sometimes they even choke the shoots. Other weeds that reduce yields include goldenrod, reeds, thistles, nettles, and dodder. In addition, there are numerous fungi.

Important: If you want to plant a piece of land with willows you would be well advised to start with a trial planting of a variety of species, which you should watch for two years. All too often the effort in terms of time and expense is underestimated, even for smaller fields.

More detailed information about soils, pests, and care can be found in a variety of reference books, some of which are listed in the bibliography on p. 347. You can also get answers to your questions from advisors in agricultural agencies or from the local extension office in your area.

38

Harvesting

When the leaves have fallen, the rods are empty of sap, and you can begin cutting.

Harvesting wild willow If you intend to get your rods from wild willows, first ask the property owner for permission. Try to find rods that are as long as possible and free of branches. Be sure that the sap is no longer running before you start cutting. The other steps are the same as for cultivated willows.

Cutting

Harvesting is done by hand or machine between November and March—or as some old proverbs put it, "In December under a waning moon."

The first- and second-year plants One- and two-year-old plants should be cut by hand with clippers, so as to avoid the possibility of uprooting the young plants. After the first two years, the plants can be cut at ground level, with small stumps left behind.

39

40

Mature plants Bundle the rods together in your left hand (if you're right-handed) and bend them toward the ground, as shown in the drawing. Now cut the rods with a scythe. Be sure to make a diagonal slice firmly and cleanly right through them. If you chop halfheartedly, both the stumps and the rods will likely splinter and allow in rain water, and in time the wood will rot. Don't harvest willow when the temperature is below freezing. Frozen rods splinter when cut. As you work, drop the cut bundles onto the ground to your left.

Machine harvesting Willow in large fields are harvested by machine. As this is done, all the rods fall down in rows pointing in the same direction.

Tying the bundles Once all the rods are on the ground, bind three to four groups of them together into a bundle with a single rod. The bundles can remain in the field for several days, leaning against each other on end. Weather permitting, they begin drying very well this way. Each of the different species should be bundled separately and labelled.

41

Sorting, or Drafting

Once you get your bundles home, clean off the weeds, and sort the rods by length.

Sorting

Sorting, or drafting, can be done in many ways, according to individual preference or habit. One simple system requires an 80 cm tall container wide enough for the willow bundle. Mark a yardstick with a line every 20 cm, and fasten it vertically to the edge of the container, as shown in drawing 42. Now, drive sticks into the ground at regular intervals. You'll place the different lengths of rods between them. Put the rods in the container, pull the longest ones out, and put them in the first interval. Do the same with the remaining rods, placing them from left to right along the ground, starting with the longest on the left and proceeding to the shortest on the right. When you've finished, you'll have rods of varying lengths on the ground in front of you. When you have enough rods of any length to form a bundle, or bolt, about 40 cm thick, bind them together in two places. The longer rods and those that you want to keep bark on should be tied three or four times.

Keep the bundles in an enclosed area where they'll be safe and dry. It's important to take care that the willows do not turn grey.

Good rod quality

• Good-quality rods are long, thin, and free of branches.
• Good-quality rods have a constant diameter along their length.
• Their wood is pliant and elastic.
• The amount of their pith is small relative to the amount of wood.

42

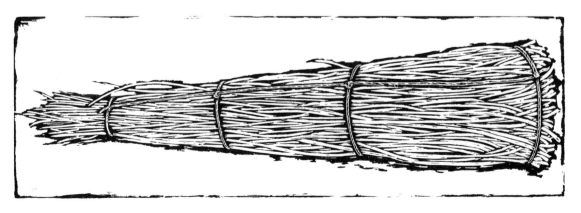

Preparing the Willow

Rods and Sticks

The willow's pliant, young rods and the heavier, more mature sticks are both used in the basketmaker's workshop.

Rods Rods are always one-year-old wood, even if they are very long. The rods that are up to 2.8 m long have grown to that length in one season. Willow rods that are 60, 80, and 100 cm long are from species that don't grow any longer, and these are woven into very delicate pieces. For the medium-sized projects presented in this book, you need 1.2, 1.4, and 1.6 m long rods. Very long rods, over 2 m, are used for large items such as wicker beach chairs, large rope-handled baskets, and for making skeins.

The willow's appearance can be radically altered by the way it is prepared, woven, and finished. We'll present the most basic kinds of preparation here, but keep in mind that the results can still be modified by further processing before weaving the rods.

Sticks By the willow stick, we are not referring to the whole plant, but rather to the rod that has been growing for 2 to 4 years and that, in this time, has reached a thickness of between 2 and 4 cm, depending on the species. These sticks are used for making hoops for casks, rings for white cooper goods, corner stakes and ribs of large woven items, frames of wicker furniture, stakes in wattle and daub (a woven building framework), corner stakes of rectangular baskets, and unwrapped crossover and side handles. The sticks can be prepared in the same way as the rods.

44

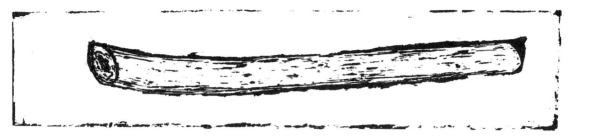

Green Willow

This term does not specifically describe a method of preparation, but rather it refers to the fresh willow rods, which are still full of sap.

The rods are freshly cut, sorted, and, without any previous drying, tied into bundles.

Storage Until the bundles of green willow are used (and they should be as soon as possible), keep them in an area sheltered from wind. After you've removed any twigs, you can weave fresh willows into rustic baskets, without first soaking the rods as you normally would.

Other possibilities The pliant rods are very easy to weave when green. Although they don't get any shorter, freshly harvested willows lose about one third of their thickness while drying, so you should beat down the weave structure often as you work. The disadvantage to working with fresh willow is that items woven green can only be used in unheated rooms. When the pieces dry out completely, the weave structure loosens, and you have work of a lesser quality. Still, you can acquire some interesting experience while making a green basket.

Weaving You might also get a lot of satisfaction out of working with material that you have collected yourself. Small, green rods can be woven into little wreaths by children or made into twine, or the bark can be carved. Youngsters can stick cuttings into sand or into soft ground to create an entire village of hedges and house facades. They can form animals and figures from bent and carved pieces. Forked and otherwise irregularly shaped rods are a particularly good sourcme of inspiration.

47

Use Even today, you occasionally find vines tied with fresh willows. Also, as mentioned on p. 28, fresh willow is woven and used as a natural building material (called fascines). The bundles continue to grow, and the deep roots hold the soil in place.

Fresh willows are the basic material used for making white willow, which is willow that has been peeled and processed to achieve the whitest possible color. The other ways to use willow are as buff willow, which is boiled to achieve a tan color, or as brown willow, which is simply woven with the bark still on the rod.

48

Brown Willow

Willow that has been dried with the bark still on it is called brown willow.

Drying The rods must dry for several months, protected from sun and rain. Once they are dry, they will have shrunk in size so much you will have to tighten the binding rods that you used to tie them together. You can tie the bundles together any way that seems most convenient for you. The dry bolts weigh about 10 kg, depending on their length. Before drying, they weigh about twice that amount.

Color Each willow species, hybrid, or subspecies has its own bark color. When the rods dry out, however, most of them lose their unique color and turn brown. An exception is the *Salix trianda* ssp. *discolor*, which keeps its solid green color.

Sorting, Storage, and Soaking For specific information about sorting and storing willow rods, see the section "Sorting" on p. 50 and the section "Storage" on p. 64. In order to process brown willow properly, it must be soaked for a long time. See the section "Soaking brown willow" on p. 109.

Weaving rods Brown willow rods, although still covered with bark, are quite easy to weave. Once the rods are well soaked, they are very pliant and elastic. For this reason, they are frequently used in indoor workshops and are very suitable for beginners. They also dry very slowly, which means that you can take your time weaving without danger of the rods' becoming brittle and breaking.

A soaked bolt can be wrapped in cloth in order to retain the moisture and further cure the rods. This process is called mellowing. Mellowed rods will remain usable in the workshop for a couple of days. The water-soaked wood has a peculiar, sour smell. Be careful, damp wood can grow mildew.

Use Brown willow rods are best to use when the effect of rough work is wanted or for objects that will not be exposed to extreme dryness. Brown-willow baskets can tolerate rough treatment, so they make good shopping baskets, two-handled laundry baskets, and garden baskets. One of the first types of brown-willow baskets that comes to mind is the round, two-handled harvest basket that is used in the garden and with which you might remember fetching wood as a child. We also recall that it made a good basket for playing all kinds of tricks—through an upside-down harvest basket, you could see very well through the openings in the weave what was going on outside, but others could not see you.

The large panniers for carrying wood are also made of brown willow. Tausen panniers, used for harvesting grapes, have handles made of twisted

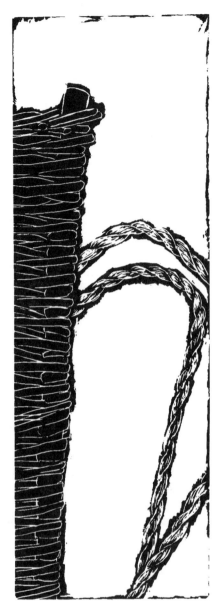

brown willow. The stiff, leatherlike cords, shown in the drawing at left, are advantageous because you can slip in and out of them easily. These containers were still being used as recently as twenty years ago in wine-growing regions. As often as possible, people tried to make these handles and other sorts of details out of materials that they did not need to buy.

49

Buff Willow

Buff, boiled, red, steamed, and cooked willow are all names for the same sort of processed willow. Buff willow is processed in the spring as soon as the weather is warm enough.

Boiling   The fresh or dry rods, held together in bundles, are placed in a large brick tank. The tank is filled with about 1000 liters of water and covered with an iron lid. The lid is fastened on in such a way that the rods are held

underwater. Under the tank is a hearth (with wood and gas). Once the water has started to boil, keep it at a slow boil for 2 to 3 hours. Then remove the willow from the bath with a fork. The tannin and other organic chemicals from the bark give the water's surface an oily sheen. The hot rods look like black glass.

Peeling When the rods are somewhat cool they are immediately peeled (for a detailed discussion of the process, see the section "White Willow," which begins on p. 59). After they are peeled, the rods are about one-half their dry weight.

Color The white wood of the willow gets its reddish brown color from the dye in the inner bark. This tannin can also provide a long-lasting dye for wool without using any additives. (It is also good for dyeing Easter eggs.)

Some people say that, if top-quality rods are used, buff willow is more durable than the others. Willows contain salicylic acids, and their color is characteristic and lasting. It's interesting to note that the bluish brown at the butt of the rod becomes a warmer and brighter tone toward the tip of the rod. Even soaking and washing cannot change the color. Only after being exposed to sunlight for many years will the colors fade somewhat.

Drying The copper-brown rods can now be tied in the middle in smaller bunches. By separating them at the top and bottom into fan shapes they can be dried standing up outside, but not exposed to direct, hot sunlight.

51

Storage and soaking You can store the willows dried this way following the instructions in the section "Storage" on p. 64. For information on soaking buff willow, see the chapter "Preparations" on p. 106.

Weaving rods Buff willow rods can be processed in the same way as white willow rods (p. 59), but, because of the boiling procedure, they are a little trickier to handle.

Use Many people like to weave sleeping baskets for their pets out of buff willow. Many of the shopping baskets, wicker armchairs, and other everyday objects you can purchase are also often made of this kind of willow. Unfortunately, these mass-produced items are usually made of low-quality willow. They are often heavily varnished to make them look more solid to the consumer, and to hide any grey or dark blemishes in the material.

White Willow

Although you can get white willow simply by peeling it immediately after harvesting, there are some disadvantages (see p. 63), and you can process only a small amount at a time. Pitting is a natural process that keeps the willow alive until you're ready to peel and use it. Start with fresh, green willow. (Dry rods cannot be used.)

Pitting The bundles, sorted by length, are stood upright in water. Find a natural pond, dig a pit, or use a large container for small quantities. The water must be 20 cm deep, and can be supplied by a hose or stream. The bundles are placed in the water, butt (or rooting) ends down, and are held upright by long poles laid across the pit, as shown in the drawing—wind, storms, or other events could otherwise knock the rods down. In addition to the poles, you'll need a 80 cm high fence surrounding and supporting the bundles.

52

Only the butt ends should be under water! In windy, dry regions, be sure the pit is on a protected site so the rods won't dry out.

When to peel   In the spring, the rods, harvested months earlier, start coming to life. The sap rises between the wood and the bark, fresh leaves appear, and long roots grow. These elaborate roots range in color from white to reddish. The growth of the leaves and the roots means that the rods are now ready to peel. If you remove the rods from the pit and leave them lying about, they'll turn spotty and grey.

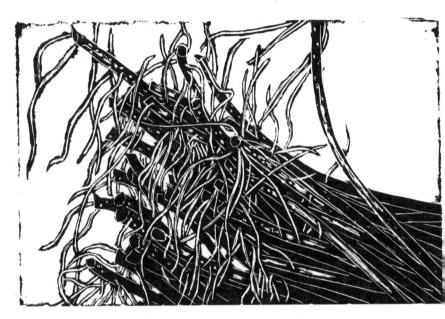

53

Peeling by hand   In the heyday of willow basketry, a reliable machine was developed for peeling, which otherwise is a lengthy process. These large, complex machines are impractical for individual use, however.

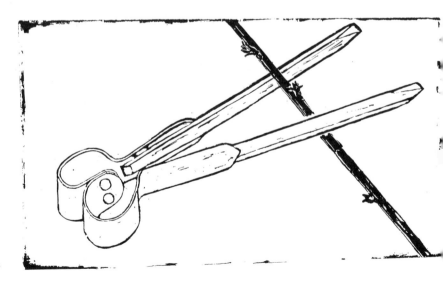

54

There are various devices used for peeling by hand. Most of them are made of iron; some of iron and wood. These tools, called willow brakes, are easy to hold and use. The basic principle is always the same: the brake has two prongs, about 25 cm in length, that grip the rod and cause the bark to split open. With one hand, you clasp the two prongs tightly together and, with the other hand, you pull the rod through the brake. Each rod is pulled through from the butt end to the tip and from the tip end to the butt. After this the bark can be easily removed. Dried, peeled rods weigh about a quarter of what they weighed when fresh.

Using a peeling post It's somewhat easier to work with the brake screwed onto a peeling post. The post can be built easily of wood. The spring, located on one side, regulates the pressure on the rod. As you work, position the unpeeled rods to one side of you and nearby so you can reach them easily. Drop the finished ones on the ground to the other side. Keep the pile of bark with the unpeeled rods.

55

Brushing Species that contain a lot of tannin, such as *Salix purpurea,* must be brushed vigorously after the rods are peeled, or they turn grey.

Drying The peeled rods can be spread out to dry on sawhorses or racks made of posts and poles. When exposed to sunlight, willow acquires a polished, bleached surface and smells lovely. If the sun is very intense, take them in after about an hour, or when the rods rustle when you move them. It may take a day or more to dry them. If they're left too long in the sun, however, they turn grey.

Bark The bark, which is full of various active agents, used to be sent to tanneries or was used for long-lasting textile dyes. As already mentioned, it also has

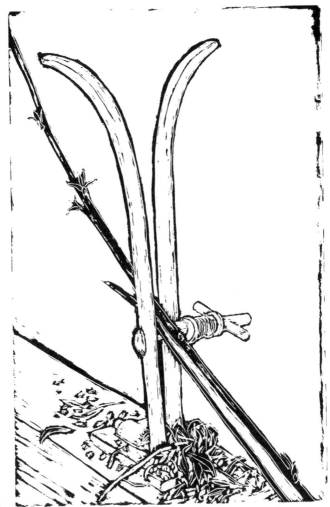

56

57

medicinal and other purposes. It can be also be composted or used as fuel. At one time, the bark was used to cover the floors of stalls, and people also made it into string out of which they wove mats.

Peeling willow after harvesting

You might ask why the rods cannot be peeled immediately after harvesting, when they're still full of sap. This is certainly possible, although you can't easily process a lot of white willow this way. In late summer, if the rods have grown to a suitable length, you can harvest and peel them. We don't recommend this, however. The remaining rooted sticks will be weakened, and in subsequent years, will yield fewer rods.

Uses

Peeled rods are good for all sorts of projects that won't be used outdoors. Coarsely woven as well as delicate pieces can be made with white willow. Like buff willow, it can also be made into skeins. White willow is a little more difficult to work than brown willow, though. Because it dries quickly, it must be used quickly.

Dyeing Rods

The only willow that can be colored successfully are white, peeled rods and skeins. Buff willow is, in fact, already colored and could only get darker by being dyed again. Brown willow will not take the dye.

When rods are dyed, they do not lose their natural texture. Certainly, therefore, dyeing is much more satisfactory than applying a thick coat of paint.

In order to get the color you've mixed, you need to bleach the willows in advance. Bleaching will not, however, make the rods pure white. The natural base color of the rods themselves combines with the final color to produce a pleasant shading. Coloring rods is difficult for a number of reasons:

• The dye must be waterfast. Otherwise the soaking water would also be colored and the tint would spread to the other rods.
• The color must be lightfast, or the dyed item would quickly fade as it was being used.
• You need a dye container whose size accommodates the length of the rods and that can be heated so the dye will be fast.

Vegetable coloring

In previous centuries, basketmakers were familiar with inexpensive recipes for long-lasting stains and dyes they could mix themselves. Preparing, weighing, mixing, cooking, settling, straining off water, and pretreating took days or even weeks to accomplish.

Before dyeing the willows, basketmakers treated them with metallic salts, chemicals, and plant extracts, which resulted in an array of strong, rich, but not garish, colors that were perfectly suited to the natural rods.

Wood stains   Today, you can prepare a dye with a wood-stain powder. Either you dissolve the powder in hot water or in warm alcohol in a double boiler (careful, it's flammable!). After the stain has cooled, you can paint, sprinkle, or dip the rods or the woven object. Without any protective coat, stains, like most dyes, are not very water or light resistant. Pure colors are sometimes available.

Tinted varnishes   Varnishes are lightfast and water resistant and allow the wood grain to show through. The oil-based colors are suitable for painting individual rods or whole woven surfaces. They require two to three days to dry. Pure, primary colors are available.

Textile dyes   You can get good and long-lasting results dyeing willow rods with fiber-reactive dyes. These dyes can usually be mixed without any difficulty to get the shades you want. When you soak the rods later, before beginning to work with them, the colors will not bleed. These dyes are also lightfast. They are quite expensive, however, because you need many liters of dye bath to dye a handful of rods. Individual rods can be dyed in a long pipe.

Store-bought rods   It's possible to buy dyed rods through a craft supplier. Unfortunately, dyed rods, especially the dark colors, run when you soak them. There are also not many colors available.

Working with dyed rods   With so many variations available in the form and structure of a basket, it's not always easy to also put the right amount of color in the right place. Color should be used either to accent the weave structure or the shape of the object.

   Light-colored rods are certainly always appropriate to use next to white, peeled willow in your basket. The light rods can be integrated fully with the soft ochre color of the willow's natural shade. You can also make baskets with two-tone and multi-colored weaves to integrate dyed and naturally colored materials.

Storage

Where and how you store your basketry materials is important. It's one of the factors upon which your success or failure depends.

Where to store willow   The best place to store willow rods is in a cool, dry location that is not exposed to sunlight or rain. Concrete structures, barns, or even a cool storage room are all ideal. Stone basements are usually too damp—the rods soak up dampness, get mildewy, or become spotted. If rods have gotten too damp, try brushing them or soaking them. Whether they will then be worth using is questionable, however.

Small quantities	Small quantities can be stored best by leaning them against a wall.
Sizeable quantities	If you have many bundles of each size, it's a good idea to build a storage frame with subdivisions, as shown below. In each section, you can put rods of one size, alternating butt and tip ends so they lie fairly flat. This also makes it easier to see what you have.

58

Very large quantities	If your storage needs are great, you might need to find a warehouse with a ramp, in which you can layer the bundles on pallets.
Pests	Keep in mind that white willows are particularly susceptible to being chewed on or soiled by unwanted animals.
Bolt sizes	When you buy willow, you buy a quantity of rods in bolts of the length and type you need. • 80 to 100 cm long 5 kg bolt • 1.2 to 1.4 m long 5-10 kg bolt • from 1.6 m long 10 kg bolt

59

Maintaining quality   You can store willow rods for almost any length of time as long as they are stored in the right place. Old-world basketmakers maintain that rods, like a good red wine, improve in quality after years of aging.

Other Basketry Materials

When you begin to consider all the materials that might be combined with plant materials for basketmaking, you quickly find that the field of possibilities is quite big. For example, consider the many different kinds of shopping bags, baskets, and garden furniture made of plastic webbing, cellophane, nylon, synthetic raffia, cellulose tapes, etc.

Materials from animals can also be used for basketry. People make weavings, nets, and strings from sinews, leather, and hair. Screens and baskets have also been woven from porcelain and other sorts of clay, glass strands, and metal wires.

These types of materials are justified by the spirit of the times and can certainly be used to develop novel ideas. In this chapter, however, we will only be discussing plant materials in detail. These plants are closely related to willow, being of the same substance, and therefore they combine very nicely with it.

All grasses, rods, and pliant parts of plants can be used for basketmaking, at least experimentally. Each plant, of course, has its own properties and construction considerations, but once you have mastered the basic techniques of working willow, you might explore the possibilities of integrating some of these other materials in your work. In addition to those described below, others, such as rushes, heather, birch branches, black alders, ash strips, and larch roots can also be easily woven.

Leafy Plants and Their Use

Seagrass or sedge
(Carex)

Seagrass is from the family of reed grasses. It grows to a height of 1.5 m and can be found in thick plots. In Switzerland alone there are hundreds of different sedges. In Camargue in southern France and in Italy, people harvest large quantities of seagrass during the summer (its French name is *sarette*).

The sharp triangular stems grow upright. The leaves are 1 to 2 cm wide and up to 1.2 m long. Seagrass grows on shorelines, in wet meadows, and in ditches.The freshly dried leaves are olive green and turn later to olive beige. The dampened leaves are used for chair weaves and as the foundation in coiled basketry. Cheaper chairs are made today with a paper imitation that looks similar. You can collect seagrass yourself or buy it in craft shops.

60

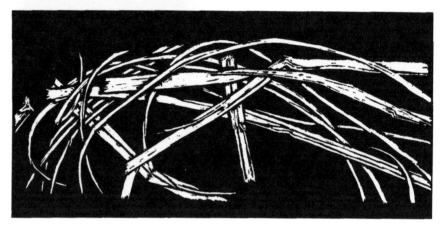

61

Seagrass string is commonly known as Hong Kong grass or China rush string. It is made of twisted seagrass and can be purchased in a variety of

62

thicknesses. This string is very strong and somewhat stiff. It is a lovely material that can be put to many uses. In the highlands of Zurich, rectangular harvest baskets and sewing baskets were often made with it. They went out of fashion long ago, however, and today have sociohistorical and aesthetic value.

Nowadays people use seagrass string primarily for weaving seats. It is very easy to work with and readily available.

Straw

63

Rye, wheat, or straw from other grains can be cut for weaving when the grain is still full of its milky sap. The green stalks are then dried and their blades removed. For weaving purposes, the growth nodes are frequently cut off. The dried material can also be bleached or dyed.

In an earlier age, Florence was the center of straw weaving. The trade later spread to the Aargau region of Switzerland (straw hats), to England (corn dollies), to France (coiled work), and to Yugoslavia (bags). In Austria's Burgenland, travellers can still find all kinds of straw weaves, especially the corndolly weave.

64

Straw braids are woven of nodeless lengths of stalks from various grain species or of the reeds from swamp plants. These strips, which used to be woven by hand in grain-producing regions, are imported today as ropes or plaits from the Far East and are woven into other materials, such as hats and bags.

Small quantites can be bought in craft shops, large amounts from wholesale suppliers. Before weaving, the material must be briefly soaked.

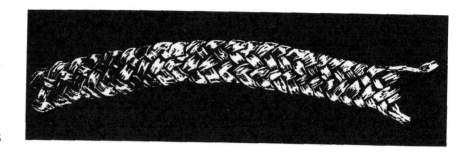

65

Rush

66

Anytime you hear soft, natural baskets discussed, you can hear the word rush. Most of the time the reference is actually to raffia, seagrass, cattails, or grasses native to the area where the object was made.

Rushes, however, are specific plants that grow in wetlands and are suitable for weaving. The weaving rush, also called Pond Rush *(Scirpus lacustris)* or Hollsteiner Rush, usually has largely leafless stems that bear blossoms and can grow up to 4 m. The very well developed air vesicles in the stems were once used to make life preservers. This freshwater grass grows in the outer regions of the grassy shores around lakes.

Rushes also grow on other continents. For example, the *Scirpus totora* in Peru is the basic material of the famous, beautifully shaped boats that are used on Lake Titicaca. The tougher saltwater variety is also used for weaving.

The dry and slightly dampened or mellowed (not soaked!) stalks are used for making chairs, bags, and soft containers. The material is easy to shape by fitching, weaving, sewing, and knotting. Pond Rush can sometimes be bought at a basketry-supply shop or from a basketmaker.

The genuine rushes *(Juncus* species) in the rush family of plants are the pointed, blossoming rods in ponds and in swampy, wooded areas. The leaf stalk is filled with a white, spongy pith, which is used especially by people in Central Europe for wrapping Easter eggs. These species are suitable for weaving and grow up to 1.5 m. The short stalks, harvested in the latter part of summer, are allowed to dry out, and are dampened just before they are woven. They are used mainly in coiled basketry and chair weaving.

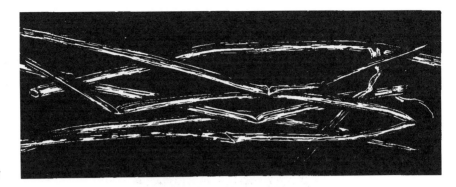

67

Cattails

People usually confuse cattails with rushes. Its 3 m height makes the thin-leafed *Typha angustfolia* the tallest of all the cattails. The decorative, felty brown blossom spikes are known to a lot of people as cannon cleaners. Florists use them for dried-flower arrangements. But only the spongy leaves are useful for weaving. The vesiculate tissue is similar to, but rougher in texture than, the Pond Rush. The leaves are about 2 cm wide, slightly pointed and several millimeters thick. The cross section of the base of the plant in the drawing below shows its crescent shape. Once dried, cattails have a lovely brownish beige hue and the stems are especially supple.

Wineries made good use of soaked cattails for tightly sealing barrel staves. The wooden barrels often had to have their bottoms removed for cleaning;

68

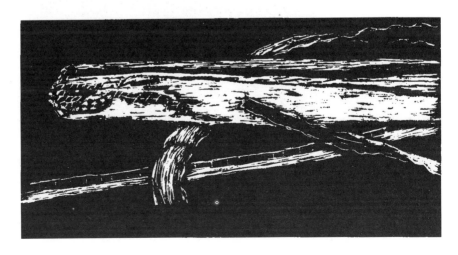

69

when the bottoms were replaced, the cattail leaves were inserted into the joins.

Bags (woven on a loomlike frame), covered bottles, as well as tied mats and hats that have been made from cattails are almost always sold as products made from rushes. These items are almost all made in Hungary, Romania, and Bulgaria. In the marshes along the Danube, cattails grow profusely. In many places here in Switzerland there are so few that they are a protected species.

Pond reed (Phragmites australis)

70

The brown seed stalks of this plant, which grows 3 to 4 m tall, resemble strands of hair standing in water. This reed can commonly be found in Austria, Yugoslavia, Hungary, and Romania, where it is used to make woven mats. In Switzerland, there were a few reed-weaving shops at least until the 1970s. In older houses, you sometimes find that reed was used as a supporting structure for plaster.

Baskets used as packaging were often woven from willow combined with split reed.

71

Corn (Zea mays)

Corn is cultivated in large quantities for feeding livestock, and the husks of the cobs can be used to create many types of woven objects. The corn cobs are beige to yellow in color and are almost completely dried out in autumn when still on the stalks.

The weaving material is cut or twisted into thick strips not longer than 30 cm. It is usually woven damp, using a braiding or knotting technique. In

many parts of Europe, people would weave corn husks into bags, shoes, sandles, placemats, and floor mats. In addition to making the well-known corn husk dolls, you can manipulate the husk into a variety of delicate or coarse creations. Often people use the corn fibers as the initial material in long braids.

72

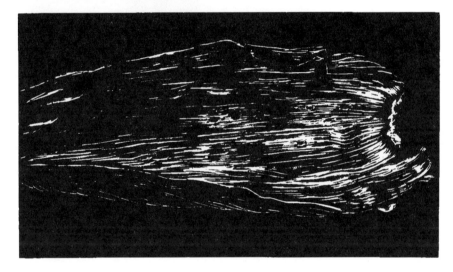

73

Esparto grass (*Stipa tenacissima*)

Esparto grass grows in southern Spain, in Italy, and in northwest Africa. It grows wild over large expanses of sand and rocky land. This very tough, thin grass grows from 70 to 100 cm tall. Its leaves bloom from March to May. The useful parts of the plant are free of nodes. Esparto grass can be beaten

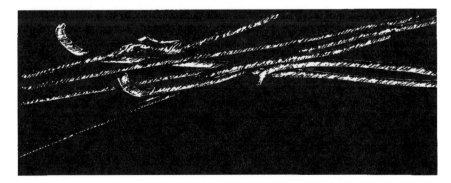

74

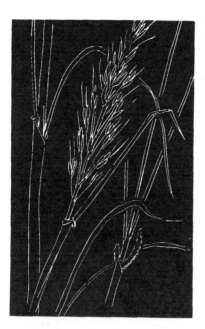

to be made pliable for weaving or it can be used as it is found. On the Iberian peninsula and in North Africa, people have made rope, mats, chairs, baskets, and bags out of it for ages.

75

Luffa
(Luffa cylindrica)

Luffa is a curiosity. The luffa sponge gourd, which flourishes in warmer climates, hides its weaving material inside itself. The ripe fruits, when left to soak in water for a long period of time, start to disintegrate. Then the flesh and the seeds can be removed, and what remains is a spongelike mesh. Cleaned, bleached, and dried, this meshlike material was dyed green and used to make Easter basket nests.

Today luffa, in itself a complicated weave structure, can be bought in drug stores as a long, cucumber-shaped massage sponge.

Palm leaf

The palms can be divided into two categories: those with pinnate leaves (resembling a feather) and those with palmate leaves (having three or more leaflets). Both can be used for weaving.

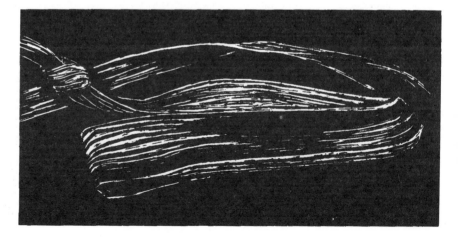

76

77

The date palms *(Phoenix dactylifera)*, found in southern Europe, North Africa, and from Arabia to India, and the Cuban Royal Palm *(Roystonea regia)* are examples of pinnated weaving materials. Sometimes the stalks of the leaves are cleverly made into containers. Basketmakers frequently take advantage of the conical shape of the leaf in the forms of their woven objects.

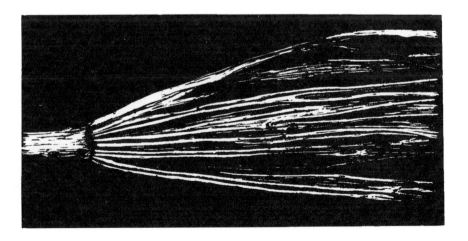

78

Among the fan-shaped palms suitable for weaving are: the Palmyra Palm *(Borassus flabellifer)* from India, Burma, Sri Lanka; the Doom Palm *(Hyphaena thebaica)*, which can be found from upper Egypt to the western Sahara; and the Dwarf Fan Palm *(Chamaerops humilis)*, which can be found in Europe. The Spanish call this mere 50 cm tall shrub *palmetto*, which means "little palm".

The leaves, which are usually slit into narrow strips, can be made into all kinds of finely woven items. Although processed fresh in the country of origin, the leaves must be cut into strips, washed, in some cases bleached, and then left to dry. Just prior to weaving, they must be dampened and kept in a wet cloth to mellow.

Raffia
(Raphia farinifera)

More than 30 other species of this genus flourish in tropical Africa, in Central America, and Brazil. The genuine raffia palm is native to Madagascar. It is

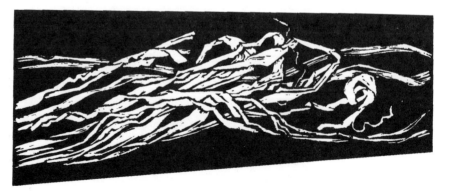

80

76

said to have the largest leaves of all plants. To harvest raffia, the natives cut off the pinnated leaves, which can grow to 20 m long. They strip off the raffia layer from the underside of each of the leaves on the stem, which are themselves 1 to 2 m long, working from base to tip. They use the raffia to create brightly colored hats, bags, and bowls.

You can buy raffia in braids or thick bunches, untreated, bleached, or dyed. Before weaving it, wet it and keep it wrapped up in a wet cloth. Similar untreated garden fibers can also be woven.

Woody Plants

Clematis
(*Clematis vitalba*) or
common Clematis

81

This native climber covers hedges, trees, and shrubs in open woods and scrub. This fast-growing, deciduous vine can climb up to 10 m high. The shoots, which grow to a length of 5 m, develop a grey, fibrous bark. In winter, the dense, white hair on the carpels form a large ball on the leafless stems. The young stems can be cut off in the cold months and wound up in a coil. You can peel these when they're fresh, but they must be cut while the sap is still running.

Thick nodes are clearly visible where the leaf attaches to the stalk. The tendrils are good for coiled basketry, and are excellent woven around willow stakes. The old, hollow stems, well known to boys and girls as smoking stalks, are not good for weaving.

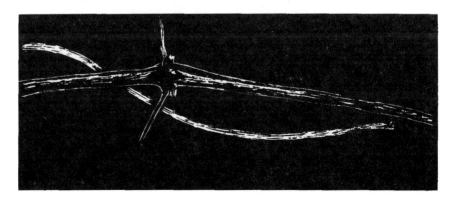

82

Dogwood

Dogwood, in particular *Cornus sanguinea*, can sometimes be used as weaving material. Identifying characteristics are the more or less heart-shaped leaves with their three or four pairs of lateral veins that meet to form points. This shrub has reddish twigs, whose pliancy makes them easy to weave. This short shrub loves sunny places in open woods and scrub, and in meadows and steep slopes.

Dogwood are especially good for making more coarsely woven baskets.

83

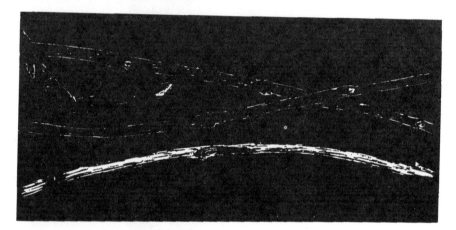

84

Blackberry (*Rubus* species)

85

Blackberries, or brambleberries, spread quickly in open woods and scrub, in hedgerows, and on pieces of land left wild. The runners grow several meters long and are fine for coiling once their thorns have been removed. To remove the thorns, put on a heavy leather glove and pull the runner through your clenched hand. The runners cut after the first frost must be wound into a coil while still fresh, or they may be cleaved and shaved to use as weaving rods.

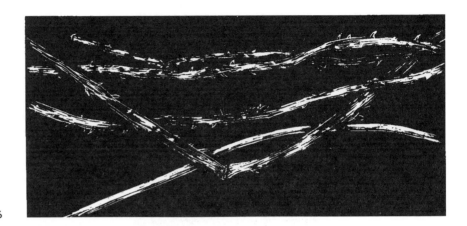

86

**Honeysuckle
(Lonicera),
Traveller's Joy or
Old Man's Beard**

87

This deciduous, lianalike climbing plant grows as high as 5 m in lightly wooded areas and hedgerows. The egg-shaped leaves are opposite. Some basketmakers like to combine these long runners with brown willow.

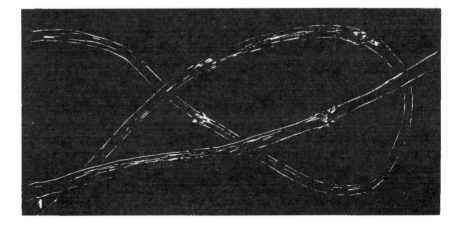

88

Wayfaring Tree
(Viburnum lantana)

89

This is a honeysuckle whose ventrally haired leaves also grow opposite along the shoot. The shrub, which grows to 5 m, grows wild in sunny locations and in many gardens. The white domed umbels (that appear in May and June) and the twigs are borne on slender branches covered with powdery hairs. The twigs are so elastic and tough it's almost impossible to break them off. When they're freshly cut, you can easily remove their bark and cleave them. Once they're dry, you can remove the pith. Soak them before you weave.

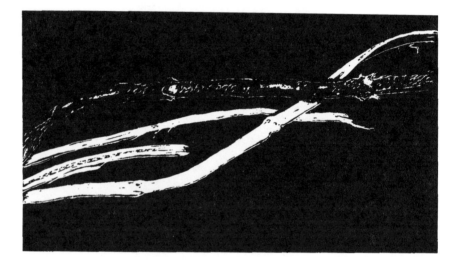

90

Birch *(Betula)*

91

Some species of this genus are suitable for weaving. They are found in moorland and heathland, from the lowlands to the mountains. The short, pointed leaves are alternate. The shrubs and the taller trees can be recognized easily by their white bark. The inner portion of the bark can be sewn like leather, glued, and woven. These birches are most frequently used in Nordic countries to make bottles, dishes, slippers, mats, and other utility items.

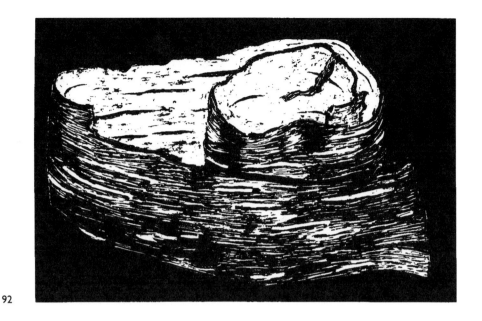

92

Norway spruce
(Picea abies)

93

Norway spruce grows in the mountains and is common to large areas of Europe. These evergreen, forest trees can grow to 50 m and often live 200 years.

The pliancy of this easily cleaved, light-colored wood makes it suitable for weaving. The tough roots and the delicate, stringlike roots are woven by the Nordic people into sturdy weaves.

The roots are cleaved, and all sorts of functional items are woven with the resulting skeins.

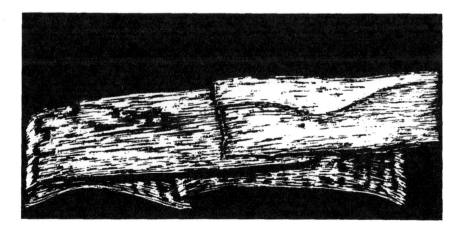

94

European filbert, or
hazelnut tree
(Corylus avellana)

95

The hazelnut tree, a pioneer plant, can be found everywhere in the Alpine foothills. The nuts grow in clusters of three or four and turn brown in autumn. Each has a light green, thorny casing.

The wood of the hazelnut tree is long-fibered, white, and hard. The straight sticks can be bent into handles, frames, and legs when fresh. Fresh, young wood can be cleaved along its growth rings and made into durable skeins, just as

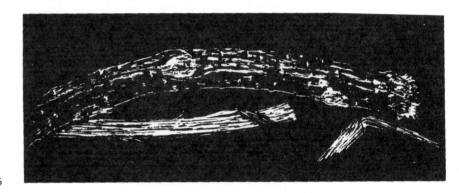

96

willow can be. They are rolled up when still fresh and soaked before you use them. In the highlands of Zurich, there is a basketmaker who is an expert in making the traditional style of large, coarsely woven baskets for harvesting berries.

Sweet, or mill,
chestnut *(Castanea
sativa)*

97

Sweet chestnut, with its edible, starchy nuts, grows in Tessin, Germany, in southern France, on Corsica, and in Italy. The leaves have a serrated border, are long and lanceolate.

For weaving rods, cut shoots that are 4 to 10 years old and are growing directly out of the ground. As in the case of willows, the stumps will generate new shoots. After several weeks of soaking, the cuttings are ready to be cleaved and woven. Young stems are cleaved when still green and warm to yield thinner skeins. These can be woven into lovely, old-fashioned melon baskets, chairs, and partitions. Oak, ash, linden, and poplar can also be processed for this sort of work. (Fruits and vegetables will keep very well in containers made of woody skeins.)

82

98

Rattan

99

83

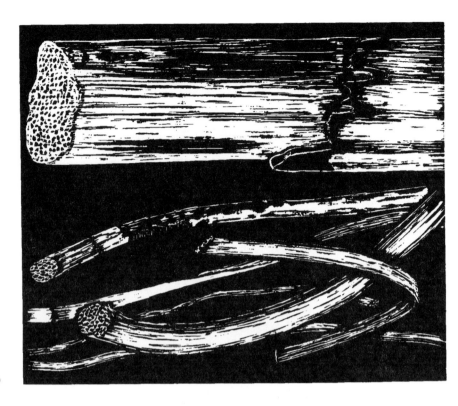

100

Rattan is probably the most popular weaving material of all. Before these vineline tropical palms are ready to be woven, they must undergo numerous processing steps. It grows as a thick, solid vine that hangs like cables, 50 to 150 m long, in rain forests on the islands of the Phillipines, Tahiti, and Manau. This climbing palm bears a scattering of pinnated leaves. The runners as well as the leaf stalks are covered with long thorns. Even the longest runners do not grow any thicker than a couple of centimeters. There are about 400 species and subspecies of this plant genus. One of the most common is the Calamus Rotang palm.

Spanish reed, as rattan is also called, is sold by different names: Malacca is thick and brown; Manila and Manau, thick and yellow; thin reed is called Boondoot or basket cane.

Once the thorny bark is stripped off, the vine has a polished, shiny surface with large and small protruding leaf nodes. The vines are heated or soaked and then bent into walking sticks, whips, wicker furniture frames, and carpet beaters.

Rattan cane   The interior of the thick rattan vine provides what is commonly known as reed. It is processed into a variety of thicknesses down to extremely thin lengths in several cross-sectional shapes (round, rectangular, oval, crescent shaped) and into strips. The material is very pliant, homogeneous in size, and porous, as shown in the drawing above, and it can be made into many types of objects.

Chair caning The remaining inner bark of the rattan vine is cut by special machines into strips of various qualities and widths. This smooth, hard, and tough material is used for Viennese-style chairs and other seating, as well as for wall and furniture coverings.

Bamboo
(*Bambusa* species) Bamboo is a giant, quickly lignifying grass that grows to a height of up to 40 m. It is the most useful plant in the world as it can be used in an infinite number of ways. Bamboo grows in all sizes and thicknesses. Its stalks are hollow between the leaf nodes, and even the thickest ones kink or split when bent. The skeins, however, can be bent, twisted, and woven in all sorts of ways. In Japan, China, Thailand, and India, bamboo is part of daily life. The plant's unique and attractive character is an impressive sight. The only bamboo park in Europe, created over 100 years ago, is in southern France, near St.-Jean-du-Gard.

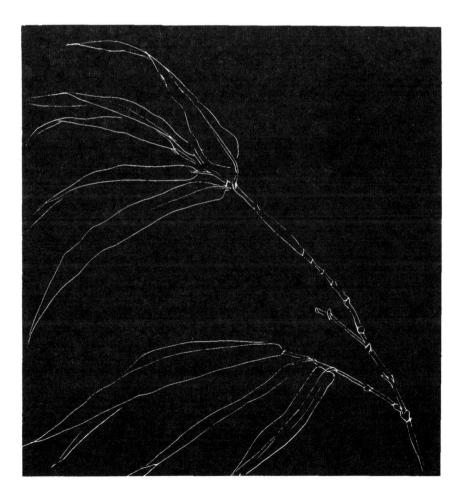

101

In the Far East, people fashion and build many different things out of bamboo. The material is long-lasting and decomposes very slowly. The hollow stalk explodes when burned.

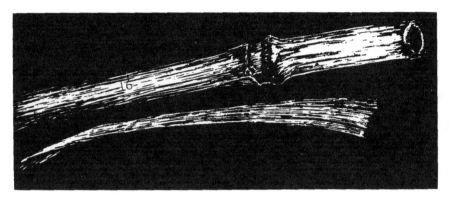

102

The Workshop

Where to Work

If you simply want to weave in your spare time, you can make do with any large area for a workshop, as long as the floor is resistant to dampness.

In the open air In days gone by, travelling basketmakers did not make a fuss about their shop. They simply worked outdoors sitting on a box.

Working outdoors is only possible if you are using brown willow. The wind and sun quickly dry out peeled willow, so it must be continually wet down.

Under shelter The travelling basketmaker moved from one farm to the next. The farmers would often let him set up under a roof overhang or in a shed. The wandering basketmaker repaired the coarsely woven, everyday baskets and also made new single-handled bow baskets and two-handled harvest baskets from pollard willow. The craftsman carried his own tools with him.

Setting up Your Shop

If you intend to spend a lot of time making baskets, however, you had better set yourself up in a roomy shop. (When the rods are stuck into the finished base, you often need about 2 m or more of space all around you.) It's not only impractical, it's a nuisance to have the rods constantly getting caught on one thing or another while you are working.

The best spot is a heated, well-lit, ground-floor room with a large entrance. In the French region of Poitou, basketmakers still work in natural caves. The high humidity and constant temperature provide optimal conditions for working with willow, but contribute to pains in the joints, rheumatism, and similar illnesses.

A corner for carpentry work, a place to write, and shelves for all your metal tools, leather, dyes, and stains are definitely necessary for an all-round basketmaker.

Floor | The workshop floor should not only resist dampness, it should also have a nonslip, nonskid surface. It takes only a little spilled water for someone to slip and fall on a smooth surface.

The ideal would be a self-made wooden floor. You can lay the flooring on crossplanks to allow air to circulate and to allow it to dry more quickly underneath. This would also provide additional floor insulation. The surface area, ideally, should be about 1.5 m by 2 to 3 m.

Lighting | In addition to plenty of sunlight, you should have a ceiling or a wall lamp, installed in such a way that your hands do not cast shadows on your work. Desk or floor lamps shouldn't be used because the rods would be hitting them all the time.

Several lights of the same intensity will create multiple shadows, which can tire your eyes and irritate you while you are working. Fluorescent lights flatten objects and eliminate shadow.

Seating | The height of the seat you should work on is a controversial topic. Depending on the regional traditions, the type of work you are doing, and personal habits, the seat height can be anywhere from an extremely low to a normal position. There are some basketmakers who simply sit on a board on the ground, made a bit more comfortable with a cushion, with their tools by their side.

We prefer sitting very low. We do much of the preparation and detailing with the work supported on our knees or thighs. This is a convenient method as you can often use your knees as a vise. A seat height of about 25 cm is fine. As shown in the drawings, water for sprinkling, the mellowing rods wrapped in wet cloth, large tools, and other necessities can remain within reach on the floor.

The bench | It's best to use a bench as a seat, rather than a stool or chair. The bench doubles as a storage place for the tools you need to keep within reach, as shown in the bottom drawing at right.

Simple seating | Two low boxes, a section of tree trunk, or something comparable, with a board attached, can be also be used to improvise seating.

If you are going to be using the seat regularly, however, it makes sense to invest a little more time in it. Cut a wooden bench measuring 80 by 50 cm. The legs can be made of two thick boards as long as the width of the bench and about 25 cm high.

Tool holder | On the end of the bench, to your right, attach a board with large holes bored into it to hold your tools. You can also screw a thick strip of wood to the end of the bench using wooden blocks and crosspieces to provide a 5 cm clearance. Place your tools in the intervals, and they are then easy to find and always within reach.

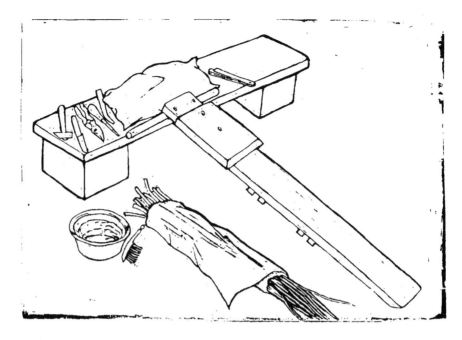

103

There's still room next to the bench for often used tools—knives, hammer, rapping irons, rulers, and a pencil. Store a yardstick, a saw, perhaps two large awls, and a whetstone behind the bench.

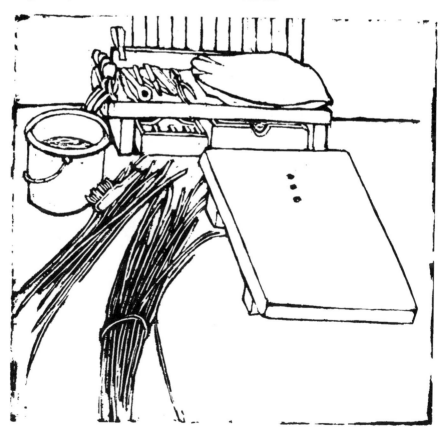

104

Seat covering   You can cover the bench with a cushion filled with wool or some other comfortable, insulating material. We don't recommend foam rubber or similar fillings. Seating close to the floor requires effective heat-insulation. Your back must also be protected from any masonry. A board propped up against the wall will allow the air to circulate between the wall and your back. You might also use the back from a discarded office chair.

Under the bench   Under your bench, as mentioned, there should be room for a couple of drawers, one of which should be divided into small, shallow compartments. Nails of various sizes and other bits can be stored there ready to use. In the second drawer, you can put your notes, paper, pencils, and pens, as well as a bite to eat! A basic first aid kit, especially for treating cuts, should also be within reach.

The work surface   The work surface is a small tablelike surface. Here, too, there are various designs possible, but basically, it should be long or high enough to reach the bench, as shown in the drawings.

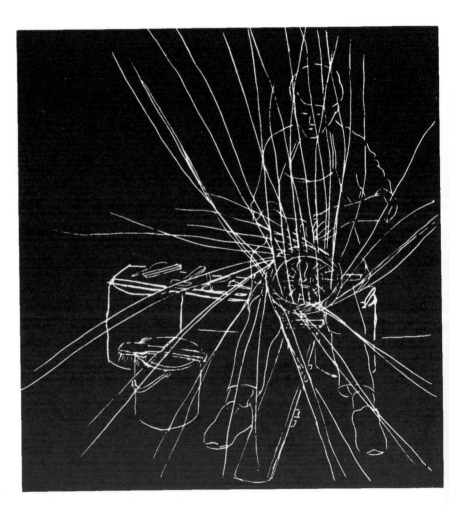

105

Simple work surface

We've developed a simple style of work surface that we use in the classes we teach. It is simply a single 1 x 0.2 m board. At one end, the board is cut at a slant through its thickness to rest against the floor. At the other end, a dowel is attached with wing nuts. The dowel can be held either under your knees or on your thighs, depending on the work you are doing. When you stow the board away, you can fasten the dowel so that it is parallel to the board. You can also attach a wider, slanted board with two holes 10 cm from the doweled end, as shown in drawing 103, p. 89. The holes are for the awls that hold the basket in place while you're working it. Nail cross strips under the board to make a rectangular base.

106

| Larger work surface | A larger work surface can be built of beech or another hardwood. The surface is tilted because the legs are of different lengths. The front two legs are only 10 cm long, the back two are 20 cm. Like the bench, the work surface is 50 cm wide and 65 cm long. Three to four holes are bored in the middle of the board's width at intervals of 5 and 8 cm. Depending on the work in progress, an awl is stuck in one of the holes to hold the base of the basket tightly and allow the work to be turned in both directions. (Some basket-makers' work surfaces are so well used there are deep furrows in the wood around the holes.) When you work the basket wall, the two longer legs are put on the bench so that the basket is raised onto your knees, as shown in the drawing on p. 91. Once you have worked enough of the wall, the work surface can be set back down on the floor. This work surface has three heights, but there are others that have a stairlike supportive frame that allow more. |

| Water | The water bucket should be to the right of your bench, with a brush for wetting down the work on the floor beside it. Don't leave the brush in the water or it will soften. |

| Soaked material | Rods taken fresh out of the soaking water can be kept on the floor between the container and your bench. If the air is dry, we keep the rods wrapped up in a wet cloth until we're ready to use them. This process of wrapping rods is called mellowing. |

| Waste | While you are working, you accumulate broken rods, picked-off tips, and butt ends. Keep all of these waste materials on the floor to your left. When the tips start piling up, bundle them together; they can perhaps be used later for smaller items or as inserts. The other waste materials can be chopped up and used for compost, or when they are dried, you can use them for fuel. |

A waste basket would get in the way of your work. Besides, stuffing waste into a basket means exerting an unnecessary effort while you should be concentrating on your work.

| Orderly or disorderly? | A busy basketmaker's workshop may look very disorderly to a visitor, but it is an attractive disorder. Leaning against the wall are bundles of all lengths of rods being used, some light, some dark. They look like tired dwarfs standing there waiting to be of service. Nearby, various finished items are about. Occasionally, a number of identical pieces are piled up and their outstanding repetition attracts the eye. Rod cuttings lie all over the floor. On a wall may be hanging crosses (for rectangular baskets) and rings (for smaller baskets); on some shelves, intriguing forms made of wood (for delicate work). |

The visitor will eventually perceive that everything has its own place and that, in fact, the shop is quite orderly.

Tools

Basic Tools

Every basketmaker must have his or her own tools. They must feel familiar and be easy to hold. A tool that is too light or too heavy can tire its user out unnecessarily. Even when making a simple basket, the most important tools are picked up and put down over and over again. The willow worker's few tools have hardly changed over the centuries. For medium-sized baskets using whole rods, the only tools you need are the following:

- knife
- whetstone
- awls
- pliers

- pruning shears
- hammer
- folding ruler
- rapping irons

An Ancient Tool

The first basketmaking tools known are from the late Stone Age. Awls, cleaves, and knives, still in recognizable condition, were discovered in the last century in Swiss ponds and lakes.

In recent times, a piece of antler dating back to 4 A.D. was uncovered during an excavation in the small lagoon in Zurich. The device, shown in the drawing on p. 94, is 15 cm long and was believed to have been a chopping tool. In our opinion, however, it could not possibly have been a chopping tool. The hole would have had to have been bored at right angles to the axis in order to hold a handle. What's more, the opening would have been cylindrical. We believe instead that this hole was used to straighten the sticks that were needed for coarsely woven structures. The extending part served as the handle. This flattened end probably also served to open the coarse weave structure to push through a rod or stick. In addition, by holding the long part, one could beat down the weave structure, which would explain why the upper end is hollowed out. A very well thought out, multipurpose basket-making tool!

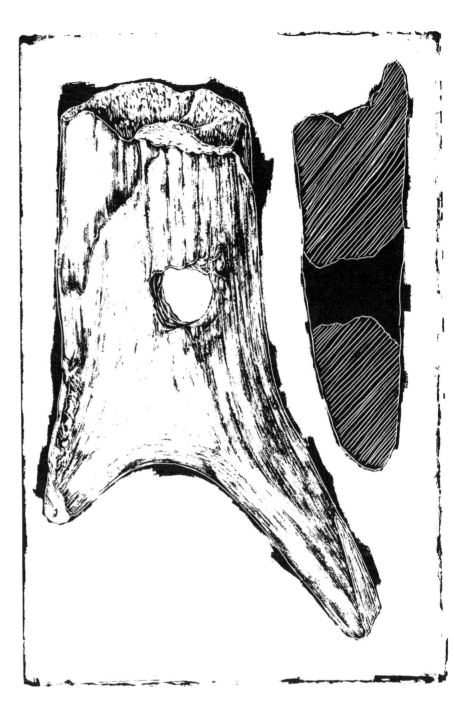

107

The most important tool, your hands

Basketmaking is truly manual work. The hand is always involved—or more accurately, both hands are. Often you use two hands simultaneously to complete one step. The hand is the most commonly used tool of them all. It does almost everything; only when the hand cannot provide enough force, where it is too coarse or too delicate, is another tool needed. Holding the tools must be practiced therefore. When cleaving rods, for example, you must know

when and how to apply pressure, sometimes only with your fingertips. Here's a short list of the hands' tasks while weaving:

Bending: The thumbs and the whole hand are good for bending thick and thin rods.

Rapping: With a fist, the ball or edge of your hand, you can beat or rap the weave to press it more tightly together.

Opening: You can use all the fingers to open up stakes.

Marking: Use the fingernails to smooth, scrape, nick, and pinch.

Measuring: You can measure a span with spread fingers; control the clearance between stakes with finger thickness; check skein thickness with the thumb and index finger.

Cutting Tools

All of your tools must be well sharpened, and anyone working with willow should be able to sharpen a knife. With well-sharpened tools, the work is easier, and there is less risk that the blade will slide off and cut you.

The curved scalloming or slyping knife

The concave edge of this curved knife, shown at top in the drawing, is the cutting edge. The point should also be well sharpened. The blade is about 12 cm long, and the handle somewhat longer. You can use this useful knife for many jobs, such as removing twigs from forked rods, taking off tips, picking off the rods at the base, and for scalloming, and slyping.

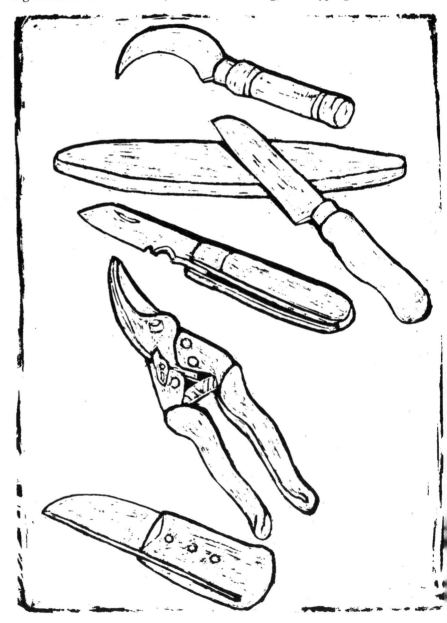

109

The shop knife   There are various types of shop knives, and a pocketknife can do the job if you have nothing else at hand. The blade of the knife is rounded along the back edge. The knife is useful for cleaving base sticks and slyping rods (although we prefer the curved knife because we find it more versatile and easier to hold).

Shears   Basketmaker's shears, shown in the drawing below, differ little in shape from the usual garden or orchard clippers, but the blades are pointed and very flat, which allows you to get closer to the woven surface. Basketmaker's shears are always necessary for picking off stakes, thick sections of the rods, corner stakes for rectangular baskets, and rods on finished borders.

Cut thicker pieces with a handsaw.

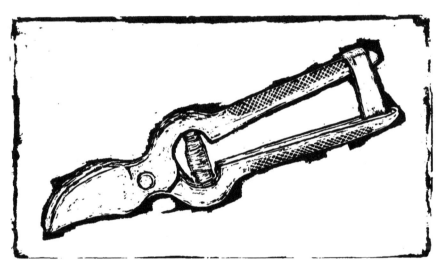

110

Picking knife   This knife, shown at the bottom of the drawing on the facing page, is also known as a picking off, pruning, or carving knife. The cutting edge is rounded and its back edge is straight. The blade is only 5 cm long. The picking knife is used for trimming, or picking off, the ends sticking out of the finished basket, although you can use an ordinary knife if necessary. The blade should always be as sharp as a razor, and using it requires some practice.

Whetstone   To sharpen your knives, you will need a whetstone, also called a grinding or honing stone, of medium grade. You can also use a grinding wheel. Whetstones are frequently finer on one side than the other.

Pliers

Pincers
The best sort of pincers are medium sized. They are used for bending and kinking nails and rods. They are also used to remove the connecting pins in the wood crosses that are used as corner supports while working on large, rectangular pieces.

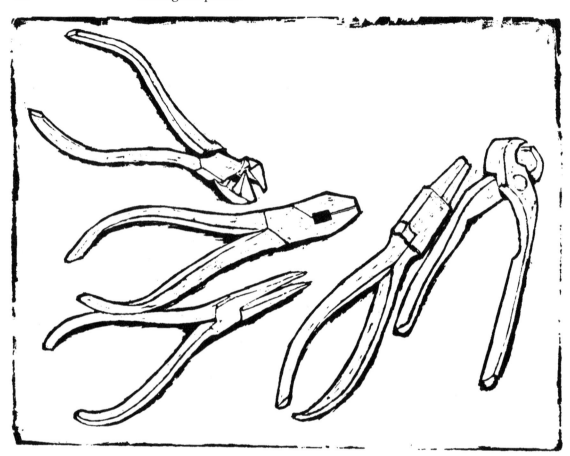

Round-nosed pliers
These pliers are about 3 cm long and, as the name implies, are rounded at the ends. In basketry, you can use them to bend the first stakes down when making a border.

Flat-nosed pliers
These pliers have a flat, angled nose. It's best to have the kind whose nose is long, narrow, and almost pointed. With flat-nosed pliers, you can press small nails through the rods very easily. They're also excellent for bending back pointed nails sticking out of the weave, pressing rods flat, and pulling willow rods or skeins out of spaces that cannot be reached with your fingers.

Common pliers
Common pliers are good for pinching, bending, nicking, and rapping woven material. The tip can be used as a clamp. You can use them also to pinch delicate wire or crimp thicker pieces of wire (for example, around a purchased bolt of rods).

Side cutters   Side cutters, also called snippers or pruners, are used to pinch thin rods and skeins in two. They're also good for picking off smaller baskets. The nose of the tool is positioned on one side of the head, in the direction of the handle. You should select a small, lightweight pair, the sort normally used in electronics.

Awls, or Bodkins

These tools are known as both bodkins and awls. A basketmaker needs all different sizes, both straight and bent. The tip is more or less wedge shaped. With large, thick awls, you can open up holes in the borders of baskets in order to make rope or crossover handles. A spacer or wedge is a large, heavy bodkin, often made of wood, which is incorporated into the basket. It's later removed, and the bow of the basket handle is inserted in its place.

You use small and medium-sized awls to hold the base of the basket on the work surface as you are working. If you need to open a path in order to anchor a rod, you can use either a small or large awl to do so, depending on the density of the weave.

Bent awls are used to finish borders, or to open a space between two rods. Awls can also be used for smoothing the rods.

112

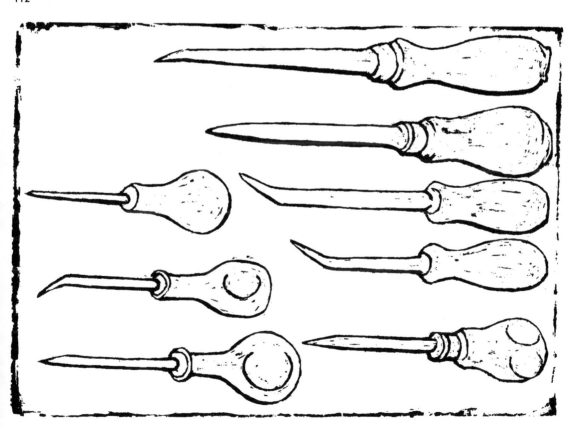

Rapping Irons and Other Tools

Rapping irons and commanders for coarse weaves

Since it is almost impossible to find them for sale, your best bet is to have these tools made by a blacksmith.

The rapping, or shop, iron is used for compressing the rows when you're working a coarse type of basket material or weaving structure. The commander has a hole in it for straightening large rods. You can also use the irons as weights on pieces that are drying.

This large tool is 24 to 30 cm long, 5 cm wide, and 2 cm thick. Depending on how you're using it, it is held at either one end or the other. A piece of hand-forged iron like this looks attractive and feels good to hold. Heavy and cold, it is a stark contrast to the weaving material.

Rapping irons and commanders for medium weaves

This rapping tool is also made of iron, but not as long and wide. It is at least 1 cm thick at its thickest point. Two thirds of it are straight, but the other third is curved and ends with a blunt tip. This iron is used for more delicate upsetting.

Tubular irons These tools are not needed often. They are used to control the bending of heavy, thick skeins that will serve as stakes. Without this tool, the skeins would easily break. In southern countries, oak and chestnut wood is frequently worked using this tool. They were at one time used here in Switzerland for making flat, coarsely woven, winnowing baskets.

Hammer A peening hammer, which is normally thought of as a basketmaker's hammer, is small and easy to hold (round on one side and with a wide, flat fin on the other). You can use this for the pegs used to fasten the bow handle to the basket, and for other tasks. You might also have use for a heavier hammer—

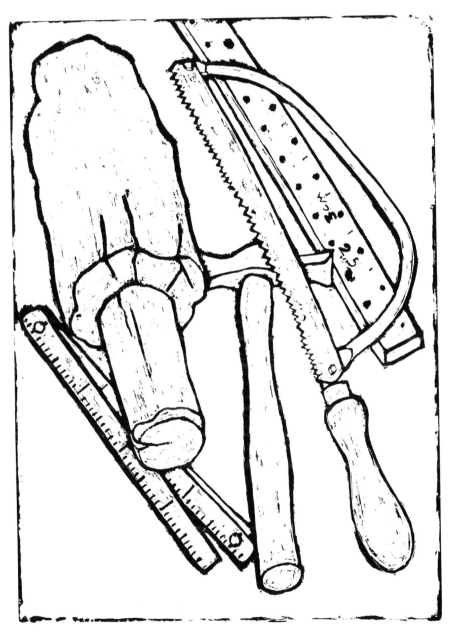

114

for example, a metalworker's hammer, about 500 gm, to hammer large pins into base strips.

Bow saw — Thick willow, corner sticks, and channeled strips, and in fact anything that cannot be cut with shears can be quickly cut with a bow saw. Notches, nicks, and grooves can also be made with this saw.

Yardstick — We hammer in short, flat-headed nails along a 50 cm long strip of wood, placing one every 2.5 cm on one side and every 3 to 3.5 cm on the other side. This sort of yardstick is a useful gauge when making rectangular baskets (to check stake intervals, etc.).

Folding ruler — This is the folding ruler used by carpenters. You can measure everything with it, and you'll use it often.

Wooden mallet, or maul — We saw or carve wooden mallets out of a stump or a piece of hardwood. A sculptor's mallet will serve the same purposes. We use a mallet to hammer awls into the work surface when holding the base of a basket in place. You can also hammer onto it or pound in pegs.

Cleaves and Shaves

Cleaves — This tool, also called a wood splitter or willow splitter, cleaves, or divides, the willow rods lengthwise into three or four pieces. These wooden tools are just long enough to fit into the palm of your hand. They're rounded in back and slightly tapered in front. Three-way and four-way cleaves are shown below. They're almost always of hardwood and sometimes of metal; formerly some were bone.

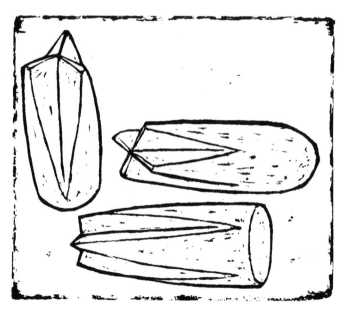

115

Shaves   After the rod is cleaved, its inner pith is removed. The tools used to do this are small shaves, or planers, often made of white beech wood. The handle makes the tool a pleasure to use. By means of the screws, the blades can be adjusted to the right height or can be removed to be sharpened or oiled.

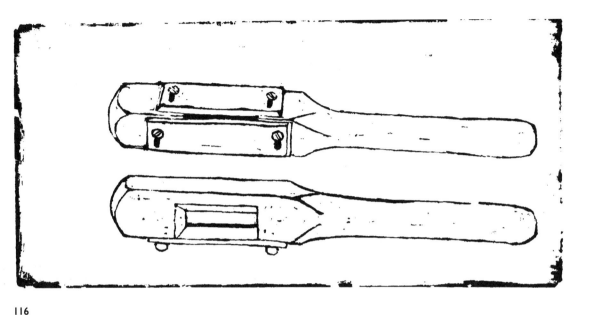

116

The year 1888 is inscribed on the shave shown in the drawing below. The curved handle makes the tool especially easy to hold.

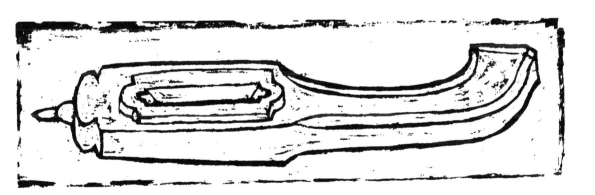

117

Large shave   This large tool, shown in drawing 118 on p. 104, is screwed onto a shaving bench and is used from the side. One screw secures the metal blade against the support; the other clamps the block tight.

The block-type shaver equipped with a hinge, shown in drawing 119, is screwed into the work surface. The wing nut allows you to adjust the blade. It's necessary to wear a leather cap on your thumb when shaving the skeins to protect it as it presses the skeins against the sharp edge of the blade.

118

119

Uprights   Uprights are used to uniformly narrow the width of the skeins. This simple, handheld tool shown in drawing 120 is rounded to easily fit in the palm. Two, parallel blades are set vertically in the wood. You'll need two or three uprights, set at different widths.

120

The upright block When this block of stationary uprights is screwed onto a shaving bench, both of your hands are free to pull the skeins through. The block contains several sets of 2 mm wide, parallel blades, which are spaced at varying intervals to produce varying widths of skeins.

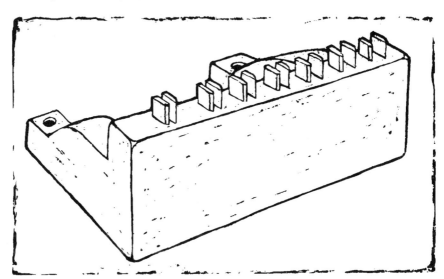

121

Preparations

Soaking

Besides hands and tools, the willow basketmaker requires two basic items: willow and water. Soaking the willow rods must not be taken lightly. You cannot create a good piece of work, even with the best quality rods, if the willow hasn't been properly soaked. When dry willow is stored, its pores open and the pith is dormant. In order to regain the willow's pliability and bring it back to life, you must soak it in water.

Duration

How long you soak the rods depends on what kind of willow you are working with: brown, buff, or white. The following factors also play a role:
- the length and thickness of the rods
- the quality of the rods
- the temperature of the water

Here are our average soaking times for each type of willow. We don't use warm water, but it will decrease the amount of soaking time required. Never use hot water! It makes the rods brittle.

	Shortest period	Longest period
Brown willow:	2 to 3 weeks	As long as 4 weeks outdoors in winter
Buff willow:	1 hour	3 hours
White willow:	1 hour	3 hours

Repeated soaking

We do not recommend repeated soakings because this will spoil the quality of the rods. If you have worked on a piece for several hours, you'll have to soak or wet the stakes again before working the border. Only the parts you'll be working with should be wet!

The water tank

A basketmaker's tank is usually made of brick and mortar, galvanized sheet metal, or even wood. Today fiberglass tanks are often installed in commercial workshops. They can be purchased in a variety of sizes and are portable thanks to their light weight. A bathtub can be used, but it is sometimes too short.

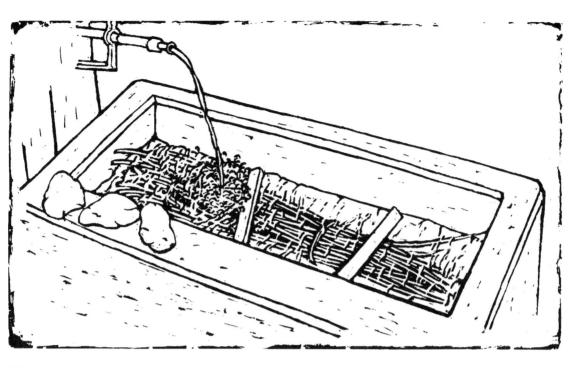

122

The most practical containers are 2 to 3 m long, 80 to 100 cm wide, and about 80 cm deep.

A professional basketmaker ideally has two or more tanks, one for brown willow and one for peeled willow.

Water
Depending on the season and the site, the water must be changed every week. The tank should also be cleaned out. Some people may be lucky enough to have a source of continuously running water, such as a small, nearby stream. This is especially convenient in the winter, when standing water tends to freeze and may crack the tank. Running water also keeps the willows clean, guarding against algae build-up and insect larvae.

Outdoor site
Formerly, large businesses would sink containers in the ground and feed them by means of a redirected stream. Brick and mortar tanks can usually be found along an exterior wall, protected from the elements and foreign materials by an overhanging roof.

If your tanks are protected from the sun in summer and from the wind in winter, it is not necessary to change the water very often. In the cold months, however, the willow may have to be chopped out of the ice, and the cold, wet rods are not very pleasant to work with.

Indoor site
The most practical place to keep your soaking tank is directly beside your work area. A standing body of water will increase the air humidity and make the rods easier to work. The tank will fill the whole workshop with the peculiar and unmistakable odor of soaking willow. The only disadvantage is that you have to change the water in an indoor tank more often because it gets too warm.

| A simple soaking tank | If you are using a bathtub or similar sort of tub, you will have to adapt it so that the rods can be held under water. Below, we've described four ways this can be done. |

<table>
</table>

A simple soaking tank

If you are using a bathtub or similar sort of tub, you will have to adapt it so that the rods can be held under water. Below, we've described four ways this can be done.

If the tank is too short to hold the full length of the rods, the tips stick out of the water. You can cover them with a wet burlap sack, which must be wet down from time to time.

A more sophisticated tank

A more useful and sophisticated type of container has the advantage of a runoff with a lightly slanted base and an overflow plug. The plug prevents the water from overflowing, eliminating the risk of disaster in your workshop. If you have a tank without a runoff, you can use a hose as a siphon for emptying the basin.

Here are several ways to keep the rods submerged:

A: Place two old stools on the willows so that they are held between the stool legs. Weight the seats with heavy stones.

Or:

B: Cut two thick boards to the tank's width. Angle the ends in opposite directions. If you push the boards down into the water and let them rise again to level, they'll wedge between the side walls. With rubber strips on the ends, they'll stick even better.

123

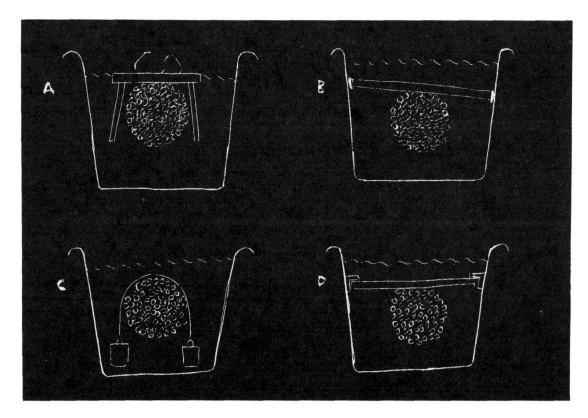

Or:

C: Fill 2 or 4 large cans (about 10 cm in diameter) with concrete. While the concrete is still soft, stick a loop of heavy wire into it. Then use the wire loops to tie two cans together to make a pair of weights.

Or:

D: Install L-shaped wood ledges along the tank's inner walls. These ledges will hold down several boards.

Soaking brown willow

Quantity: Before you soak brown willow rods, estimate the quantity you need. You should either know which baskets you want to make, how many, or how much time you have to work. (Include a few extra rods for adjustments or errors.)

Filling the tank: If you are soaking a lot of willow, place the longest rods on the bottom, the shorter rods on top. Alternate the butt and tips ends so that the pile is relatively flat. The device for submerging the rods is placed directly on top of the shorter rods.

Water: Once the rods are in the tank, fill it with water. Check the position of the holding boards while the water is running in. Once the tank is full, it's almost impossible to adjust them because the rods push up hard against them.

Time: Jot down the date in a safe place on the tank (experienced basketmakers can do without a reminder). If you intend to work with brown willow over a long period of time, it's a good idea to put new rods in regularly. During the weeks of soaking, tannin forms a skin on the water surface; leave this undisturbed and there won't be as strong an odor from the standing water. You don't need to change the water.

After soaking: Now remove the largest bundles from the water, let them drain a little, and wrap them up in wet burlap. They're ready for immediate use.

Long-term storage: If the rods are not used within a few days, they start to form a slimy, shiny skin. This skin, which is unpleasant to touch, can be washed off before you use the rods. If kept damp for any longer, they'll quickly start to rot, especially in warm weather, and will be useless.

Repeated soaking: Brown willow will crack and peel if resoaked.

Soaking white and buff willow

Quantity: The soaking period is short, and so you should soak only as much willow as you can use within a couple of hours. Carefully consider how many rods you need and how long they must be. For a single-handled shopping basket, for example, you will need about 1 kg of willow. The sticks for the slath, the crossover handle, and other parts must also be soaked, somewhat longer than the thinner rods. Stack the shorter rods on top, as you would for brown willow.

Water: Put the rods right into the water. You need not change the water every time you soak. The rods should never be put into warm water. They may become flexible more quickly, but they also lose their elasticity shortly thereafter. You must allow the material enough time to get ready for the stress and strain of being woven.

Time: The rods are properly soaked when they can be bent and kinked without breaking. Check this simply by taking one rod out of the water and trying it out.

Too little soaking: If the rods haven't soaked long enough, they'll be difficult to work. Trying to bend them will hurt your fingers. Often they'll kink in the wrong spot or snap.

Too much soaking: If the rods soak for too long, their quality suffers. The wood and the pith will be so saturated with water that the elasticity of the rods is poor. They'll be frayed and too brittle to be rapped down with the rapping iron, so the resulting weave structures will be second-rate. Oversoaked peeled rods have a reddish color.

After soaking: Take the rods out of the tank, wrap them in wet burlap, and place them next to your work area, with the butt ends toward the bench. The rods cannot remain in water any longer, but by wrapping them, they can be kept damp for a couple of hours. This mellowing process prevents oversoaking and keeps the rods as pliant as possible while you work.

Storage: Be sure to keep the rods covered when not in use. Rods must never be kept damp an entire day or longer, or they will become grey and spotted.

Grading

Do not underestimate the task of grading the thickness of the rods before you start to work.

In the bundles of sorted willow, there are rods of various thicknesses. Each thickness has its particular placement in the woven project. The general rule is, the butts of the stakes should be thicker than the weaving rods. The rods used for the upsett should be thicker than the weaving rods in the wall, but somewhat thinner than the stakes (see p. 120).

You can grade an entire bolt before soaking or you can grade small quantities after soaking. For the projects in this book, you can grade the rods after soaking them.

You might try grading simply by picking rods out of the bundle one by one, but this would soon lead to chaos.

With the technique described here, you can grade four different thicknesses at once, holding one thickness behind each finger of your right hand.

Drawings 124 and 125 illustrate how to grade rods of two thicknesses. Grading more at one time is difficult for beginners.

Technique   *Initial grading:* Locate the bundle with the rod length you want, remove the lowest tie and a handful of rods. Hold the rods in your left hand and pass them to your right. Separate them by thickness into two groups as you do so. Hold the thick rods between your index finger and thumb, and the

124

thin rods between your index and middle fingers. With practice, you'll work quickly and accurately. Lay the thick rods to your right, thin to your left, with tips in the same direction.

125

Second grading: Once you've sorted a certain number, separate the thicker and thinner rods within the two piles you have on the floor. These four bundles can be tied with different-colored strings to label them for their specific purposes.

Measuring thickness by eye is the fastest way to work, and the skill is a useful one to develop. Not only will accurate grading give you better results in the final product, but you'll develop a good eye for spotting damaged or defective rods as you work.

Cleaving

A rod or a stick can be split into two, three, or four strips before being woven. Split willows are also called clefts.

Brown-willow rope-handled laundry baskets or storage baskets often have upsetts made of clefts. These baskets are lightweight and easy to handle, but not very durable. Disposable packaging for flowers, cheese, beans, etc., also used to be made of cleft willow.

Clefts are more commonly made from peeled willow. If they are also shaved and uprighted, they have a delicate and refined quality that can be used to create artistic treasures.

Splitting sticks for the slath
Splitting sticks is part of the procedure for constructing the slath for the base of most baskets.

When making the shopping basket described on p. 175, one half of the base sticks are split open. The picking knife, or another sharply pointed knife, is inserted into the stick, not quite in the middle of its width, but exactly halfway between its ends. Once the point is through, you can twist the blade slightly to open up a slit in the base stick. By turning the blade slightly at an angle, the slit is kept open long enough to insert the remaining base sticks that form the crosspieces.

Splitting rods in two
You can split a rod entirely in two with a knife. When doing this, you must be sure that the blade runs straight down the middle. Any sawing action of the knife will tear the wood fibers. Splitting rods is easiest to do when they have been soaked and then allowed to dry a bit.

Three-way or four-way cleaves
Cleaving requires the special tool described on p. 102. A cleave divides the willow into either three or four clefts, depending on the tool's design. Large-scale shops have machines that can do this work quickly and well.

We recommend that beginners start with the three-way cleave.

How to use a cleave
Cleaving requires that you cut with the grain, not against it. For this work, lovely, spotless, nearly dry, thick sticks are best to use (the most suitable are those from the American, or Universal, Willow).

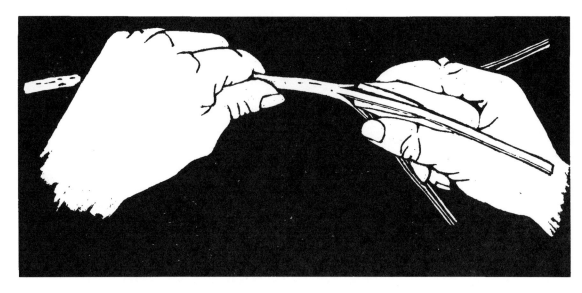

126

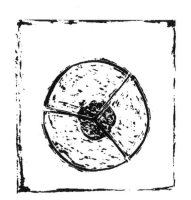

127

Procedure: Cut about 25 cm off the tip of the rod, and make three or four cuts in the end. Press either the three-way or four-way cleave into the cuts. Hold the cleave in your right hand (if you're right-handed). Let your left arm rest on your knee and hold the rod horizontally in your left hand, about 7 cm in front of the cleave. Press the cleave to the left into the rod. The cutting edges must always intersect the center of the pith. If the tool slips to one side, all is lost. The cleaved piece will be too short and unusable. As you slide the cleave along the length of the rod, move your left hand down the rod as well. Don't move it too far away from the cleave, or the rod will bend, and you'll end up with more firewood. If you want to master cleaving, relax, concentrate, and be patient and careful.

If your cleave keeps slipping, try to find out what's wrong and make the needed adjustment. If you can't get it right, perhaps put it off until another day.

Cleaving develops your sense of touch. Your fingers learn to sense tiny irregularities and the slightly spiraling wood grain.

The rods are pushed through the machine, butt ends first, one at a time. (You can also hand-cleave by pushing the rod into the stationary tool.)

Practice exercise

You can make the fan shown in the drawing below to try out the various ways of splitting rods. The handle is a stick split several times with a knife. You use a cleave to make the clefts that are woven into it. This same simple weave structure can also be used to make a spoon or a dish shape, if the stick is left whole on both ends. With a long stick, you can make a lawn rake.

The open border requires waling or holes drilled into the stakes to hold the last weaving rod. Instead of adding stakes (bistaking), where the weave widens, we split the existing stakes. When making a coarsely woven item like this one, there's no need to process the clefts any further.

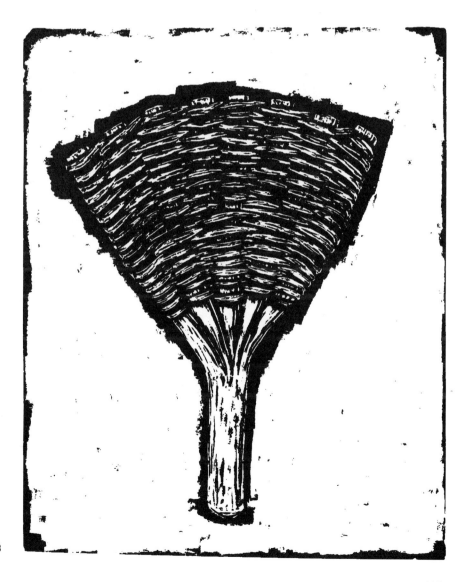

128

Shaving

The cross section of a split willow rod is shaped like a piece of pie, as shown below. The pith forms the tip of the wedge. Along the curved edge of the wood is the bark, if the rod is unpeeled.

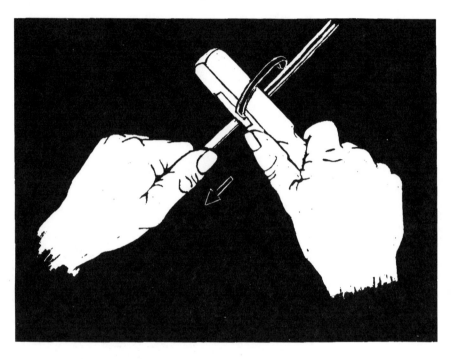

129

To produce a skein, you must remove the pith from the cleft so that only the outermost portion of the rod remains. There are a number of tools used

for this work, as described on p. 103. The simplest of the shaving tools fits easily in your hand. Its blade can be adjusted so that you can remove, or shave off, the necessary amount of willow. You can remove the pith and only a very thin sliver of wood or you can make a skein as thin as a sheet of construction paper—or thinner.

130

Using a handheld shave

Hold the piece you're shaving in your lap with your left hand. Hold the shave in your right hand, with the blade facing down. Press it down on the willow, against the pith, pulling the rod smoothly to your left. Repeat until you have the thickness you want.

Using the bench shave

With your left thumb, protected with a leather cap, pull the cleft through, between the plate and the blade. The right hand pulls it smoothly through. Don't shave too much off at one time.

Shaving by machine You can set the precise cutting thickness and shave the clefts one at a time by machine. These are used in large shops.

Uprighting

If you want to weave with unusually even and fine willow, you can upright the shaved skeins. Each skein will then have an even width along its entire length. Often skeins are uprighted to a width from 3 to 8 mm.

Using this tool is very tricky and demands a lot of practice and patience.

Using a handheld upright Hold the tool in your right hand and press the skein down firmly with your right thumb, as shown in the drawing. Pull the skein through the blades

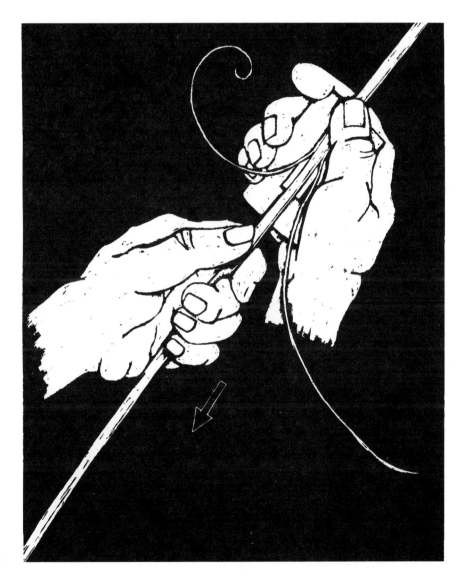

131

132

smoothly and firmly with your left hand, without stopping or jerking. The shiny side of the skein should be facing up. Repeat this process until the skein's width is uniform along its entire length. Each time the skein is uprighted, the tool's blades should be slightly closer together.

Using the upright block The work is basically the same, but because this tool, shown on p. 105, is secured to a workbench, you can pull the skein with both hands.

By machine As for shaving, there are also machines designed to do the work of uprighting.

Cleaning Clean off any bark still on the skeins with a small knife. Be careful not to damage the shiny surface.

Basic Techniques

Glossary of Terms

Here's a short list of frequently used terms. There's a more extensive glossary at the back of the book.

1/1, 1/3, 2/2, etc.: Weave-pattern abbreviations. For example, 2/1 indicates that a rod is worked over two stakes and behind one stake.

Base cross: The cross of sticks, also called a slath, which marks the central starting point of the basket, and around which the initial rows of weaving are made.

Bistaking: Adding more stakes alongside existing stakes to increase strength and stability or increase diameter.

Butt: The thick, bottom end of a rod.

Core: Stick or thick rod covered with stitches.

Dome: The upside-down, saucerlike shape of the basket base.

Fitching: A two-strand weave, in which the rods originate at the back of the work and are twisted to hold stakes in place.

Foot: An extra border to elevate and protect the base of a basket, which is both decorative and functional.

Insert sticks: The base sticks that are inserted through split sticks to form the cross of the slath.

133

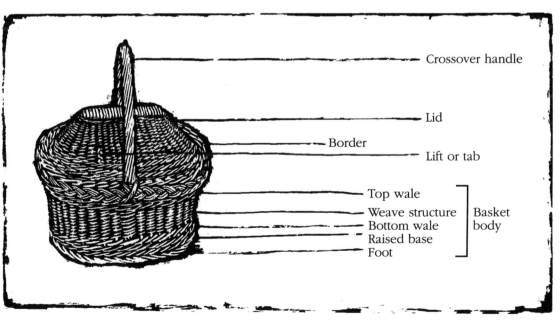

- Crossover handle
- Lid
- Border
- Lift or tab
- Top wale
- Weave structure
- Bottom wale
- Raised base
- Foot
- Basket body

Opening up: The groups of base sticks, positioned in a cross shape, are separated and spread out after two or more rounds of weaving, to open up the base.

Pairing: Working two weavers so that they cross each other in a twist resembling an S around each stake.

Pricking up: Using a knife or awl to open up a rod so that it will bend without cracking.

Randing: A weave pattern in which one rod is worked in front of one stake and behind the next (abbreviated 1/1).

Rapped work: A weave structure whose rows are beaten tightly together with a rapping tool.

Rib randing: A weave pattern in which one rod is worked in front of two stakes and behind one stake (abbreviated 2/1), where the total number of stakes is not divisible by three.

Slewing: Working two or more weavers as one.

Slype: A long, slanted, diagonal cut.

Slyping: Cutting rods at an angle.

Split layer: The sticks in the slath, which are split open, and into which more sticks are inserted to form the base cross.

Stakes or spokes: The rods that stand parallel to each other or radiate out at regular intervals to form the framework, or warp, for the weaving rods.

Stroke: A full stroke is made in front of and behind the stakes until one full repeat of the pattern is completed. The shortest stroke is in front of 1 behind 1 (1/1, in abbreviated form).

Tapering: Cutting rods at an angle (slyping) two or more times.

Tie in, or tying the slath: The first few rounds of weaving to secure the sticks at the center of the base.

Tip: The thin, top end of a rod.

Turn down: The way each stake is worked to make the border.

Upsett: The outer edge of the base where the stakes are woven vertically to form a side or wall.

Wale: A weave pattern worked with three or more rods.

Warp: Stakes, or framework elements.

Weaving rod, or weaver: The material woven between warp stakes.

Weft: Rods or other materials woven between warp stakes.

Whole, or full, rods: Rods that have not been cleaved.

Resiliency A weave structure is held together through counterpressure, that is, the tension created by the arrangement of the rods. The resilient, woven rods try to return to their original straight shape, which creates the pressure that gives the weave structure its stability. Willow rods acquire their resiliency in the course of a single summer. Each rod resists wind and weather and turns toward the sunlight and warmth. Rods that have been in very rich soils contain too much pith and are unsuitable for weaving.

134

Limits of the material

When beginners face, for the first time, the task of overcoming the willow's stubborn nature, they start to perspire, their fingers ache, and the rods break. After a while, they discover the easiest ways to manipulate the material and how to work with it instead of against it. If you expect too much of the rods, poor results will be quick in coming. People who have cultivated, processed, and prepared their own rods will have less difficulty getting a feel for the material.

There are references throughout the book for more specific information, but the following discussion is an introduction and provides some practice exercises before you begin the projects at the end of the book. The beginning basketmaker will soon have acquired so much knowledge that looking these things up will no longer be necessary. (The shopping-basket project on p. 175 also describes in detail the procedures discussed here.)

Weaving willow is somewhat final. If a basket is taken apart, the rods hold their woven shape and can't be used again. So only minor changes can be made in a finished piece of work.

Bending

Bending rods

In fact, most rods are bent, as they are continually being woven over and under the basket stakes. Because rods kink as they cross the stakes, however, they're not the best example of bending.

The trac weave, described on p. 155, however, consists entirely of truly bent rods.

Often the rods have to be hand-manipulated into a tight curve or angle in order to insert them in the proper place.

Procedure: The tip of the bent rod is inserted into the weave and is ready to be drawn through. Grab the loop of the bend with the other hand as you pull the inserted end through and anchor it. Move your fingers out of the way as you tighten the rod.

Practice exercise Bend the rod, using the thumb of your right hand as shown in drawing 137. You can work bent rods to make loose rings or small platters in a variety of designs.

135

Bending sticks Special care is required to shape thicker rods and sticks into loose rings, platter frames, or circles.

Fresh material: The best and easiest way to learn how to bend thick rods and sticks is by using fresh, unsoaked willow. Brown willow, hazelnut, and chestnut have an elastic bark that does not split, even when made into a circle. Rings made of fresh material can be easily bent and stored for later use. Tie them up with cord to keep them from opening while they are drying. Once they have dried, remember, you can no longer modify their shape.

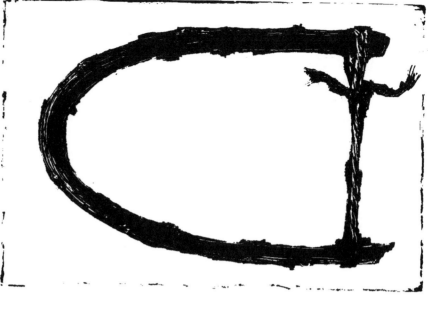

136

Dry material: You can put bends into dry material if you soak it in advance. In this case, however, you need more sensitivity to and knowledge of the material, as well as patience.

Bending: The goal is to make a curve not an angle. You're bending, not kinking. This is the problem when you're just beginning. Bending willow has to be done quickly and precisely, or the work springs back into its original shape.

137

Procedure: First, you work on the fiber. Starting at the thick end, press your thumb as opposing pressure against the inner side of the bend being made.

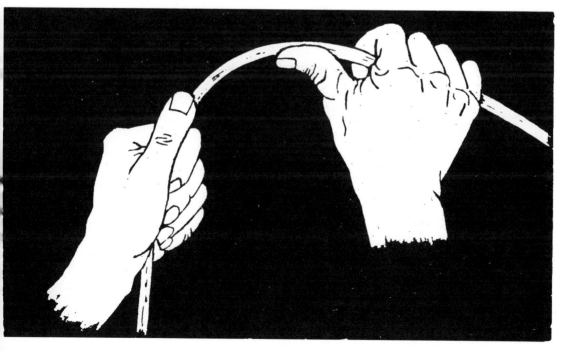

The resiliency of the butt of the willow is greater and requires more pressure. The fibers on the outer edge of the curve lengthen and are pushed outward by the pressure exerted by the thumb. They have to span a greater distance. This also makes room for the fibers on the inner curve, which are being compressed together. Continue to bend the stick, working the entire length methodically, centimeter by centimeter. As you progress, the bow will start to take shape.

As you get closer to the tip, be careful because there is more pith in this part of the rod. The first 50 cm of the tip are not used for weaving. Wrinkles may form on the inner curve, but they shouldn't. The curve must be evenly shaped and contain neither straight sections nor kinks. Kinks can't be repaired, so if you have any, discard the stick. The curve shouldn't be worked too much either, or it will soften and lack the resiliency it needs to act as a bow handle or comparable part.

While you're working the bend, don't rotate the stick, or you'll get a spiral that will keep it from lying flat.

Bending aids If you know the size oval or circle you want, draw a pattern on a 1/1 scale. Then you can check the work in progress against the drawing. It's preferable to bend the material somewhat smaller than the final shape, so that it will look better when adjusted.

Other shapes You can make other shapes too by sawing blocks, constructing the shapes and curves you want, and screwing the blocks onto a board to make a form. The sticks are then fit within the blocks. If you cut blocks that are thick

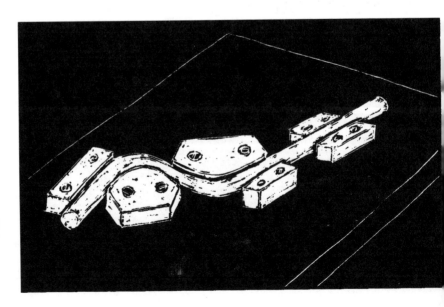

138

enough, you can make a form to shape several sticks into the same shape at one time.

If you cannot leave the sticks on the board to dry, nail them to a strip of wood, remove them from the board, and put them aside to dry.

Practice exercise To bend a stick into a half circle, cut a rectangular opening in each end, as shown in the drawing. Insert another piece of willow, shaped to lock the two ends in place. The resulting form is that of a wooden bell collar, which used to be found throughout the Alps. Bow shapes are also used for other things.

139

Cutting

The first principle of cutting is keep your knife sharp. Cut surfaces should be smooth and clean. There are a variety of cuts used in basketmaking, and there's a great deal of trimming, shaping, tailoring, cutting back, cutting out, picking off, etc.

Honing the knife There are two steps in properly honing a knife. To sharpen the blade, you use the coarse side of the whetstone. Move the blade in a circular motion at a low, constant angle to the stone, adding water. Once the blade is sharp, remove the rough burr on the cutting edge with the fine-grade side of the whetstone.

Straight cuts For various tasks, you need to make a straight, perpendicular cut. This can be accomplished in a variety of ways.

With shears: A basketmaker's shears are used to cut the base sticks to proper length or trim a few centimeters off the butt ends. Sticks can be picked off the finished base with shears, too, but the tool squeezes the rod somewhat so don't use it too often, especially if you want crisp ends.

With a knife: For a straight, undamaged end, it's best to work with a knife. Decide where you want the cut and hold the blade perpendicular to the rod at that point, as shown in the drawing below. Turn the rod or stick until you have cut a groove about halfway through the diameter. The piece can then be easily snapped in two. If necessary, smooth the cut surface. One use of straight-cut rods is for basket lids.

140

With a saw: Very thick sticks have to be cut in two with a saw. For example, sawing is necessary for corner sticks of rectangular basketry and furniture frames.

Slanted cuts   You'll need to cut the butt ends of the rods at a slant in these basketmaking situations:

With the scalloming or picking knife:
- Inserting the weaving rod of a wale; butt is replaced by butt.
- Working a rand on a form; the weaving rods must be cut before they're set in, in order to have enough room between the stakes and the form.
- Staking up.
- For large, rectangular baskets whose corner sticks must be anchored in the base.
- For German-style braided borders, which require diagonally cut bistakes.

- For crossover handles and side handles, which must be inserted as deeply into the weave as possible.

With the shears:
- For picking off finished work quickly.
- For picking off the ends on finished borders.

141

With a picking knife:
- For picking off finished work.

Practice exercise   If you want some cutting practice, you can make a set of short, sharpened game pegs. Instead of being set apart by color, they are differentiated by the number of cuts. At one end, the rods are cut straight; at the other they're slyped one or more times.

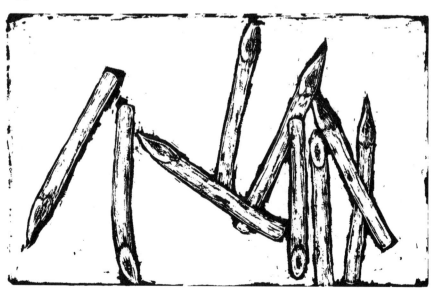

142

Slyping

Slyping rod ends is usually required before inserting rods into a base or staking up the basket wall. You also slype rods to insert crossover and side handles into a weave and to taper the pegs that hold handles in place. Slyped rods can have one, two, or three, long or short cuts, but the points must always be firm.

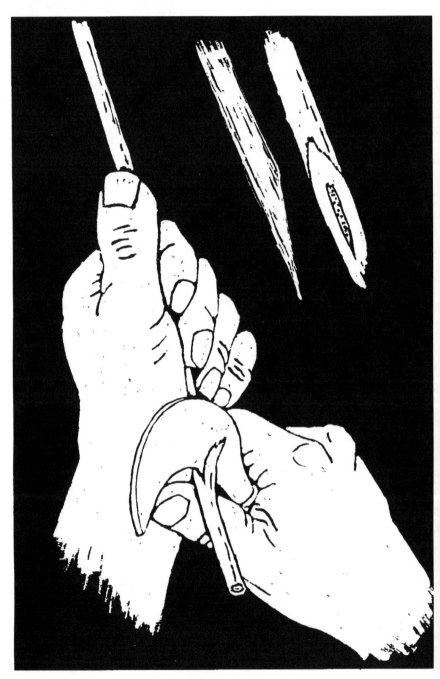

143

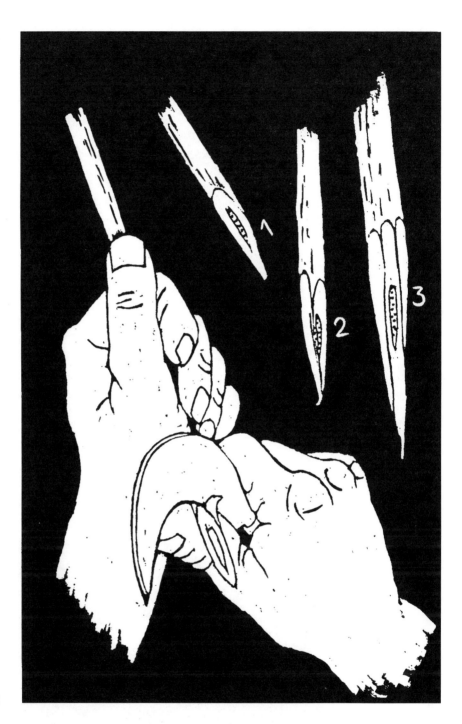

144

The first cut Your knife and your thumb work together as a shave when you slype the end of a rod, as shown in drawing 143. Keep a distance of about 1 cm between your thumb and the cutting edge of the knife. Adjust the angle of the blade to get the cut you want. You can slype off thick or very thin shavings. Your left hand holds the rod on top of the thumb of your right hand and under the blade.

You can then pull the knife in your right hand toward your body in one short, quick motion. In the process the thumb is raised a bit, but the blade never comes into contact with it. This first cut require some practice. Rods with only one cut can be used as stakes in large rectangular bases.

The second cut Still holding the rod in the left hand, give it a quarter-turn and repeat the cut described above, as shown in drawing 144.

The cut must contain an edge of the pith of the previous cut and the woody point. This will create a strong and sturdy point that can be inserted easily into the weave. If the point consists only of pith, you have to repeat the cut. The cut should be 2 to 2.5 cm long. If the point is too short, it's difficult to insert and secure; if too long, it breaks easily. Stakes for round bases must be slyped twice to fit the space, which is usually conical.

The third cut Thick sticks may be irregularly shaped. Frequently, when they are harvested, they crack at the butt ends.

We slype them three times firmly. The cut surfaces make up three quarters of the rod's circumference. Crossover and side handles that will be wrapped must be slyped three times.

Working with the natural curve Every rod or stick has a curved butt end. As the willow grows toward the light, it sends its shoots out from the stump and produces this natural curve.

If the basket wall will be at a right angle to the base of the basket, then the butt of the rod must be cut on the back, or outer edge, of the natural curve. Then, when the point is inserted (the flat cut angled upward), the rod stands straight.

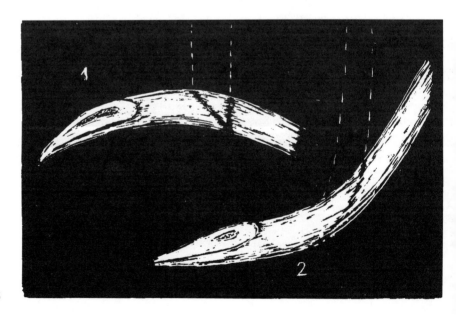

145

On the other hand, if you intend to make a rounded or spherical shape, cut the slypes on the inside of the natural curve to further accentuate the natural curve of the rod.

Scalloming

A very long cut along the length of one end of the rod is called a scallom. This can be made in a number of ways.

Straight scallom   To make a straight scallom, the rod is split and smoothed into a skein for 30 to 40 cm of its length. To do this, you use a sickle-shaped, scalloming knife. Cut halfway through the rod and then split it down to its end to form a long, curved taper.

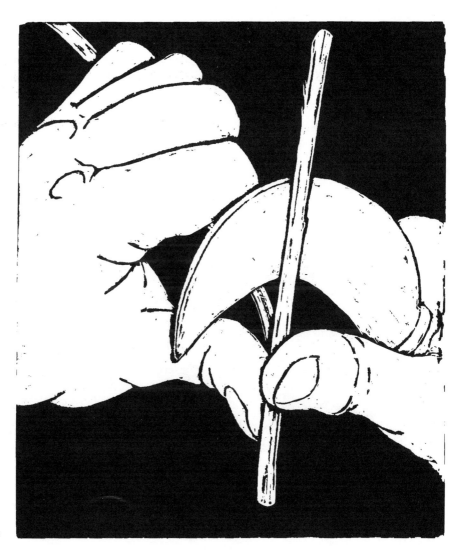

146

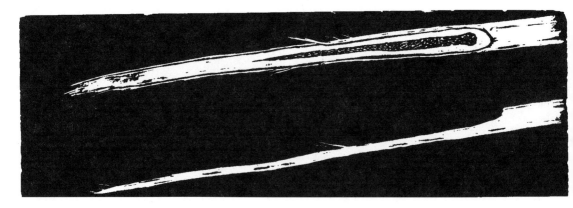

147

Use: This skeinlike end can be used on ribbed, or frame, baskets to connect the center stake with the ring (see p. 244). For rings around platters, give the ends overlapping, diagonal cuts so they fit together tightly and smoothly.

Domed scallom   This scallom, which is somewhat more diagonally cut, consists of three parts, as shown in the drawing below.
A: Shown here in side view, this cut dips. This is the area that can hold a section of rod in place, as illustrated.
B: To make this second part of the domed scallom, the edge of the knife cuts back through the diameter to form a belly. This section stops the rod being held from slipping out.
C: The heel thins all the way to the end. It strengthens the scallom and gives the surrounding rods purchase on it.

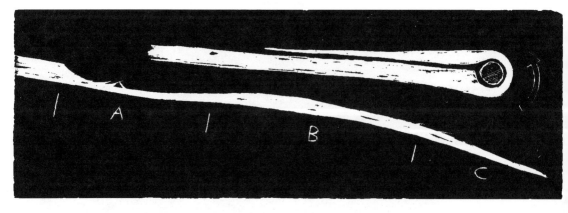

148

Use: The domed scallom is needed for the platter project on p. 230. There are also openwork and skeined baskets whose stakes are tied to the outer edge of the base ring with domed scalloms.

132

Marking

Nicking the rod is a traditional way to mark the height of the weave on the stakes or for marking the total height of the basket's wall before the border is made. This method of course is quite easy when working with brown willow. You cut the bark once deeply and take off a bit of bark to mark the spot. You only need to make a couple of marks around the basket.

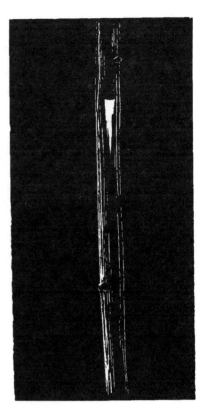

149

Pricking Up

There are various ways to do this. Each particular method is designed for a specific purpose in basketmaking.

With your thumbnail When working delicate baskets, press a groove into the damp rod with your thumbnail. The rod can then be turned up easily.

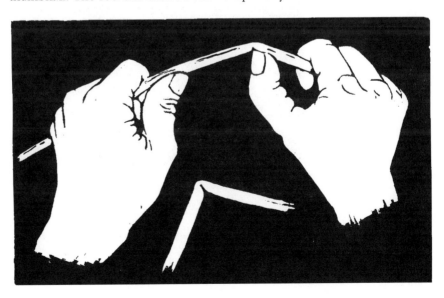

150

With the awl   An awl is used to prick up thick rods, including those stakes that must be inserted into the base and bent at a right angle. Applying a little pressure, bore a small hole into the rod with the awl at the point where you want to make the bend. Rock the awl back and forth before removing it. If the rods have been properly soaked, they should not break.

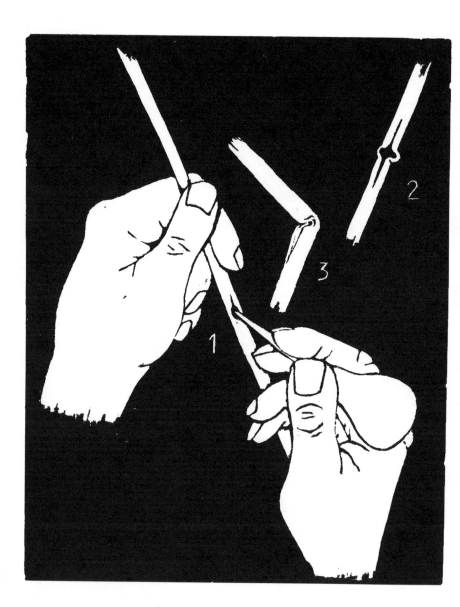

151

With a knife   For a rod that will need to be bent into a 90° angle, you first cut a V-shaped chip out of the wood. (Of course, you can make the cut any angle you require.) This method for pricking up can be used in any project that requires a rectangular frame, for example, some lids and handle cores.

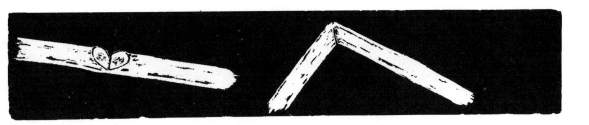

152

With pliers If you have marked the exact dimensions of the piece you are working on, you can easily pinch a cross into the rod with pliers. This pinched rod is ready to bend. This is the method used for furniture and supporting frames.

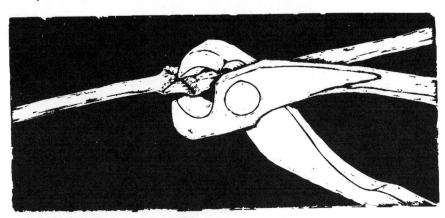

153

154

With round-nosed pliers Pricking up is part of the start of a border. The first few rods at the rim edge are pinched with round-nosed pliers, allowing you to neatly and easily control the bends and the spacing. You can also finish the border more easily.

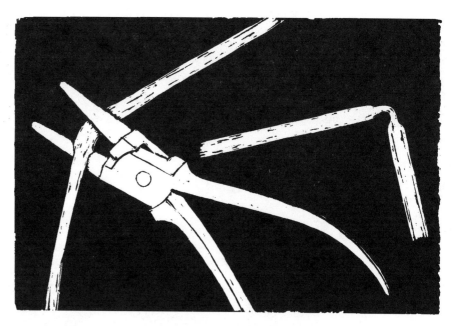

155

Bending by weaving Every basketmaker is aware of the fact that each time a stroke is made, the rods naturally kink slightly. The kink should occur at the point where the weaver meets the stake. When it is off the mark, the results do not have an even, professional appearance.

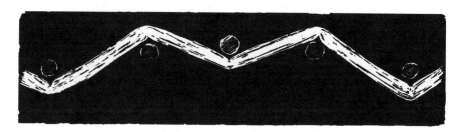

156

Practice exercise

157

This simple willow triangle can be made with rods of various lengths or diameters. You can also pinch more than one round, which results in one triangle's overlapping another. Several of these together can be used to make a mobile. Experiment with the various ways of pricking up as you make it.

Rapping

Rapping is an important part of making many kinds of baskets, regardless of whether they are tightly or loosely woven. Rapping reduces the intervals between the woven rods. This technique creates a solid, durable weave structure with a uniform appearance. Whether you use multiple whole willow rods for French randing, or single rods for weaving ribbed baskets, you need to rap them down. If the weave structures are not rapped, the rods loosen as they dry, and the baskets lose their shape.

Rapping sticks
Basketmakers used to rap their work with a rapping stick made of ash or another hardwood, as shown in the drawing below. The wood tool was easy on the rods and didn't damage them, but you had to use more force to compress the weave structure successfully.

Rapping irons
Today, basketmakers more often use rapping irons, whose weight makes them easier to use and more versatile.

The edge of your hand
You can also rap a weave structure down with the outer edge of your hand. This is especially effective with brown willow.

158

Fingertips	If the basket's weft is made up of skeins, you need to rap more gently. Simply compress the weave with your fingertips.
Heavy irons	At the other extreme, a block weave requires frequent rapping with a heavy iron. In this dense, 2/2 weave, the rods completely cover the stakes.

Cranking

Cranking is a pretty tricky technique. You'll produce quite a bit of waste when you try it for the first time.

Cranking, also called twisting, makes the willow less fragile and more pliant. Depending on the purpose, you can crank either short sections or whole rod lengths.

159

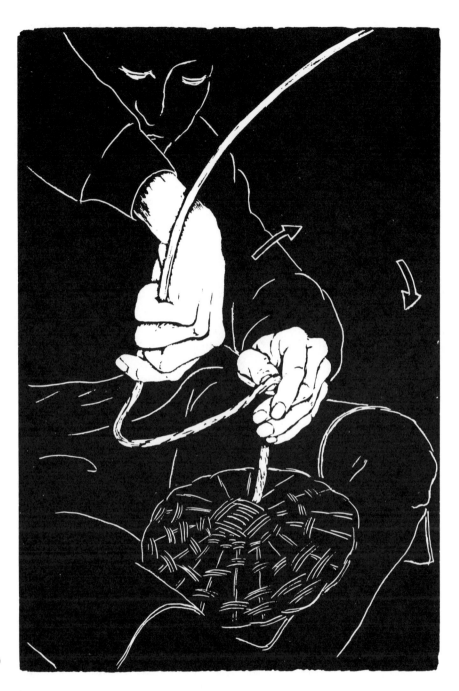

160

Single twist   We put a single twist into a rod before inserting it into a basket's base to start the bottom waling. Rods are also twisted in openwork when starting a fitch. We'll also twist a rod if it accidentally splits during weaving, or before it is worked in difficult spots where it might be likely to break, for example at the start of a border, or within a braided or roped border.

Twisting whole rods

Whole rods are cranked to make a variety of crossover handles, side handles, and hinges. One end of the rod is anchored in the weave structure in the body of the basket. The left hand acts as a vise and an axis, loosely holding the rod vertically and allowing it to turn. The right hand holds the rod about 30 cm above the left hand and cranks the rod around from left to right, as shown on pp. 138-139. The fingers of the left hand should allow the twist to climb up the rod—don't block it. Slowly slide the cranking hand up the rod until the whole length is twisted. Leave the final 20 cm of rod behind the right hand untwisted. You will insert that untwisted length later into the weave; if twisted, it would be too soft to do so. This technique is mainly used for rope handles, closures, loops, and hinges (see p. 325).

Both the rod and your fingers must be wet while you are working. Once you have twisted the rod, don't let it go. If you do, the twist will come out, and you'll have to start all over again. If the rod starts to double up on itself and form knots, you've twisted it too much.

A twisted rod gives the weave structure unbelievable pliancy and robust character. You can see this in lidded-basket handles, which are made of one twisted rod that is then double-plied.

Variation: Many basketmakers prefer the reverse way of twisting. They let the work hang from the rod that is being twisted and rotate the work so that it twists the rod. If you use this method, you might find it useful to stand with your feet apart and suspend the work in front of you, between your legs.

Practice exercise

The knot shown below was made simply by twisting one end of a rod. Bundles of sorted willow were often bound with a twisted rod and a knot like this. Its simplicity invites you to experiment.

161

Double Ply

When two strands of yarn are twisted together the result is called a double ply. Willows can be double-plied as well.

Use   Double plies are often used to make the loops found on woven trunks and suitcases. They are also used to make side handles, as added decoration on openwork, and to make certain kinds of crossover handles, as well as to reinforce and hold the various styles of borders with unwoven stakes.

Procedure   Usually, you anchor two rods that are well soaked and of the same thickness beside each other in the weave.

First rod: One rod is cranked clockwise, as described on p. 139, while holding it tightly between your knees.

Second rod: Work the second rod the same way, cranking it in the same direction. Now, hold one rod in each hand. Stretching the two rods taut,

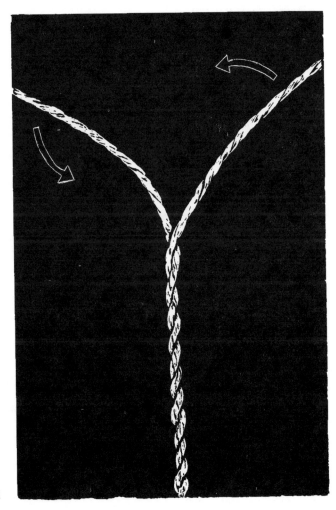

162

wrap them around each other from right to left (counterclockwise), in other words, in the direction opposite the direction of their individual twists.

Don't let go of either rod while plying them together. Keep them taut so the twist will be even. A well-made double ply will look like twine or cord—full, without any gaps. Keep the rods and your hands wet while working.

Another method

The double ply for crossover handles and rope handles is made somewhat differently. Both ends of the first twisted rod are inserted into the weave structure. The "second rod," in fact, the continuation of the first, is twisted and then wrapped around the first to create the double ply (see p. 225).

It's fun to see how two common willow rods can be made into a cord with all the characteristics of twine. Double twists can of course be made from the rods or stalks of other plants. In Tibet hanging bridges are made completely out of double-plied plant fiber. This gives you some idea of how strong an otherwise fragile material can be when plied.

Practice exercise

Decorative loops and flower shapes can be made from double-plied rod tips, as shown in the drawing, using these same techniques.

163

Wrapping

Use   Wrapping is done mainly with skeins, more rarely with whole willow. Crossover handles, bridges on two-lidded baskets, base or lid centers, furniture frames, and decorations are often wrapped. A favorite wrapped object is a ring, sometimes in oval form. These rings are used as closure loops, side handles, dainty crossover handles, chains, and decoration on baskets. In Oberfranken, arm bracelets are wrapped with extremely delicate willow skeins in a wide variety of patterns. Skeined baskets are frequently finished with a wrapped border.

A large wrapped item, typical of Switzerland, is the Alpine horn. In the old days, it was held together naturally with willow skeins, which were uprighted by hand. Today, it's wrapped with flat cane and varnished heavily, and so has lost its original character.

Procedure   The following technique for wrapping a bow handle contains all the details necessary to understand the wrapping process. To begin, you need something to wrap. One or several rods positioned side by side will do; a thick shaving or a stick can also serve as the core.

Place the end of a wet skein, inner side up, on the surface of the core, and parallel to it, as shown in drawing 164. Bend the skein at a right angle (the outer, bark side will now be facing up) and wrap it tightly around the object. The next wrap is positioned directly beside the first. If you are wrapping a bend or a curve, you will require more material on the outer edge than on the inner edge. Allow the skeins to overlap by about one-third their widths on the inner curve; then they'll fit snugly on the outer curve.

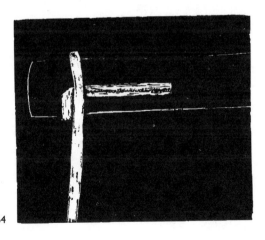

164

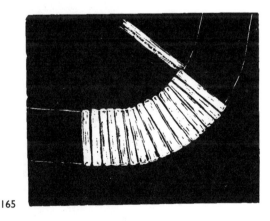

165

Decorative patterns   If you want to make a more complex, decorative pattern, work in crosspieces of tips or thin skeins, as shown on p. 144. The wrapped skeins can be worked over or under these. Choose materials and patterns that complement the style and design of the basket.

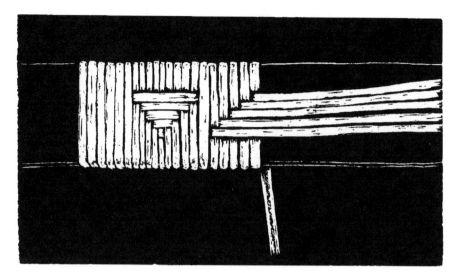

166

Adding on   Skeins are limited in length, so you'll often need to start a new one. When you add on a new skein, the one you are working must still be long enough to make about another four to five wrappings. The new skein is placed, inner side up, parallel to the core, in the same way that you started the first skein. Now wrap the first skein over 4 cm of the new one. Twist the old and new skeins together in such a way that the new one has its outer, bark side facing up, and the old one has its inner side facing up. Continue wrapping the new skein, covering the end of the first skein as you work, as shown in the drawing below.

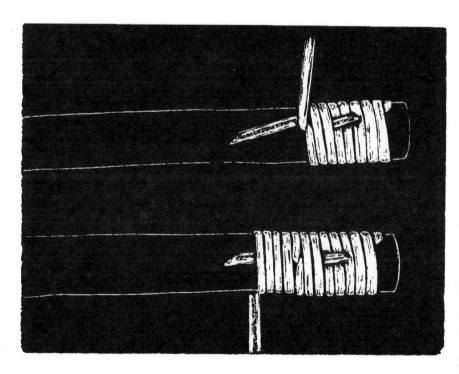

167

Rings present basketmakers with endless design possibilities, through varied skein widths and colors, core diameter and thickness, and techniques of layering and crossing.

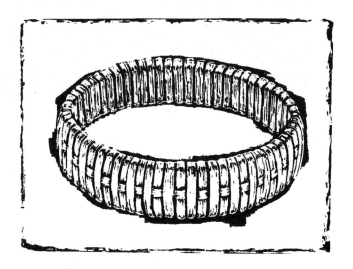

168

Lashing, or Sewing

You can also stitch with willow, and you don't even need a needle. Where the material is too tightly packed, you can use an awl to bore a hole through the material.

Sewing connects, fastens, covers, and has ornamental value in your willow basketmaking. The technique can even by used to create complete surfaces.

"Lashing" is a more precise term for sewing with willow, which results in bound or secured basket parts. Lashing involves some wrapping, combined with the sewing motion of working down and through one woven surface and up and through the adjacent one.

Where lashing is used

- On delicate baskets and bowls, basketmakers often sew on a foot made of one rod or skein to stabilize and protect the base.
- If skeins are used as stakes in a project, the border is not made with the stakes, but rather with other skeins that are sewn on, as shown in drawing 339 on p. 270.
- In the assembly-line, mass-production of willow baskets, one worker makes bases, which are then sewn onto finished bodies, which have been made by somebody else.
- Lashed, or so-called tied-on bases, are found on more delicate basketry. Drawing 169 on p. 146 shows the underside of a lashed base. The slath is held together by the lashing and the warp stakes are fastened to each other at intervals. The whole is then lashed together through the stakes. On the far left and right, two stakes are lashed together as one.

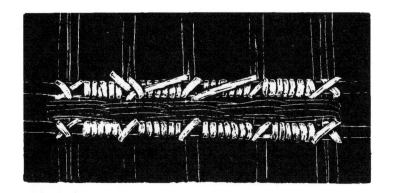

169

- Entire surfaces can be designed with lashing. If you decide to use this technique, form a spiral around the basket with a weaving rod, which is then lashed to the warp stakes. This results in what is known as an open weave.
- Willow skeins are sometimes used to sew together brown willow containers.

Procedure Fine or delicate stakes, whether they are skeins or thin rods, are frequently lashed onto the base of the basket. They may be too soft to insert, so they are sewn, or lashed, on with a sewing skein. Two clefts are used to hold the stakes in place, as shown in the drawing below. With an awl, open up the weave a couple of rows from the outer edge of the finished base. Insert the wet skein downward through and then up around the two clefts encircling the edge of the base. Now, clamp one stake between the two clefts and make a second stitch like the first. There should be one stitch between each of the stakes, which also provides clearance between them.

The bodies of these finer baskets are often made with the help of a wood frame, because it's impossible to work the soft, wet, skein stakes without one, as they lack stiffness. (There are also wood forms, or molds, around

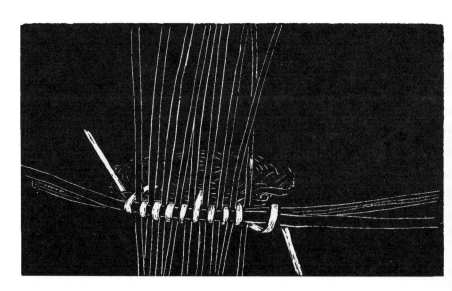

170

146

which you can weave baskets. They consist of several parts so they can be removed more easily once the basket is finished. Some have only an upper and a lower part.)

The small skein basket shown on p. 256 has lashing at the base of the siding. It strengthens the basket and is decorative.

Broken Rods

Warp stakes

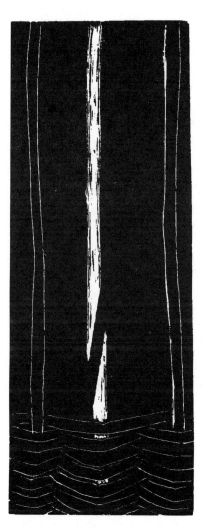

171

Split, broken, or otherwise damaged stakes must be replaced as you weave, although they should not have to be replaced very often.

Procedure: If a stake breaks off at the edge of the work, unweave one weaving rod. Slype the broken end of the stake, and weave up to the edge of the slype cut. Then position a replacement stake, which has been slyped at the complementary angle, against the broken rod to form a straight stake, as shown in the drawing at left.

Weft rods   To repair broken weaving rods, leave the broken end behind the weave (inside the basket). Find a section of rod with the same diameter as the broken end and of the same length as the piece that has broken off. Start the new piece at the stake at which the broken rod ends, and continue weaving.

147

172

Border   Weaving rods are easily broken when you're working a border. Cut the broken rod close to the top of the woven surface. Insert a new, slyped rod to the left of the cut end, as shown in the drawing above. When turned down, the new rod will cover the small mistake.

173

Staking Up

The closer the stakes are set together and the tighter the weaving rods are compressed, the denser the weave structure will appear. (This is, of course, only true when the materials are of consistent thickness.)

The purpose of staking up is to add stakes in order to allow the form of the basket to expand. The additional stakes provide more warp to support the weave and strengthen the basket.

Where staking up is used	We stake up round bases that have large diameters and oval basket bases that start with a strip of wood (such as that of the openwork laundry basket, as shown on p. 288). Stakes are also added to the frame of the ribbed-basket project, as shown on p. 248.

Some baskets whose shapes widen also need to be staked up. If you are working a shape that gets narrower, however, you may need to reduce the number of stakes in the frame.

Staking up is almost always required as part of working the upsett of the finished base, before you begin the basket's siding. One or two additional stakes are inserted alongside each of the original base stakes (as for the projects on p. 175 and p. 211)

How to stake up, or bistake	When the stakes have spread too far apart (which depends on the weaving pattern and the thickness of the material), it's time to add new stakes. They must be as thick as those already in the frame, and slyped twice (p. 129). Be sure your hands are dry. Insert the new stakes on one or both sides of the existing stakes. Depending on the basket's shape and how strong a weave structure it requires, you may not need to insert new stakes at every existing stake, but be consistent in the patterning. Open up the new and old stakes to make room for the weaving rods. You can also work the paired stakes as if they were one stake for one or more rounds. These bistakes give the weave a uniform tension and resiliency.

174

Insert thicker stakes	To insert thicker stakes into the basket, you need to work with an awl, as described on p. 199.

Effect	Bistakes can have a design function as well as a structural function. They can be used to intentionally create special effects in the surface of the woven structure.

149

Wetting Down

The following descriptions will mention wetting down repeatedly to maintain the rods' pliability. This is accomplished by sprinkling, brushing, soaking, or mellowing (wrapping rods in wet cloth after soaking). The drier the air, the more wetting down the rods will need. Peeled willow, in particular, must be kept damp, and you'll need to wet it down often while working. When buff willow begins to dry out, you'll notice the color lightens. Brown willow, because of its long soaking time and its bark, doesn't dry out as fast.

Tools A dustpan brush is a very practical tool for wetting down the work. The water drips come off the brush in a spray. Unlike a sponge, the brush also provides some relief for your hands, which are already wet much of the time. A sprayer can wear out your fingers.

175

Hand Positions for Weaving

Using your hands well is a matter of practice. In order to get successful results and avoid weariness, it's essential to position your fingers properly. Speed, precision, and rhythm all depend on this. How you move your fingers also determines whether or not the basket's weave is even. Willow basketry requires the maker to work quickly and purposefully (which is not to say at breakneck speed). The longer you work on a basket, the drier the willow becomes, and this affects the quality of the finished basket.

Even the bright, flat rattle of the rods slapping together can convey whether the work is being held properly or not. The sound is evenly interrupted by the light "tang, tang" of the rapping iron.

176

The five fingers of the left hand are also necessary tools. In general, the left hand supports and moves the work, corrects the stake intervals, and holds the rods about to be woven.

The right hand does the actual weaving. In order to work a series of rands, the thumb and index finger carry the weaving rod (or rods) behind a stake, from the left side. The middle and ring fingers of the right hand catch the weaver on the right side of the stake and position it in the next interval. Throughout the process, the right little finger steers and supports. Once the rod is in position, the left thumb and index finger press the rod against the previous rows of weaving. The thumb presses in such a way that the rod gets a light kink where it crosses the stake. The rest of the left hand is in an interval to the left, pressing down on the already woven rods. These movements should be fluent and have their own up-and-down rhythm.

This may sound complicated, but with practice, the sequence of moves become understandable and eventually mastered.

Picking Off

When the weaving is finished, we pick off all the ends that are sticking out of the basket. This step should not be underestimated. Finished work that is cleanly picked off reflects good-quality workmanship and professional pride. The fact that picking off is often neglected has lead to a common belief that basketry items are somehow second-rate. After all, aluminum and plastic goods don't have these rough ends. The picked-off ends, especially those below the border, are a visual continuation of the rods beside them, and their irregularity adds interest to the weave structure.

Baskets that will be used should not have any leftover bits of rod sticking out of the weave, either inside or outside the basket. If you intend to line the basket, plan so that all the ends are left inside the basket (behind the weave). For other items, you may choose to leave all the ends outside (in front of) the weave.

Trimming the ends

We use the picking knife (pp. 96-97) to remove all the ends protruding from the basket's base and wall, inside and out. As you work, be careful not to damage or cut through the neighboring rods. If the rods are clipped too much, they'll slip through the weave structure and create a hole. On the other hand, if the ends are not cut flush to the surface, they'll annoy the basket's user.

Checking your work

Run the palm of your hand across the woven surface to check for any remaining protruding ends. This will ensure the basket won't later catch on clothing or nearby objects.

Letting the ends protrude

There are some instances in which you would leave all the ends lying untrimmed inside the basket. For example, there is an old form of basketry-covered bottle that had a straw or hay lining between the bottle and the basket. The lining was held in place by the uncut ends, and the fragile container and its liquid contents were well protected.

Some designers intentionally use untrimmed ends as a design element in their basketry.

Weaving Techniques

There are numerous basketry techniques, and you often find many used together in the same basket in such as way that it is difficult to clearly distinguish and classify them.

The basket projects described and shown in the second part of this book are all examples of "stake-and-strand" weaving. This style of weaving is characterized by a rigid framework (or warp) that supports the rods (or weft) that pass over and under it.

Stake-and-strand weaving is the most widespread technique for working willow. Other basketry techniques, such as coiling or diagonal plaiting, are often integrated into stake-and-strand to create borders, feet, and crossover and rope handles, and to loosen up the structure of the weave.

The techniques of wrapping and lashing, discussed in the previous chapter, and the technique of upsetting, explained in the description of the shopping basket that begins on p. 175, are also weaving techniques. Unlike the other techniques explained here, however, these cannot be combined simply as you wish.

The following is a summary of the most well known willow-weaving techniques. The list begins with those structures in which the material is simply woven over and under (as plaiting), and is followed by structures in which a single passive stake is locked by an active strand (that is, stake-and-strand).

Weave structures made with whole willows are referred to as coarse, medium, or tight, depending on how loosely or tightly they are woven.

The Corndolly Weave

This weave structure, which is derived from a netmaking technique, is marginal in willow basketry.

Traditionally, it's used on the ends of chair legs, as well as for lid handles, basketry decoration, baby's rattles, and sometimes also as walls for small baskets. Some people use the technique when weaving straw.

The technique   The corndolly technique begins with a star-shaped arrangement of rods, which together form the weave. The first rod is turned down to the right,

over the two beside it. The second rod passes over the one already turned down and one more. The work continues and the materials assumes a spiral shape. Use very flexible, thin rods.

Form The corndolly weave can be used to form a spiral-patterned disc, a screw-like cylinder, or a cone.

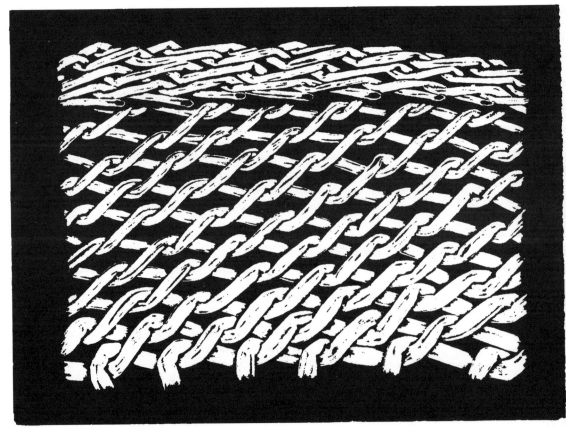

The length of the rods limits the size of the woven object. They cannot be woven back and forth. The technique can be used to make a loose or tight weave structure.

The Trac Weave

This is a specialty technique that was once very widespread. The weave structure appears dynamic and open. The trac weave (or Madeira border) is related to diagonal weaving, but its unique characteristic is the fact that it creates its own border.

Although many northern European basketmakers are familiar with it, the trac weave is more popular with basketmakers in the Mediterranean areas. In Spain, they work trac weave to make baskets with a high foot, which the women carry on their heads. (A wonderful, four-strand fruit basket is depicted in a painting by the artist Caravaggio, dated 1596.)

Technique A trac weave can be combined with another weave structure by staking up a base with several stakes added beside each original base stake. These new stakes must be as thin, long, and as pliant as possible. Working from one direction to the other, all the stakes are turned down so that they are at the desired

height of the woven basket. Then, their tips, which are now pointing downward, are woven diagonally over and under the groups of adjacent butts.

In drawing 179 on p. 155, reading from right to left, you can see the following: A group of four rods is turned over the group of rods to the left, then under the next group, then over the next. The rod groups bite the tails, so to speak, of the ones lying beside them. The work continues in this way until all the groups are woven, and the structure is manipulated so that the groups lie more or less together. The rods in each group must always remain neatly together, so that all the tips are at the outer edge of the base. Some people also use trac weave to make a braid or a foot.

Form In its purest form, trac weave can be constructed flat, in the shape of a platter, or into a gently sloped, bowl shape. The size will depend on the length of the rods. In trac weave, you use only one rod length; the weave cannot be increased or extended.

A particular style of carpet beater is made with a similar weave called the knot weave. The knot weave, however, requires that the weaving rods start and end in the same place. The bowl in the drawing is made with a knot weave with six groups of five rods.

The most well known way of using trac weave is as a basket wall with a border or foot. The base can be round, oval, or a flared oval. The technique is not suitable for back-and-forth weaving.

180

Texture Trac weave can be woven tightly or loosely, depending on the amount of tension you maintain. Generally, the groups include two to eight rods. The angle at which the rods cross may also vary from a gradual to a very sharp angle, depending on the length and number of strokes. This allows for great variation in the finished effect.

The Open Check Weave

This weave, known also as basket weave, could be considered the most basic weave of all. The warp and weft elements are simply interwoven to create an interlocking structure.

This type of weave can also be worked in a diagonal direction, as shown at far left in the drawing on p. 158, or in three or more directions, as shown at right in the drawing. In multidirectional weaving, no one direction is predominate.

Using this weave, delicate willow skeins can be worked into bowls, sieves, capped flasks, lidded boxes, trays, or furniture.

Another variation is the closed, crossed weave made of skeins (plaiting), shown in the wrapped pattern in drawing 166, p. 144.

181	**Technique**	The skeins are placed in one direction on a frame or on a wood form, or mold, of a basket body. The crosspieces are woven over and under them. Especially when weaving items on a form, the passive elements can become active and the active passive. It is simply a matter of interlacing all the elements equally.
	Form	With an open check weave, surfaces can be woven back and forth. You do not work more than one skein in any one direction.

You can create the base of the basket with another type of weave structure and incorporate the open check weave into it.

If stakes are attached for weaving to be done parallel to the border, large basket bodies constructed with open check weave could almost be considered a type of stake weaving. A basketmaker might also use open check weave to create a circular weave, or might use staked and circular techniques on the same basket. Spiral-shaped weaving is also possible, but is not used very often.

Texture The surface of open check weave is smooth and therefore good for the items mentioned on p. 157. The round profile of whole willow is not suitable for this pattern. Flat materials can be worked closely enough together to create a closed surface, but whole willow can't.

The most popular stroke is the shortest—over one and under one (1/1). This pattern will create a surface that can be embroidered or embellished if the basketmaker chooses to do so. Randing patterns, in all their variations (2/2, 1/3, 2/5, and progressing each row by one or more), are also possible to work in those structures whose skein intervals are not too large.

Color The flat, smooth surfaces of open check weave make it easy to introduce color into the patterning. Colors can be combined to create effects that themselves become the predominant design.

Coiled Work

Coiling is an extremely old technique. In areas where there is an abundance of willow, the wrapping skeins needed for coiled work often are made of unpeeled clefts. Raffia bast, palm leaves, rush, and hazelnut skeins are also sometimes used. The core or foundation consists of straw, seagrass, rush, wood shavings, round cane, brambleberry shoots, or other plant materials.

Coiling was used to make old-fashioned beehives, baking bowls, storage containers, and stitched bowls, which are fine shapes completely coiled in willow. It was also used to make mugs and flasks that were then sealed with birch resin.

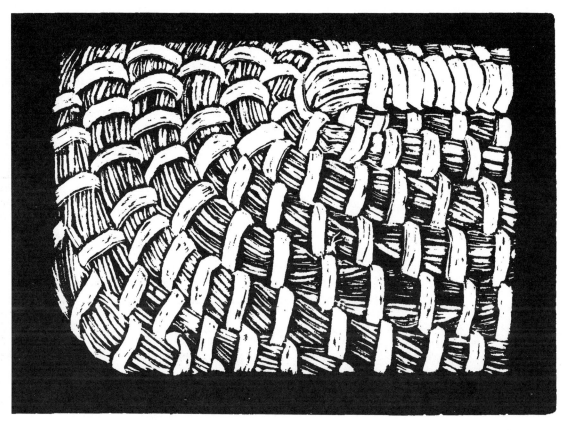

183

Technique   The technique of coiled work involves sewing, or lashing, the core or foundation with a "thread," that is, the skein.

The skein wraps around two or three coils and pierces the sewing skein just under it, or is inserted through the previous coil and secured to it. (The core in drawing 184 consists of thick shavings of wood.)

Coiled work might also involve a type of knotted lashing. The technique is very popular and widespread, among those working with palm leaves, for example, because it is very sturdy. The interlocking stitch is like the hemstitch made when sewing fabric.

159

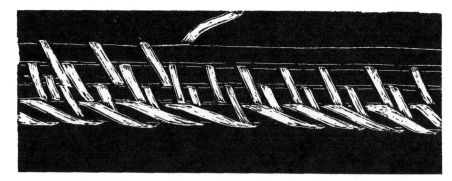

184

| Form | The coil forms a spiral, which starts at the center of the base of the woven piece. It can be used to produce round, flat platters or shallow bowls with a raised edge—either circular, oval, or oval with cornered edges. Coiling can be worked back and forth, but this is rarely done. |

| Texture | The core or foundation can be thick or thin, smooth or bristly, round or flat (flat cores usually consist of bundles of shavings). Usually the coils are closely packed together, but they can also be separated by knots (this is known as mariposa stitch or palm-leaf work). Coiled skein work can be worked so that the foundation is completely covered or open, with widely spaced stitches. Pattern variations can also be created by different stitches and colors. |

French Randing

French randing is also simply an over-and-under weave. It is the most commonly used weave structure for the bodies of willow baskets. It is a weave par excellence—sensible and advantageous—for working whole willow. The round rods are angled slightly in the intervals between the stakes.

| Technique | For detailed descriptions of how to work a French rand and examples of its finished appearance see the shopping-basket project, p. 190, and the lidded baskets on p. 215 and p. 223. |

| Form | The French rand is a 1/1 weave, in which one rod is added in each interval to the left of the previous rod. It produces a compact weave structure with an upward, diagonal line. It is not generally woven back and forth. |

| Texture | The texture of French randing is that of rounded thin and thick sections, unless the basket is worked with clefts or skeins.
To give the basket rigidity and strength, basketmakers usually start the rand with the thick butt end of the rod. The second band, begun when the first is entirely woven, is also started with the butt end. The resulting effect of the changes in the diameter of the rod from butt to tip is that of wavelike repetitions (especially visible on tall baskets), which create a lovely rhythm. |

185

The individual bands of randing can be emphasized or intentionally broken up with waling or other weaving techniques.

Planning The thickness and length of the rods, density and circumference of the basket, number of stakes, and shape of the basket all influence the height and the diameter of the bands of French randing.

Number of rows Two rows of randing of the same size spoil the overall appearance. They seem to divide the basket in two. A whole and a half row would look better. You can also separate bands with another pattern.

French slewing French slewing is French randing with more than one weaver. In the interval between each stake, there are two or more weavers, stacked on top of each other and woven as one (see p. 207).

Stake pattern Basketmakers who enjoy adding a decorative touch to their baskets frequently add stakes, with the help of additional rows of weaving. They insert the slyped ends of the stakes into the bottom waling and then into the top waling of the finished weave at regular intervals, as shown in the drawing on p. 154. These added stakes cover the crossing rods, and create an attractive vertical line along the wall of the basket.

186

Color   The weave structure's plain surface allows the creative use of dyed rods.

Randing

As the German name for the weave (literally, "fence weave") suggests, fences, gates, and walls were often constructed with this weaving technique. Many are illustrated in copperplate prints and paintings from the Middle Ages. Woven fences have stood for hundreds of years, and today they are viewed both as property demarcations and artistic creations.

Randing on a round basket can also be worked as a chase weave, and so, the two terms are often combined (chase randing). People also refer to weaving rods as "fence rails," which wind around "fence posts." Harvest baskets (broad and oval, round, or rectangular) also remind one of fencing around crops in a field.

Technique   The directions for a tray made using randing begin on p. 305. The technique is quite simple and rustic in finished appearance.

Form   You can best use this weave for squarework (rectangular bases and lids for baskets, paravents, and furniture). It can also be worked on round lids and bases, and on ribbed shapes. Block weave is a variation on randing.

187 **Texture** The tapered, round form of the thick and thin willow rods gives the weave structure its randomly varied appearance. The weave pattern is 1/1.

Block weave

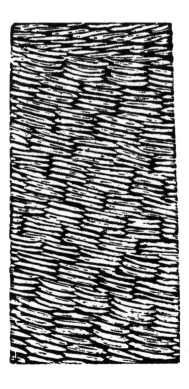

If you work a block weave, which is over two, under two (2/2), the weave structure is so dense that the stakes are completely enclosed and covered. After a certain number of rows, the point at which the rods cross advances by one stake to begin a new block. Block weaves are ideal for using up tips and leftover rods, which will not reduce the solid quality of the surface structure. A basketmaker can use the block weave to create a number of varied designs.

188

Randing with skeins   Skeins can be randed, over and under stakes, back and forth as well as round and round. They can also be used for chase randing, as is the skeined-basket project on p. 267.

The stakes can be either thin whole rods or heavy skeins. The weaving skeins are woven around the stakes, which are positioned more closely together if they are thin rods than if they are skeins. Skeined stakes are lashed to the frame, as shown in drawing 170 on p. 146.

The delicately corrugated structure, often interrupted with rows of waling, lends itself well to decoration with woven motifs. These motifs are usually 1/1 patterns, but there are endless design possibilities. The width of the skeins, the density of the weave, and the color are also variables for consideration. There are also innumerable types of finishes, rings, crossover handles, feet, and basket shapes to choose from. Then there are so many options, it's important to know which one (or several) you want to emphasize.

Skeins woven in a randing pattern create a much denser structure than skeins woven in an open check weave.

(You'll find more examples of twill variations woven with skeins in the top two drawings on p. 338.)

189

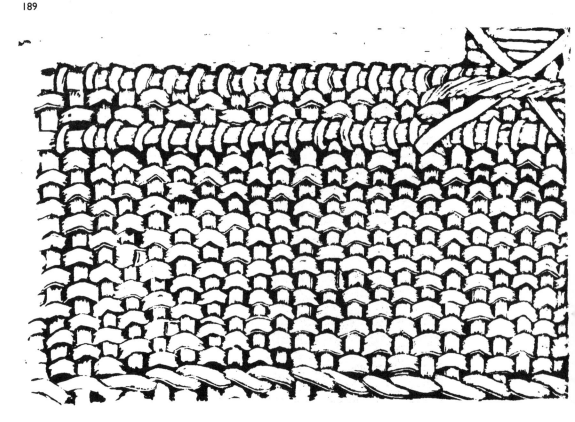

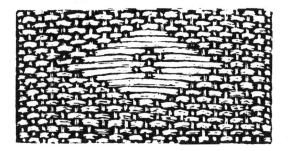

190

Flat skein weave   One might consider the flat skein weave as the most noble of the weave structures. The bases and lids of finely constructed baskets are frequently woven this way. In days gone by, jewelry and utility baskets were worked completely with this time-consuming method.

The twisted-skein weave is particularly attractive. The skeins are set on edge in such a way that the light that filters through the surface appears bright or subdued, depending on the vantage point of the viewer. The surface is a texture of dense, flat waves. The difference between this and other randing patterns is that the skeins are woven on edge, not on their flat surfaces. The frame and the stakes are concealed. Flat skein weaves are usually woven 1/1.

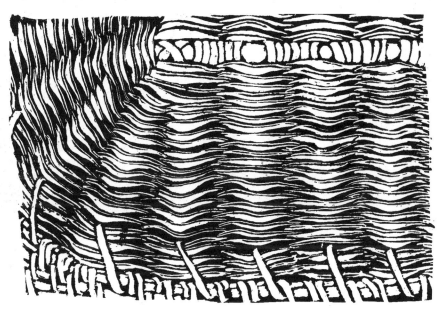

191

The Ribbed Basket Weave

The ribbed basket weave has a rustic character if it is worked with brown willow, and brown willow is the best material for it.

You can also work the ribbed basket weave with buff and white willow. Clefts, shavings, or skeins made from hazelnut, chestnut, ash, or fir roots create baskets that appear more uniform and lighter than those made of whole willow.

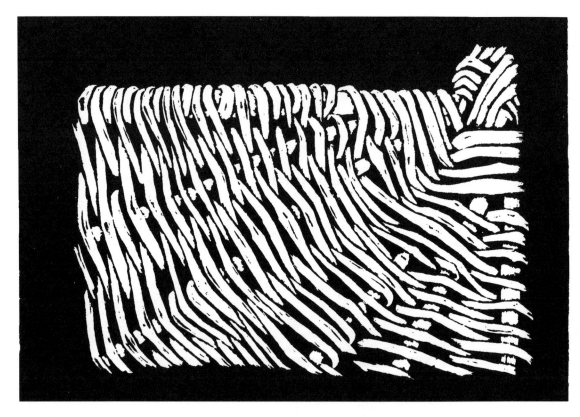

192   **Technique**   This can be worked back and forth, and so is considered a plain plaiting or rand. The ribs (warp) radiate from one end of the basket and converge at the opposite end. As the ribs draw closer together, they disappear one by one under the weaving (see p. 251).

Form   The special feature of the ribbed basket is that it doesn't need the usual base or border. It could be called a one-step basket. The oval is the most common shape; then round and rectangular oval.

Texture   The density of the weaving rods is usually greater than the density of the ribs. When worked back and forth, the pattern is usually over one and under one (1/1). Longer strokes cannot be worked as well. The texture appears more or less ribbed and corrugated.

166

Openwork

This open weave structure is found mainly in France and other Mediterranean countries. Openwork is often used for packaging for shipping fruits, vegetables, and small animals, and to construct cages for chickens and other fowl. Furniture and partitions are also made of openwork. Its construction is surprisingly rugged, despite its lightweight, loose appearance.

193

Technique The way in which you tie openwork is by fitching, or, as it is called in the textile industry, "twist-tying." The warp stakes are held in place by two rods, regularly spaced and positioned at a right angle to the stakes. Because there is no actual weave structure, this fitching is given a half-twist between the stakes to secure the frame. For large-scale production, basketmakers use wire rings to give the basket its shape and to maintain uniformity. The rings are removed after the basket is finished.

Form Openwork—whether round, oval, rectangular, or other—starts with a frame or ring. The platter on p. 230 has been made with openwork. The stakes are held to the base ring with scalloms (see p. 235).

194

Solid bases made of whole willow can be used on a basket with an openwork wall. The contrast of the closely woven base and the widely spaced wall is very attractive, and the effect is more dramatic than when both are done in openwork. Some items have no bases at all—for example, the willow fish trap shown in the drawing above. The functional form is determined solely by the natural lengths of the rods.

When you make tall baskets of openwork, several rounds of regularly spaced fitching are often necessary. Traditionally, the end of one row leads into the next, resulting in a upward spiral. When the rows of fitching are connected in this way, the wall of the basket is stronger and more attractive than when they are worked as separate rows.

Texture   Openwork textures are light and airy by definition. The number of stakes in the structure can vary. The density of the staking affects the density of the fitching. You can fitch stakes in pairs or in groups of three.

In a more complex variation, openwork can be worked diagonally as a continuous spiral. Whether the fitching is worked in several rows close together or in single rows depends on the final results you desire.

Sometimes sections of openwork alternate with woven surfaces. In this case, you must decide in advance where you want to weave and where you want to fitch, and how much you will do of each.

Design

Creativity in Basketry

The many, traditional basket projects presented in this book (beginning on p. 175) do not have very novel shapes. Rather, they have been known for thousands of years. So how can we design creatively? The material is determined, the shape is a given fact.

Yet we still continue to make baskets. For what purpose? To what end? Does some instinctive impulse to collect and shape material push us on? Whatever the answers to these questions, our goal is not simply to produce large numbers of baskets. As makers, we would like to become ever more intimately acquainted with the material and aware of its hidden design potential.

In addition to your manual skills, your perception and imagination will also be required. Almost every movement of the hand can give expression to a creative impulse. It's up to the basketmaker to take advantage of it.

Structure

A weave structure is not a random mass of material. It consists of individual elements that together make a whole with a specific texture.

If you consider today's home furnishings, often you'll find that smooth surfaces dominate. Structured surfaces may occasionally appear, but textured, relief surfaces are likely to be nearly absent. A woven object does not need to have a rough or engraved surface intentionally applied to it. Its very construction creates a lively surface texture.

There are many kinds of textures possible, as well. The determining factors are the material, its preparation, the weaving technique, and the varied results of the combinations of these:
- tight or open structure
- rough or smooth surface
- glossy or matte finish
- bright or dark coloring

The many types of willow plants available, discussed in the chapter "The Willow Plant" (p. 22), also opens a whole world of possibilities. In some cases, these materials can be incorporated into the basketry projects found in this book. The questions are: Which material should I select? Where is it most suitably used in the basket? How much should be used, and how frequently? Think carefully, and avoid unsuitable materials.

Let your hands be guided by your heart and head. This will invigorate the finished basket, and you will create a convincing work.

Surface and Shape

The metamorphosis of flexible, fragile rods into a woven surface or a strong basket that can carry objects or support weight is really something special. One should not just take it for granted, but rather experience it fully with the senses while weaving.

You can also look at other objects in this new light, and your perception of basketry will further be changed. When you are weaving warp and weft, you are partitioning space. These partitions can be considered as basic geometric shapes.

If you're working on a basket with a potbelly shape, you are not simply making a section of a sphere that extends outward. There are many considerations. The dome shape can form an arch or it can be made at a slight incline. Its highest point might be in its center, in the upper half, or in the lower half. Will the dome be circular, flattened, or sharply pointed? Is the diameter of the base larger or smaller than the diameter of the top rim?

The forms of natural objects also provide a rich supply of design ideas. This doesn't mean that you need to weave the specific shape of an apple, for example, but rather to sense the essential qualities of the fruit's surface and shape and to create a woven object that reflects those same qualities—without losing sight of the intended function and size of the basket you're making.

These basic, natural shapes will also determine how the baskets are constructed. The baskets on the next pages are grouped by shape and not by the weaving techniques used to make them.

Geometric shapes The cone—in fact, the up-ended base of a cone—is the shape found most frequently in basketmaking. The next most common is the cylinder, which usually opens up slightly toward the border (otherwise the shape appears to narrow toward the top). The sphere, or rather a segment of a sphere, can be seen in the ribbed basket shown on p. 253.

Oval baskets are as popular as round baskets. Drawing 196 illustrates a rectangle, which is the basis for the shape of the squarework baskets (p. 304) and the stool (p. 326). The obelisk with its trapezoidal sides is the foundation for harvest baskets, wastepaper baskets, and baby carriages.

The rectangular, truncated pyramid may be found more frequently in finely woven baskets, made with skeins.

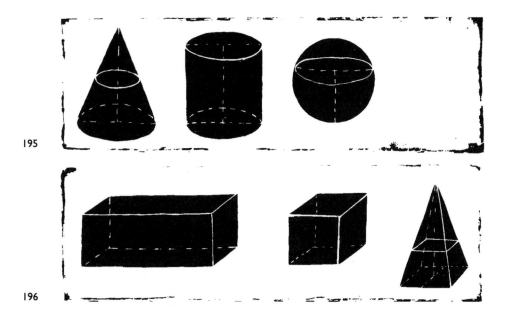

195

196

The severe, rigid, geometric forms appear softer and more organic when they are woven. In willow basketry, you rarely find sharp edges and corners, largely because of the rounded nature of the material itself.

The clear and precise rules of geometry allow us to analyze and categorize basket shapes. This knowledge of the underlying geometric shapes helps you to understand, design, and draw them.

Even if you do not succeed at first in making a basket that meets your expectations, or even the drawings you've made, don't lose heart. Try to get a little closer to your goal with the next basket you make.

Accurate basketry work requires practice, determination, and technical ability. The more mastery you have of the weaving techniques, the more time and attention you can devote to the various subtle features of the design.

Proportions

Proportions can of course be calculated in precise measurements, but these are of limited use. The texture, color, and form have just as much an influence on the effect of the finished basket. In general, good proportions for a basket are achieved when the length is twice the width (2:1). You can also work with the ratios 3:2, 3:4, 4:5. As a tool in establishing these ratios, we use "the golden pattern cut." Construct a square, bisected by a straight line, with a circular and triangular shape enclosed, as shown in the drawing below. The line A is the longer; line B is the shorter. For a basket with a 2:1 ratio, A would be the basket's length and B would be the basket's width. The height of the basket would correspond to the length of A plus the length of B. Of course these three dimensions are not the only elements that must be considered when making a basket. The basket's appearance as a whole is also determined by the proportions of foot, border, lid, and handle.

This rule of thumb simply provides an opportunity to exercise your ability to judge proportions. Measuring gadgets are certainly not what has helped us to establish our sense of the best proportions for a basket.

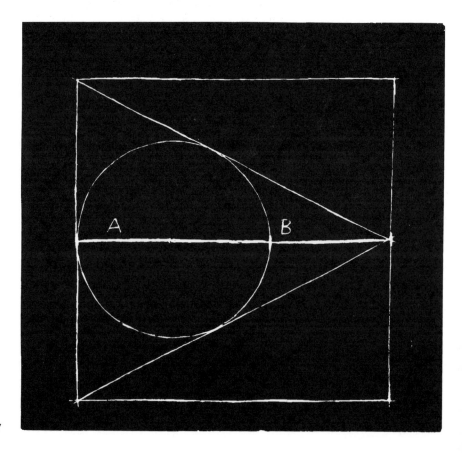

197

Color

Trees of the same species of willow frequently have different leaf and bark colors. The bark colors of subspecies and hybrids mix with the others. Some rods have a soft, whitish film or residue, which reveals that they have been undisturbed in nature. Some rods turn reddish or change color as they mature on their upper sides (the sides facing the sun); others change color toward their tips.

Rods can become brown and dry, having lost their fresh color during storage. The butt end of the buff willow rod is usually somewhat bluish, and the copper shade turns to a warm reddish brown towards the tip. The tone of the white peeled willow is a bright, warm yellowish beige. This lightest color willow is very popular, probably because of its fresh appearance.

People often combine white and buff willow; the nuances of the brown willow are less easily used for color design. When a white rod is woven here and there, however, the result is a spotty, tutti-frutti-colored basket, which is great to use as a fruit or garden basket. You might also accent the edges or surface with color.

The way the color is distributed can accent the weave structure, create optical illusions, or even conceal the weave. A common technique for forcing the weave structure to retreat into the background is called *La jambe de Suisse* ("The Swiss Leg"), a reference to the striped trousers of the Swiss Guard at the Vatican. It is achieved with randing, working alternating light and dark rods in the stake intervals, to create vertical stripes. These stripes look best on tall baskets.

The youthful yellow beige and hints of green in a freshly woven basket appear even richer in sunlight. Willows lose their precious golden color as years go by, but they turn a respectable, interesting grey.

Round Baskets

When most people talk about baskets, they're probably talking about round baskets, perhaps with a handle. These are the most common forms of baskets. The shape can be described as a cylinder or as a cone with its pointed end cut off. In willow basketry, the usual way to start a basket like this is by making the round base.

Generally, a basket's construction consists of two parts: the separately woven base and the basket wall, which is worked up from the base. The border, as the top edge is called, is usually made from the stakes, which function as the warp in the wall.

An exception to this rule is the woven platter.

The Single-Handled Shopping Basket

Who is not familiar with the single-handled basket? In days gone by, it was an indispensable item in almost every home. The paintings by Albert Anker, which document "the good old days"—daily life in the nineteenth century—often have a single-handled basket displayed in the foreground. One, delicate and fine, holds someone's knitting; another, coarse and robust, is being used for work in the field.

The construction and pattern of the basic single-handled shopping basket seem so simple, it is difficult to imagine how demanding and time consuming it is to create.

Over the centuries, the form and weave structure of this style of basket have remained unchanged, yet the finished item is still attractive and fashionable. The basket need not decorate a home like a relic rescued from the past. Ecology-minded people use it for shopping; others find it handy in the garden and around the house. Once the basket has outlived its usefulness, it will, like all organic fibers, return to ash or rich soil.

Material

For the base: The slath requires about ten, thick, 1.6 m to 1.8 m long rods. The weave requires a handful of thin, 1.2 m long rods, of similar diameter. (These and all other materials must be soaked.)

198

For the wall: For the stakes and upsett, you need at least 60 1.6 m long rods. The weave requires a handful of 1.4 m long rods.

For the crossover handle: You'll need a stick as thick as your thumb, and 10 to 15 1.6 m long rods.

The Slath

There are many ways to weave a round base. This particular style of basket base is the most common one made in Switzerland. It consists of a center cross, or slath, which is secured with rods. The rods are then woven to form the separate base for the basket.

Slath 4/4

Trimming: Cut off the butt ends of the thick rods. Next, cut a length from each rod that is about 10 cm longer than the planned diameter of the base.

Slitting open: After an hour of soaking these rods, use the picking knife to split one lengthwise a little below the center of its diameter, as shown in drawing 199. The rod will be flatter on one side of the slit than on the other.

Inserting: Thread four rods through this slit, as follows: the first, butt end first; the second, tip end first; the third, butt end first; and the fourth, tip end first. The slit will be opened to the same width across all four rods

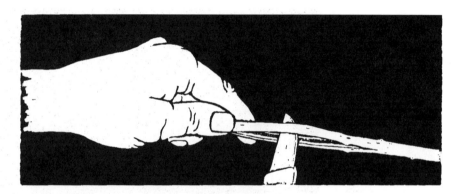

199

200

To make the opening a bit larger, bend the slit rod slightly. Insert the four rods in a steplike formation, as shown in drawing 200, to make it easier to next slip on more split sticks.

More slit sticks: Slit open the remaining rods for the base. Alternating butts and tips, slide them one by one over the four unslit rods. Line the slit rods tightly next to each other, and arrange all eight base sticks evenly to form the shape of a cross.

Tying the slath The slath is held firmly in place by tying it. Choose two rods with equal diameters. The butt ends of each are scallomed along a 20 cm length (see p. 131).

Inserting the scalloms: Place the slath, dome side down (you are now looking at the underside of the base). With the cut surfaces of the scalloms facing upward, the two rods are inserted next to each other into the slit in the four base sticks, as shown in the drawing below.

201

First stroke: Fold the rightmost rod to the right, as shown, so that it lies parallel to the slit sticks.

Turning the work: Turn the work so that the dome side is now facing upward. Turn the first rod again to the right so that it crosses over the four unslit rods and behind the slit rods.

First stroke, second round: With the dome side still facing up, fold the second rod (from the underside) to the right so that it crosses and locks the first rod in position to form a corner. Lay the second rod on top of the four slit sticks. (Drawings 201 and 202 both show the underside of the work.)

Further rounds: Continue to work, turning the cross. The rod tips move alternately, one over and one under.

202

Reverse pairing or fitching

This series of strokes you have made by twisting two rods around each other in the stick intervals is called "reverse pairing" or "fitching." Pull the rod tightly with every stroke. The second rod worked always crosses the previous rod in the interval.

Opening up

After three full rounds of reverse pairing, divide each of the four groups of sticks into two groups of two. Continue to work over and under the pairs of sticks, as shown. (The drawing shows the right side of the work).

203

Second layer of opening up: After two more rounds of reverse pairing, separate the pairs of sticks so that the weaving rods can be worked over single sticks. The 4/4 slath will then have 16 intervals.

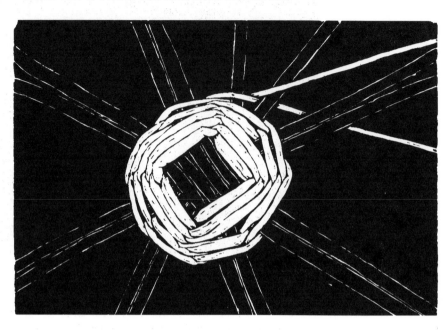

204

Replacing the weaving rods

When the rods being used to tie the slath are almost completely worked, join two new rods to the work. The rods on top of the work are moved slightly to the left to allow you to insert the tip of the new rod from underneath the weaving, as shown in the drawing below. Now continue the work with two double strands until the first rods are used up; leave their ends on the underside of the weaving. Keep the work taut so there are no gaps between rounds.

205

Joining the butt ends: Once the rods have been worked down toward their ends, make another join—butt end to butt end. This time, because the ends are thick, you won't weave with double strands.

206

207

Weaving the base   Before the last round of opening up, you could begin another type of weaving, such as triple weave (2/1), instead of continuing the reverse pairing. If you use reverse pairing for the whole base, however, the surface will be uniform and very strong.

Continue weaving until the base is finished, retaining the circular shape while you work.

Finishing: The tapered form of the rod allows the outer edge of the finished spiral to be flat. End the work with tips. To prevent the work from coming apart, simply anchor the two tips into the previous row of weaving.

Checking your work: Check that the shape of the base is uniform by measuring its diameter in several positions. If necessary, you can even the shape with a few raps of the rapping iron.

Picking off	Remove the protruding rod lengths with side cutters or a picking knife, close to the woven surface. The base is finished. As is, it can be used as a trivet or mat. If you're not planning to use the piece as a basket base, don't cut the rod ends too short.
Dome	The dome side of the slath should be facing upward to give the basket a flat surface against which to rest and maximum strength.
Calculating the slath	We'll use the drawings below to illustrate the general principles of calculating the number of base sticks you'll need in the slath. The largest circumference of the basket is divided by the stake interval to determine the total number of stakes needed. In general, plan on stake intervals two to three times the diameter of the stake (usually between 2.5 cm and 3 cm). Because each base stick is bistaked, divide the number of stakes by two to determine the number of stick ends. Divide that by two to determine the number of sticks in the slath.

Example: 30 cm (Diameter A) × 3.14 = 94 cm (B) ÷ 3 cm (stake interval) = 32 stakes ÷ 2 (bistaked ends) = 16 ends ÷ 2 = 8 base sticks. These are arranged in the drawing as a 4/4 slath.

The first base you make will very likely be somewhat bent or misshapen, but the important thing is to carry out each step. It's a good idea to construct several bases in a row to gain some experience. Use the best ones for your baskets. Depending on how you work, you may choose to calculate before you soak the rods.

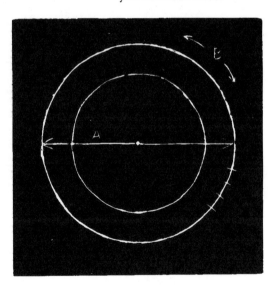

208

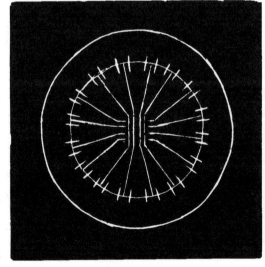

209

The Stakes

The rods for the sides of the basket must be inserted into the base. The angle of the upsett (that is, the transition from the base to the wall) gives the basket its profile and stability.

Choice of material

The stakes should be selected from the thickest of the soaked willows (see p. 110). Split and branched rods cannot be used for the upsett. The number of stakes when bistaking is generally four times the number of sticks in the base.

Slyping

In order to be inserted easily into the base, the rod ends must be slyped (see p. 128). For straight basket walls, we cut the rods twice on the back of the natural growth curve of the rod.

Inserting the stakes

Insert the soaked and slyped rods on the left and right sides of each base stick, alternately, pushing them in as deeply as possible. You will likely need to use a thick awl to open up the surface of the weave structure first. The cut surfaces of the stakes must face upward.

Once all the stakes have been inserted, you will have what looks like an enormous, dome-shaped sun.

210

Pricking up

We use an awl to prick up the stakes about 1 cm from the edge of the base (see p. 134). If the rods have dried, spray them with water to wet them down again.

After the stakes are standing in the desired upright position, we tie them at a point halfway up their height. Be sure that the stakes are tied so that they are exactly centered over the base so the finished basket will be symmetrical in shape.

211

Rapping the stakes

Pound all pricked-up ends of the stakes flush to the edge of the woven base with the rapping iron, so that they are well anchored.

False Foot (or Foot Wale)

Waling with sets

These strokes cover the cut ends of the base sticks. They also provide a simple way to make a lower border without having to make a genuine foot.

When making smaller objects, we work with one set of rods; for larger baskets, we work with two sets, in order to get an even upsett all around the basket. For this shopping basket, you'll need two sets of four soaked and slyped rods, of equal length and diameter. Open up the weave structure with an awl and insert four rods on the right sides of four stakes, butt ends first. Prick up the rods with the awl. Next, do the same with four rods of the second set on the right sides of four stakes on the opposite side of the base. Each set will span half the basket's circumference.

Inserting rods

212

Stroke placement

213

Second stroke

214

Third stroke

215

216

First set: The first working rod is the one farthest to the left, as shown in drawing 213 on p. 185. Carry this rod over the three others and in front of three stakes, behind the fourth stake, and out again. This four-rod wale is abbreviated as 3/1. Repeat the stroke with the remaining three rods, always working the leftmost rod to the right, as shown in drawings 214-216. Always pull the rods taut so there are no gaps between the base and the upsett. Work the pattern over the first half of the basket's circumference.

Second set: When the rightmost rod of the first set is in the same interval with the first rod of the second set, stop weaving the first set and begin the four-rod wale with the second set. (The rightmost rod of the first set is marked with an X, as in drawing 217 on p. 188.) Continue the 3/1 pattern with the second set around the rest of the basket's circumference, until the rightmost rod is in the same interval with the leftmost rod of the first set. Also mark this rightmost rod of the second set with an X.

First set: Cut off the X-marked rod of the first set. Work the remaining three rods 3/1 for one stroke per rod to create an even transition. Repeat on the other side. Secure the basket to the work surface with an awl to turn it easily (see pp. 90-91). Now you'll work with the remaining six rods.

Second set of
four-rod wale

217

218

The Three-Rod Wale

The three-rod wale is the easiest way to weave an upsett, and it creates a stable basket base.

The remaining three weaving rods from the first set are now worked in front of two and behind one (2/1) for half of the basket's circumference. The second set of three are worked the same way.

219

Joining the waling

Once you've worked the rods to the tips, you need to add new rods. As shown in the drawing below, lift each of the three rods in order to insert three new tips from the outside of the basket. Continue working 2/1 around. Now join new rods to the remaining set of three, tips to tips.

220

When necessary, join the butt ends of the two sets of rods with the butt ends of new rods, finishing with tips.

Finishing   The upsett is finished with the tips that are left outside the basket. The whole circumference of the basket is first rapped down with the rapping iron (see p. 137) to tighten and level the top edge of the work.

Finishing determines the final form of the basket, so keep the desired shape in mind while you are working the upsett. If you're making a cylinder, for example, keep the stakes as vertical as possible. If you intend to make a conical form, you should lightly press each of the stakes outward to open the form as you work the upsett (or inward if you want the shape to narrow).

Number of upsett rounds   The bottom waling also influences the overall appearance of the basket. In general, you should work two to four rounds. A wider upsett makes the basket look and feel heavier. The intended shape of the basket may sometimes allow a very wide upsett—for example, a very open basket that flares suddenly at the base, where little or none of the bottom waling is visible.

French Randing

Structure   While you are working it, a French rand is basically a wreath of willow rods. One rod is inserted in each interval, butt end behind the stake. Carry each rod over one, behind one (1/1). Continue working the pattern around the basket, beginning each new rod in the interval to the left of the previous one, until all the rods are woven to their tips. French randing creates an upward spiralling pattern. The walls must be the same height all around. Turn the work slowly, but continuously, to the right as you weave.

Starting to weave   Select a handful of soaked material of the same diameter. Do not cut off the butt ends.

Inserting the weaving rods   The rods are inserted between the stakes from right to left, but each rod is woven from left to right.

The weaving rods should be similar in length and diameter. Beginners should use rods whose butt ends are somewhat thinner than the stakes, otherwise the work is difficult to control.

When working a round basket, the first rod is inserted in any of the stake intervals. For oval and rectangular baskets, however, a straight side is a more convenient place to start. Beginners should not start where the bottom waling or upsett was ended; this might lead to confusion about where to insert the last rod. The inserted ends protrude about 2 cm behind the stakes into the basket. Try to stagger the butt ends of new rods.

221

222

Working the weave The first six rods are worked one stroke—in front of one, behind one and through (1/1). All the rods are left in front of the basket. The seventh rod is worked for two strokes of 1/1 and left at the front.

223

Initially, you will also complete two strokes of 1/1 with the eighth and all subsequent rods.

In order to insert the next to the last rod you raise the first one a bit and slide it underneath. This last rod is worked just like all the others (1/1).

Be sure you have inserted one weaving rod in each interval. You can check this best by looking at the inside of the basket. If each stake has a rod behind it, you have inserted enough rods.

The double strokes that begin with the seventh weaving rod are needed to make room for the weaving to continue. When the last rod has been worked, the first six rods, which are worked 1/1 once, finish the visual progression of the round. In one round the unevenness is corrected; in the subsequent round, this pattern is worked again this way.

The weaving rods are worked so that they travel around the stakes in a zigzag path. This keeps the stakes locked in place so as not to deform the shape of the basket and the weave structure.

Rapping down

For a stable weave structure, you need to rap down the weaving with the rapping iron after each three to four rounds, or sooner if the weave appears to be uneven.

Finishing the French rand

Once the rods are woven almost to their tips, the French rand is finished. You can end the work earlier if you want a shorter basket. The walls should be the same height all the way around. Find the lowest spot in the weave structure and rap down anything higher than that until the basket has a uniform height. Use the rapping iron carefully, or the thin lengths of rod will split. The walls should also have a uniform shape all around, like a piece of pottery. Otherwise, you have to reweave it with new, unkinked rods.

The remaining ends left in front are picked off and cut so closely to the surface of the basket that they slip inside.

Another band of French randing For a taller basket, you can insert another row of rods all the way around. A second band or even several bands can be added to the top of the basket in this way. Choose thinner rods for subsequent bands than were used in the first. The stakes at this height are not as thick as they are at the base, and you want the basket to appear lighter at its top edge.

The Four-Rod Wale (2/2)

Shape, stability, and the desired height of the basket are all affected by the top waling. It divides the body into sections. Our four-rod wale is classic, but it is also functional and good looking. For this wale, you'll need four rods, which will be worked 2/2. You can make one or two sets, depending on the desired height of the basket, but primarily on its finished diameter.

Beginning the waling Remove 20 cm from the tips of four wet rods. Then insert one rod tip in each of four stake intervals, working from right to left. Leave the butt ends in front of the basket. To begin the 2/2 waling, hold the rod farthest to the left in your right hand, carry it in front of two stakes, over the other rods, behind

224

two stakes, and back out through the next interval. (Keep this position in mind for orientation.)

While you are working the wale, there are always four rods in neighboring intervals. The right hand now takes the second rod, carries it in front of two and behind two. After all four rods are worked, you return to work the first one again. This weaving pattern creates a very smooth texture that emphasizes the roundness of the basket. On the inside, it covers the picked-off ends of the randing. The structure looks the same on the inside and outside.

Joining : Once the four rods have been worked to their butt ends, we join the rod farthest to the left with a new butt end. The rod that is ending should be pulled to the left to make an opening for the new rod. Work the rod 2/2. Replace the other rods the same way. For a smooth surface, be sure to join butts to butts, tips by tips. There are mechanical reasons for this as well—a thick butt end worked adjacent to a thin tip will create gaps in the weave structure.

Finishing the waling : The waling must be finished with the tips of the rods. Its height is more an aesthetic consideration than a practical one. Two bands of waling of equal width provide an unobtrusive framing for the weave structure. You can't go wrong if you make the top waling somewhat narrower than the bottom waling. Visually the basket will look settled, rather than top-heavy. Never forget to rap the weave down, measure height, and keep the materials damp. A basket that leans to one side is not a properly finished piece of work. Allow yourself those few minutes to make the top edge evenly horizontal all around. Once the border is finished, nothing can be changed!

Wetting down : If you've worked a long time on the randing and waling, you'll probably now have to wet down the basket in order to continue working. Turn it upside down, and leave the unwoven stakes and the waling in water for at least one half hour.

The Three-Rod Border

The basketmaker uses the stakes that protrude from the woven walls of the basket to lock the weave structure. These remaining lengths of warp are woven together to form the border.

The three-rod border (3/2): This border requires a certain manual dexterity, an ability to remember the pattern, and a thorough familiarity with the strokes. These skills will enable you to join the beginning to the end of the border so regularly and uniformly that the work blends evenly together.

194

Pinching with round-nosed pliers

With round-nosed pliers, pinch four stakes about 1 cm above the waling (see p. 135). The 1 cm long interval allows you to turn the stakes down and fit them more easily into the border.

225

Starting the border

The first pinched stake on the left is turned down behind the two stakes to its right and then it is left in front of the third stake. The same is done with the other three pinched stakes.

Now carry the first rod in front of three and behind one (3/1), leaving it in front, as shown in drawing 227. Don't pull the rod tight; you want to leave room for the last stake in the border.

226

227

First pair

Now turn down the next vertical stake behind two and into the same interval where the first rod, which you just worked, was left. The first pair is now complete (see drawing 228 on p. 196).

Second pair

The second pinched and turned rod now moves in front of three and behind one. The next upright stake is turned down behind two to share the same interval, as shown in drawing 229, making the second pair.

195

228

229

Third and fourth pairs Work the next two pairs in the same way. *Continuing the weave:* When all four pairs have been created, continue to work by repeating the same procedure. Take the rightmost rod from the pair farthest to the left and move it in front of three and behind one (3/1). The next vertical stake is turned down behind two, and is left in front. The whole border is worked like this until the end. (Once the whole border is finished, the leftmost rod of each pair will be picked off.)

230

The two rods in the pair must not be on top of one other, or you can easily make a mistake. The second rod worked should be parallel with and to the right of the one worked before it.

Wetting down If you're using peeled willow, be sure to dampen it before and during the work—especially the stakes you haven't yet turned down.

Final strokes When you reach the stakes you pinched when you first started the border, you'll weave them in using the same method described above.

196

231

Working the last rods

In order to weave a perfect border, don't hesitate to murmur the strokes to yourself as you work (in front 3, behind 1, turn down behind 2, and out). Working the end of the border is easy when you've had some practice, and it's good training for your memory.

You now have four pairs to the left of the first pinched stake. Carry the rightmost rod of the pair farthest to the left in front of three and behind the first pinched stake, leaving it in front. The next upright stake is turned down and threaded out from behind through the same interval to create another pair.

The last pair

The rightmost rod of the pair now farthest to the left and the last upright stake are woven as described above to form the last pair. At this point all the stakes have been turned down. (You'll need the awl to open up and maintain space for the rod to be pulled through, as shown in the drawing below.)

Now there are four pairs left, sticking out from under the border. The rightmost rod of each pair should be woven in 3/1.

232

233

When the border has been completely woven, one rod tip sticks out of each stake interval under the border. There should never be two beside each other, or you've skipped a step.

Picking off: Pick off these remaining ends with a knife. Don't cut them so short that they slip through the woven border!

234

The Twisted Bow Handle

This twisted bow, or crossover, handle, consists of a thick willow stick wrapped with thinner rods. It's the most common method for constructing a bow handle.

Anchoring the first end

First of all, the core, that is, the stick that will be covered, must be positioned properly. It shouldn't be placed just anywhere. For aesthetic reasons, you should be sure that the bow is parallel to the four split skeins in the base slath and is straight across the basket. Because the core must be inserted next to the stakes that are exactly in the middle of the basket, the bow itself is never located exactly in the middle.

To make the opening for one end: Insert a large awl into the border, to the left of the basket's center stake.

Anchoring the second end

You can simply count to locate the corresponding stake on the opposite side. If the base and the body are not woven accurately, however, the handle might end up some distance from the middle. An incorrectly positioned handle not only disturbs the eye, it can also be detrimental to the basket's function. In a case like this, choose a stake off to one side to visually balance the placement.

To make the opening for the other end: Give the basket a half-turn. With a long awl, make a hole on this side, again to the left of the center stake and as deep as possible. Be careful not to damage the weaving.

Selecting the bow: The bow can have a diameter of 9 mm to 12 mm, depending on the diameter and height of the basket.

Slyping: Slype the stick for the bow on one side three times to make it easier to insert (see p. 128).

Bending: The stick is bent to the bow's desired shape (see p. 121).

Inserting the stick   Insert the bent stick as deeply as possible into the weave alongside the stake (after removing the awl). Don't use pliers or any other tool, because the bow may break at the border. Wet your left hand and hold the stick about 4 cm from the end. The right hand, made into a fist, hits the left hand twice, firmly. This way the stick is inserted easily and painlessly.

Proportions: The height of the body, the circumference, and the thickness and height of the bow together have a great impact on the basket's overall appearance. A good sense of the right proportions is necessary (see p. 172). One much-used rule (which, however, does not always apply) is that the distance from the highest point of the bow to the basket's border should be the same measurement as one-half the diameter of the basket's opening.

Marking: Position the free end of the handle on the other side of the basket, at the spot where the awl is still inserted. Move the end along the outer edge of the wall and mark the height you want with a pencil.

Cutting and inserting: The bow should be cut and slyped about 15 cm beneath the mark. Insert this cut end as you did the other.

Bow shape   The inside of the bow should align with the basket wall, as if it were simply a continuation of the wall emerging from the border.

Now decide on the bow's final shape. Generally, bow handles are shaped into a slightly flattened circle, which can support more weight. If the shape of the basket seems to require it, you can shape the bow nearly into a right angle. There are other ways of making angular handles, however. Willow cannot be wrapped around an angular bow as closely as around soft, rounded shapes.

Checking your work   Check the handle's shape by looking at it from the side and along its profile. Often it is somewhat twisted, but with a lot of counterpressure, you can correct it. The profile of the bow handle must also be at a right angle to the border.

Inserting the rods   Now insert a medium-sized awl into the border to the left of the bow-handle end. Choose ten high-quality, uniform rods from the rods being soaked. The tips must not be broken off. Insert the butt ends of two of them into the opening made by the awl, and insert two more into the border directly in front of the bow. All four rods should be well placed around the core, but not on the right side of it (or you'll get lost in the wrapping process later on). Position four rods at the opposite end in the same way.

Wrapping the core   Now you must work quickly and precisely.

First wrapping: Hold the basket firmly between your knees, keeping the bow handle in profile. Hold the four inserted rods in your right hand, parallel to each other. Bend them back toward you and to the right, as shown in drawing 236. The rods, kept parallel and pressed together, can now be moved as a unit around the core, working to the left.

235

236

237

Second wrapping: Give the basket a quarter-turn, move the rods once over
the handle, somewhat to the left of the center.

Third and fourth wrapping: Once again under, over, under and through,
with the tips left inside the basket. The intervals between the wrappings
should all be of uniform size. Wrap the handle core a total of four times
with the group of rods.

Second band of rods: Work from the other end of the bow in the same manner.
(If the interval is too wide, you can add a fifth rod.) The core must be covered so that there are no spaces between wraps. Because the outer curve
of the handle is longer than the inner curve, there will be thin openings,
but the rods must not lie one over the other or have kinks. Leave one set
of tips in the basket on either side of the handle.

Fastening the rods　The ends must be wet down. Insert a thick awl vertically under the highest round of waling between the handle and the first stake to its right. Spread the handle and stake well apart. Thread the tip of the rod closest to the bow through this space from the inside out. The rest of the tips follow in order, one beside the other.

239

238

Fastening the ends　There are many ways to fasten the rods wrapped around the core. Some are eye-catchers, others are less conspicuous. Perhaps you can eventually develop your own method. The manner of fastening shown here is commonly used, easy to do, and decorative as well.

Wrapping　Wrap the rod closest to the handle to the left, around, and to the right. Make an opening with the awl to the left of the handle at the same height as the opening to the right. Insert the rod you've just wrapped through and pull it tight. Wrap the rest of rods in the same way. The tips should all be positioned inside the basket.

240

Tying up   All the tips are twisted together tightly to lock them. Between the first and the second stake to the left, make an opening in the weave through which you can thread the twisted tips to the front side. In the next interval, thread all of them back into the basket. Pick off the tips as close to the surface as possible.

The other end of the handle: In the meantime, the tips of the rods at the other end have fairly well dried out. Wet them down thoroughly before you start to work.

The French refer to this way of fastening as a "fish bone." Perhaps it once had symbolic meaning.

Pegging   To make the peg, slype one end of a piece of rod about 10 cm long and about as thick as a pencil. With the large awl, open up a hole in the core of the handle at the level of the first and second rounds of top waling. Drive the peg in with a hammer until it is flush with the surface of the basket wall. Pick off the protruding length on the inside of the basket, and use it for the peg on the other side. The pegs bear the weight of the basket's load. If you don't peg the handle, as is often the case in commerical basketry, the wrapped ends begin to unravel as the basket is used.

241

242

243

244

205

Base strips   Baskets to carry heavy loads have their bases reinforced with two strips of wood. These strips (also called rails or skates) can easily be cut from scrap lumber. The ends must be angled to correspond to the base shape. To attach them, use long nails that protrude up into the base and bend the ends over with a hammer.

Note   To get the proper feel for this work, a beginner would be well advised to make several of these single-handled shopping baskets, one after another. In past centuries, people often made sets of five or more baskets that could be nested one inside the other to save space. The baskets fit together like the peels of an onion, as shown in the drawing below. These little "onion baskets" also have differing proportions. The baskets can be made in such a way that, when they are together, all their borders are flush with one another, or so that the border of the smallest basket is the highest, or the lowest.

245

The lower the basket sides, the wider the basket appears to be. These handles have all been made the same way. You can, of course, take basket height into consideration when making the handle—for example, the tallest basket could have the lowest handle. Carefully consider the overall appearance when deciding on handle length.

246

247 Shown here is a progression of sizes of cylindrical baskets and baskets with flared walls. All of these baskets have the same proportions. In order to fit into one another, their diameters must increase relative to the thickness of the basket walls.

248 The proportions of these cylindrical baskets vary. The diameters and handles are all the same. The weave structures are also the same, with the exception of the tallest basket, which has two bands of French randing. Cylindrical baskets should be made slightly and gradually wider toward their top borders; otherwise, as a result of a trick of the eye, they appear to grow narrower.

The Lidded Basket

Lidded, or covered, baskets are frequently used to keep foods that require air circulation. These baskets also keep grains, onions, peas, and other foods protected from sunlight and mice.

249

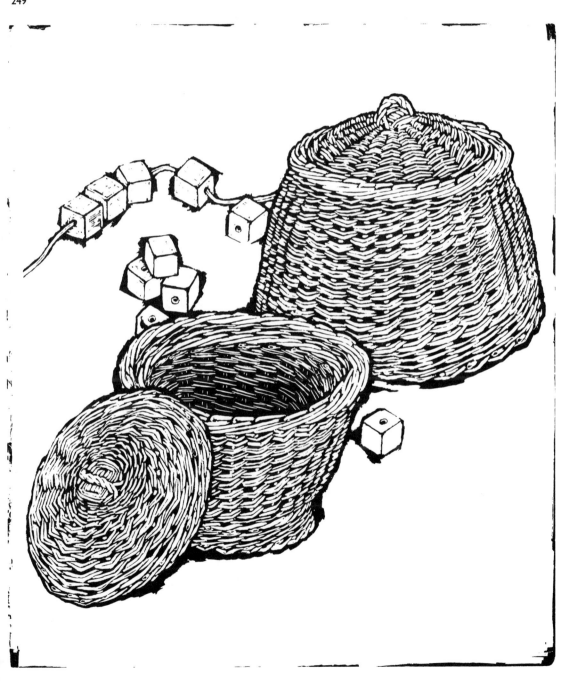

The lidded basket with a handle was traditionally used for shopping in the marketplace as well as for shipping articles. It is an object deeply associated with the past, as seen in the paintings of Joachim Beuckelaer (1530-1574). The loveliest little lidded baskets were among a lady's accessories for special occasions. Merchants carried all kinds of small domestic animals and merchandise into the city in rectangular, covered, woven containers.

Today people use lidded baskets mainly for their dirty laundry, as sewing baskets, and as small trinket holders.

The lid can be made differently than the one shown here—for example, it may have the shape of a semicircle or two semicircles joined in the middle by a bridge. The hinges can be located just as well on the basket's border, especially on rectangular baskets. There are also overlapping, flush, and inset lids.

The lid can swing, drop, slide, or be completely separate from the basket. It can be lifted by a knob, a loosely fastened ring, a hole, or a twisted handle. There is also a variety of fastening mechanisms and hinge attachments.

The lidded basket presented here has a woven base that is staked up to create the wall. The inset lid is made in the same way as the base, except it has a small handle in the middle.

If you have not yet made at least one bow-handled basket, don't attempt this basket. The steps already described in detail in the previous chapter will not be explained again here. Beginners will also have some difficulty making a lid that fits properly.

Material For the basket's 20 cm wide base and wall, you'll need approximately 500 g of 1 m long rods. You'll need at least 15 thick, 1.4 m long rods to construct the base and lid slaths. Select rods of uniform diameter and length and soak all the material.

French Randing the Base

The slath can be constructed in a 3/4 configuration. Three rods are split open in the middle, as was done for the shopping basket (p. 177). Four rods are threaded through the three slits. Be sure to pay attention to which is the dome side of the slath. The slath is worked in the same way as the slath for the shopping basket, except that opening up occurs at the start of the fourth round.

Slath To tie the slath, work two thin rods from their scallomed butts to their tips. Wet down the material.

Refer to pp. 179-180 of the shopping-basket instructions. Begin opening up at the start of the fourth round.

The weave Work the base as a French rand, inserting the butt end of one wet rod into each interval. Because there are 7 base sticks, you'll need 14 weavers, all of uniform diameter. Insert the first butt end in any one interval, and carry it over one, behind one, over one; then insert the second rod, in the interval to the left of the first. Continue randing until you are 2 cm short of the diameter you want. Continually dampen the willow as you work.

250

251

Twining   Twine two rods of equal diameter until the base has the right diameter. Finish the work with tip ends. In the drawing below, two new rods are being joined to the weaving (see p. 180).

Measuring: Check the dimensions of the base at several positions. Eliminate any bulges with the rapping iron.

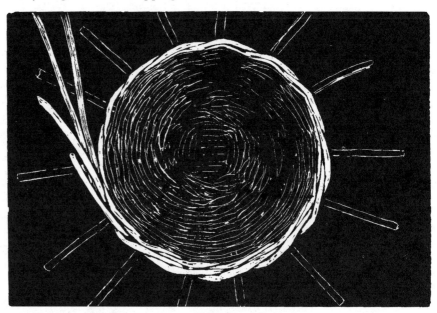

252

The stakes   Slype the soaked rods on the back of the curve at the butt ends. The rods must be of uniform thickness. With cut surfaces upward, insert one to the left and one to the right of each base stick end (work with the dome side up). There will be 28 bistakes. Pinch and turn them up. To secure their upright position, bind them near the top around their circumference (see drawing 106).

253

Bottom waling This is a three-rod wale (2/1) and is worked with two sets of rods, one set on each side of the base (see p. 189).

Joining: The first set of rods ends with butt ends. The new rods are inserted butt ends first so that the waling can be completed with the tips. The two rounds of bottom waling will require 12 rods. For a tight, level, stable foundation, you must rap the work down often. Wet down as needed.

Slewing

Slewing gives the work a special character. The procedure is the same as for working the shopping basket's French rand. Instead of inserting only one rod between the stakes, however, you insert two or three rods into each interval, as shown in the drawing below. The rods should be somewhat thinner than the stakes. The more rods you insert in each interval, the faster the work is completed around the basket, but the more difficult it is to retain the basket's shape. You'll need quite a bit of experience before you can get a perfectly shaped basket wall slewing six rods at a time.

Brown-willow containers for flowers, cheese, and seafood used to be woven this way. These early examples of disposable packaging were constructed quickly and loosely, but they were attractive. Today, we would probably not throw them out.

Some types of ladies' handbags also feature the diagonal direction of a slewing weave structure. These items are usually made with planed and sized skeins, worked on wood forms.

254

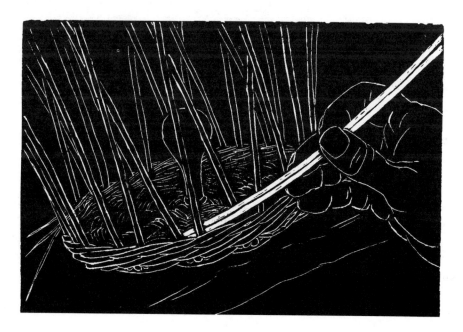

Start slewing with the butt ends of the rods. At the moment the primary concern is controlling the basket's shape. The pair of rods that are inserted in front of each stake are strong, and it will be necessary to bend them around the stake with each stroke. At the same time, the stake—or several stakes in a row—has to be kept in its original position. Wet down the rods. They should be rapped down lightly and regularly after each round (see p. 191).

Work the 1/1 weave pattern with two rods the first time. Be particularly careful not to make any mistakes when starting a repeat of the pattern. Continue working this pattern until you have reached the rod tips; you can end earlier if you want a lower basket wall, as long as the top of the weaving is even.

Checking your work: Check the wall all around the basket and rap it down to a uniform height where necessary. The height of a lidded basket's wall must be particularly even. The next step is to make the inside ledge that supports the lid.

Don't forget to dampen the willow again if it needs it.

255

The Waled-In Ledge

By waling, you can easily add a kind of sill, counter, or ledge to the basket. This projection can be used for various purposes and can be attached on the outside or inside of the basket wall. For a basket whose lid fits into the basket's opening, the ledge is made on the inside of the wall. The lid is somewhat smaller in diameter than the opening of the basket. Without the ledge, the cover would simply fall into the basket. A waled-in ledge is made with four, five, or seven rods, depending on how heavy it needs to be. A piece of luggage made in the traditional manner has a lid that rests on a ledge that protrudes on the outside of the basket wall. The core of the ledge is a rod, which is covered with the waling to create the strong, solid ledge such a large item would require.

Preparation   For this lidded basket, you'll work four rods without a core. Take 8 to 10 of the thickest, most uniform rods from a soaked bundle. Measure from the tip ends of four rods to a length somewhat longer than half of the basket's circumference. Cut them to this length. The others are left as they are.
First group: Insert the tip of the first of the four trimmed rods in one interval, and the other three to the right of this one. Each of four intervals are holding one rod, as shown in the drawing below.
To create the ledge inside the basket, the four-rod wale (3/1) is worked in reverse, that is, in front of one, behind three (1/3).

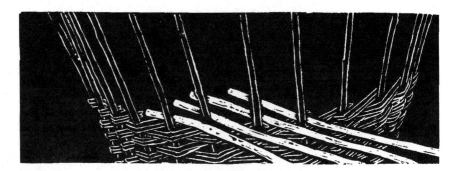

256

Waling   The first rod that you inserted (the leftmost) is carried to the right in front of one stake and behind the next three (1/3). Leave the rod outside the basket.
   Weave the next three rods in the same way, working from left to right. Continue the pattern until one half of the basket's circumference has been woven. Be careful not to kink the rods as you work them around the stakes.

257

258

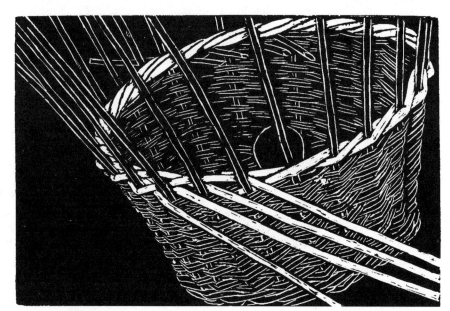

259

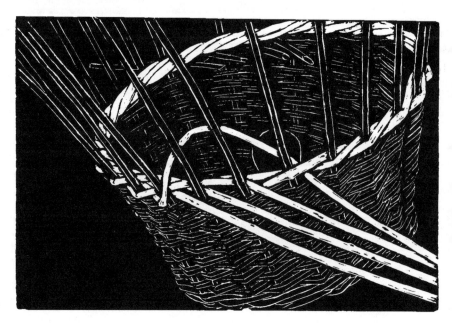

260

Second group: Now take four of the wet rods that were left at full length. Insert their butt ends, rod by rod, in the intervals in which the first rods have finished. Continue to work the 1/3 pattern, but as you carry each rod to the front of the basket after a complete stroke, thread it under a rod from the first group, as shown in drawing 260. Adjust it so it lies next to the rod sharing the interval. Continue working until the ledge is completed around the circumference of the basket, rapping down gingerly to keep it evenly horizontal.

Top waling   To allow some room for the lid to sit between the ledge and the upper border, we add another round of waling. The inner ledge will also protrude a bit more. If you were to make the top border right after making the ledge, the lid would not remain in place.

   With two sets of two rods, work a round of 1/1. Rap down the weave and soak the unwoven stakes for about one half hour.

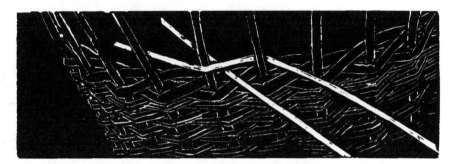

261

The Four-Rod Border

This border is worked in almost exactly the same way as the three-rod border for the shopping basket (see p. 194).

   Turn down five stakes behind two, as shown in the drawing below. Next, work the rod farthest to the left in front of four and behind one (4/1). Turn the upright stake to the left of it behind two and out the same interval as the previous rod to create a pair. Work the other four turned-down rods 4/1, and make pairs by turning down upright stakes behind two. The right rod of each pair is worked 4/1, and the stakes are turned down behind two until you finish the border.

262

263

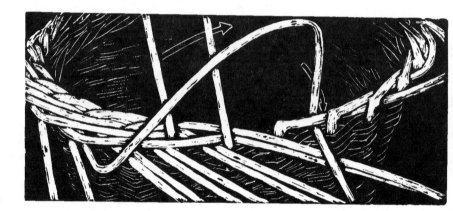

264

265

Thread through the remaining five rods on the right of each pair. You may want to rap the top edge level. Also, check for mistakes in the border. The end should merge invisibly into the beginning so the border appears continuous.

Remove the basket from the work surface and turn it upside down on the floor in front of you. Now pick off protruding ends, inside and outside the basket.

Adding a Foot

Many baskets are made with a foot to increase their stability or improve their usefulness, or for reasons of design.

Stakes The short rods left over from making the border can be used as stakes. Slype one and insert it to the left of a base stake; insert another to the right of the next base stake, etc. The foot stakes should be at fairly regular intervals, parallel to the side stakes.

266

Weaving The short foot siding consists of waling. Three damp rods are anchored at their tips, and each is worked in front of two and behind one (2/1). You need only one group of three. Join new rods at their butt ends and finish with the tips. If you rap the weave down properly, you should have an inconspicuous seam between the added foot and the basket. Wet down the work.
Foot shape: The border can also be worked higher and in a conical shape—simply press the stakes lightly outward while you're working. The basket will then appear to sit on a pedestal.

267

Border The foot's edge is finished as a 2/1 border. Turn down each of three stakes behind two, then work each 2/1. Turn the next rod down behind two to make pairs (the active rod is on the right). After working around, make sure the basket stands properly on the floor.

268

269

The Lid

To make this lid, you'll use the same procedure you used to make the basket base. You'll shape the lid's dome shape as you work.

Make the slath for the lid as for the base, but with eight sticks in a 4/4 configuration. Work three complete rounds, then open up the work, as described on pp. 179-180. Work two complete rounds, then open up the individual stakes.

270

271

Slewing Now you'll fill the spoked frame with the same slewing technique used for the body of the basket. Start the work with wet butt ends for the best over-all appearance. Make sure that the stakes are evenly spaced to ensure regularity in the weave structure and an even border. The finished lid will then fit properly onto the inner ledge of the basket—and be neither too loose nor too tight.

Lid size: The slewing is worked to a diameter 4 or 5 cm less than the diameter of the basket's interior. The waling and border will take up the remaining amount, but some slight space must also be left for the lid to slip in and out easily.

Waling After slewing, work a few rounds of waling to give the lid stability. Depending on the size of the stake intervals, you may need three or four rods. Start with the tips and make the joins with the butt ends, but always end the waling with tips. (If you finished the work with butt ends, it wouldn't be possible to make the cover neatly round so that it would fit into the basket. The thick butt ends of the rods cannot be pressed into shape.) Lock in the ends, and rap the edge to even it out in the form of a circle.

The sticks are picked off almost flush to the edge of the finished waling. Only a little bit should protrude.

Border The sticks in the slath are so stubborn that they cannot be worked to make the final border; you have to insert bistakes solely for this purpose. The thick end of each rod is slyped, and one is inserted to the right and left of each base stake. Make sure the stakes are long enough to work the border strokes. In front of two and behind two (2/2) is a suitable border pattern because it

223

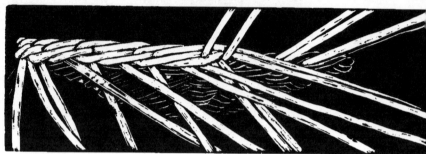

creates a smooth, rolled surface. Long strokes, such as 4/2 or 5/2, are not solid enough for inset lids. They also get caught on the basket's edge, which makes opening and closing the lid a nuisance.

Leave the picked-off ends on the outside of the lid. Work with the domed side facing you. To anchor the stakes as deeply as possible, rap the border firmly towards the middle. The border should completely cover the ends of the stakes.

Size Precision work is necessary when making inset lids. A lid that is too large cannot be simply reshaped to fit by making the dome higher nor can the material be packed any more closely together. It's just as impossible to fix a lid that is too small—there's not enough material in the weave. Making a lid of the right size is easier if you work on a form, or mold, but it also presents other difficulties, because you need uniform materials and exact spacing.

One-Rod Handle

For this handle, you'll need one soaked, 1 m long rod. The finished lid is kept with its dome side up.

Fastening: Working from the underside of the lid, the butt end of the rod is inserted between the base stick and the weaving to the right-hand side of the slath, as shown in drawing 274.

Twisting: The rod is next pricked up level with the top surface of the weave structure with an awl and twisted, or cranked, three quarters of its length, clockwise (see p. 138).

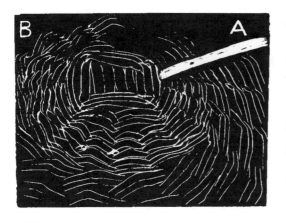

274

275

First loop Working on the top, domed surface, insert the rod end between the first and second base sticks in the slath on the left-hand side of the lid, outside the rounds of tying in. Insert it at the center of the lid, as shown in drawing 275. Then pull the rod until there is a loop about 2 cm high. Poke the rod back to the top surface between the third and fourth base sticks—now there are two base sticks between the two rods protruding on that side of the lid.

Second loop If necessary, wet the work. Twist the free rod end clockwise again. Then

wrap it counterclockwise around the first loop. Bring it through the loop twice, finishing on the right side.

Note: Unlike the crossover handle, all the rounds in this twisted handle must be intertwined to make a proper cord. Reinsert the rod two base sticks away from the other handle end on that side. Wet down as needed and give the lid a half-turn.

276

277

Third loop

278

279

Wrap the two loops along their length as you repeatedly twist the working rod. Then, to secure the tip well, insert it into the same place in the weave from which it already emerged. Fasten it using a 1/1 stroke between previous rows of weaving on the slath and around the base sticks.

Important: If you want an attractive finished handle, you must twist the rod into a uniformly shaped cord each time you make a loop. Also, pull the rod tight along its length each time. Remember that the rods will lose some of their thickness when they dry. Pick off any leftover ends.

Twisted handles such as these can also be used on lightweight baskets.

280

281 The foot can modify the shape of the basket and its proportions. If the foot has to be very high for aesthetic or practical reasons, you can add another row of French randing and finish it with waling. (The leftover rods from the basket border would be too short for this work.) The French randing in the foot should never be as high as the randing in the body of the basket. If it is, the overall appearance of the basket will be very boring.

282 The device of progression, a very commonly used element in design, is illustrated by the varied lids of the baskets shown here. The effect could just as well be created in the handles, the French randing, slewing, or in the shape of the baskets themselves. Progressions are created by making a series of planned modifications in dimensions by various degrees.

229

The Platter

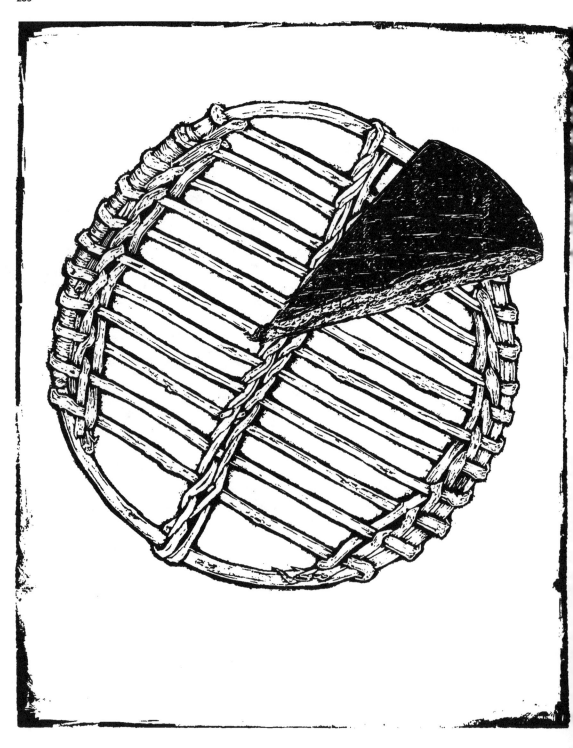

This construction is completely different than the others presented so far. This platter is a round, open, scallomed frame. A platter can also be made as an oval, rectangle, or square; more complicated shapes are usually not as attractive. To construct frames for squares and rectangles, you make right-angled cuts, as shown in drawing 152 on p. 135. Large constructions may be used as room dividers, wall coverings, and decorative window displays.

Round, visually divided, open surfaces are especially suitable for cake, fruit, and cheese boards. They're also useful as trivets for hot pots and in pantry bins. The bases of openwork baskets and seats on stools are very commonly made this way. Rattan, hazelnut, and chestnut can also be used for this type of object. The strength and pliancy of these woods ensure the needed stability.

The kitchen-size platter is ideal for a first attempt at weaving. In the following text, we'll tell you all you need to know. There aren't any complicated techniques.

Material

For a platter with a diameter of approximately 30 cm, select one finger-thick, well-proportioned rod. (This mature rod can come from wild willow.) For the ring, you need only the center portion of the rod. The material can be used fresh or dry (if soaked again). For the stakes, you'll need 1.4 m long rods, whose diameter is as constant as possible. (See p. 111 for information on grading rods.) Soak about 30 rods. You'll need at least two for fitching.

Forming the ring   Beginners should draw the finished shape, full size, on paper. While making the bend (see p. 122), put the ring on this template to check its dimensions. The line drawing corresponds to the inner circumference of the ring.
Marking: Carefully bend the rod to the size you want the platter to be. Mark the overlapping sections about 15 cm from their butt ends. (This mark later indicates the middle of the doubled section.) Mark the overlapping section again 10 cm to either side of the first mark, as shown in drawing 284 on p. 232. This 20 cm length remains doubled.

Straight scallom   *Thick rod end:* On the inner side of the curve, scallom the marked distance of the butt end so that it tapers to the end (see p. 131). The other, thin tip of the rod should be scallomed on the back of the curve. Position this second scallom against the inner side of the circle. The scalloms must be even in cut and taper.

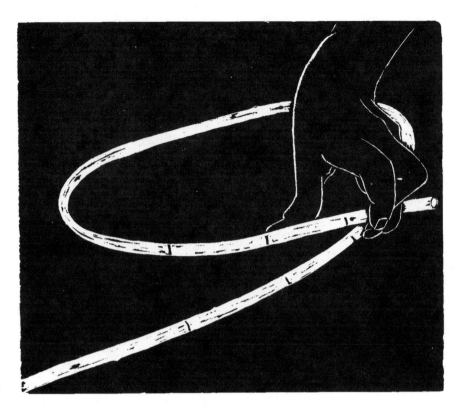

284

285

Join   Now place both scallomed surfaces together, aligning the two center marks, as shown in drawing 285. With pliers, push a 25 mm nail into the rod at the mark, and bend the tip over on the back side.

Checking your work   Before you insert any more nails, check the ring against the template you drew earlier. The shape should be evenly round, have the right diameter, and lie flat on the paper's surface. If the shape and size are right, hammer a 15 mm nail at each end and lock them in place by bending the tips over.

286

Wrapping the join To reinforce and cover the join, you'll wrap it with a skein. The skein should be somewhat tapered at one end. Slip that end lengthwise under the tongue of the scallom where the ring begins. With the bark side up, wrap the skein tightly, leaving no spaces. After wrapping about 20 cm, insert the end under the last wrap, and fasten it with a small nail. Pick off any leftover material.

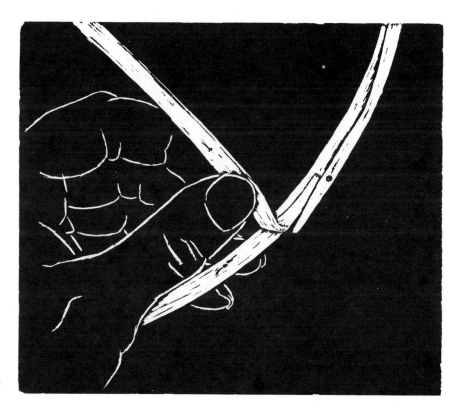

287

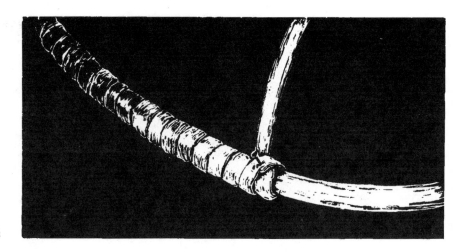

288

Laying Out the Stakes

The rods are arranged along the periphery in such a way that the surface looks striped. The spaces between the scallomed rods contribute just as much to the whole appearance as the willow rods themselves. You can space the rods in a variety of interval patterns, for example:

- intervals as wide as the rods are thick
- intervals that are consistently larger than the rod diameter's by a given quantity
- intervals of widths that vary, but planned to form a intentional pattern

Rods haphazardly spaced contribute little to an attractive whole.

Sketching Check the shape of the ring. Section the finished circle into quarters, marked at the positions that correspond to 3, 6, 9, and 12 o'clock. One of these marks should fall at the middle of the wrapped section of the ring. Starting at this mark, make five equally spaced marks to the left and five to the right, all on the wrapped ring. These marks indicate the intervals of 11 stakes.

Scalloming Take 11 rods out of water to use as stakes. (Generally more stakes are used for a larger platter and fewer for a smaller platter.) The size of the interval between stakes, the distance from the last stake to the ring, and the thickness of the rods must also be considered. Scallom ten rods along 12 cm toward the butt end. Scallom the eleventh rod along 25 cm (see p. 132).

Attaching the rods With the wrapped section of the ring toward you, lay one rod on the mark farthest to the left, with the scallomed surface resting on the ring. Wrap the scallomed end around the ring, to the left side of the rod, over the rod, and then to the right, parallel to the inside curve of the ring, as shown in drawing 289. Keep it taut! If you must put down the work, secure the scallom with a clothespin. Work the second scallom at the adjacent mark in the same way. This second rod secures the end of the first rod. Work all ten rods.

The last rod is worked in the opposite direction. The 25 cm long scallom holds the tenth end tightly. Wrap the end over the ring, to the right of the rod, over, and under the rod to the left. Work over and under to the second rod. Cut the end short under the work.

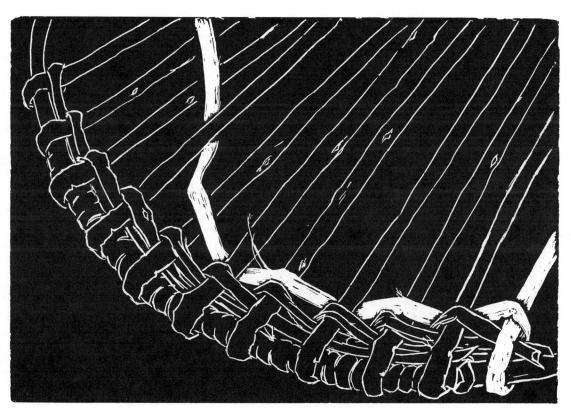

Fitching

By fitching, you'll divide the platter at right angles to the scallomed rods. The necessary marks have already been made (at 3 and 9 o'clock). It's not easy to fasten all the stakes at the same height in a straight line. If it doesn't work, you must cut away the fitching and try again.

The weaving rods Work with two well-soaked rods of equal thickness. In each hand, hold a rod about 30 to 35 cm from the tip. Bring your hands together so that the rods form an X, as shown in the drawing below.

291

Twisting Twist the two rods together clockwise, as shown in the drawing below. Then fold them over in a U-shape.

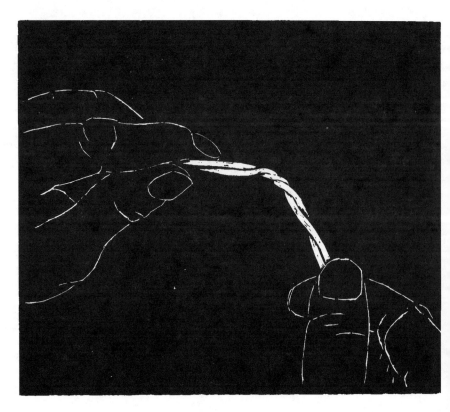

292

Tying up	Cover the mark on the ring with the U created by the twisted rods. Secure the two strands tightly on the ring with a single twist. Each strand consists of a tip and a length of rod.

Work position: The platter should rest on your knees. The hands hold the fitching strands as shown in the drawing below. In this way, the thumb of the right hand can easily press the stakes down so that they are tight against the ring.

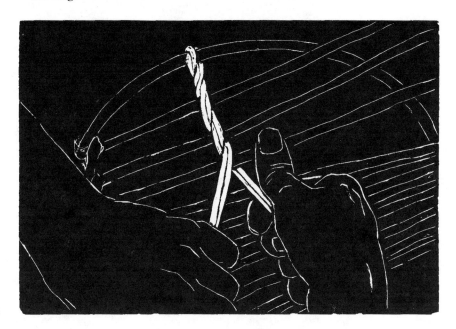

293

Twisting	Twisting continues counterclockwise. If you were twisting thread or yarn, the twist would be called a Z-twist. The twists must be so tight that the stakes cannot be budged. Between stakes you make only a half-twist, so the rod that was underneath at one is uppermost at the next. When the tips are too thin, you have to leave them behind, continuing to twist only with two single rods.

Position of the stakes: Make sure that the stakes are at a right angle to their scallomed ends and parallel to each other. The finished work will look nicer.

Fitching back	Once you work to opposite edge of the ring, twist the strands once. Do not turn the work. Work the fitching back across the ring again, on the same side, from right to left (see drawing 295).

Ending the fitching	End one rod on the underside of the ring, the other under the first spoke. The platter now has its form. There are only a few more hurdles to overcome.

Fastening the stakes	On one side, the unattached stakes still protrude beyond the ring. You'll connect these ends to the ring in the same way as you did the others at the start of the project.

Trimming: Cut the tips of the stakes 20 cm beyond the ring.

Note: The last stake, which was the longest of them to begin with, must extend beyond the outer edge of the ring by a distance equal to the diameter of the platter. Wet down as needed.

Turn the platter so that the unfinished edge is toward you. The stakes should now be under the ring. This next step is complicated, so be patient.

Scalloming You need to scallom the unattached ends of the stakes in the same way as you did the other ends. Be careful not to cut completely through the rod

296

when scalloming! Your thigh, with a good protective covering, is an ideal work surface for this tricky business. The hand holding the knife can move along the inside of your leg to guide the cut. The surfaces to be scallomed should be facing up.

Attaching the scallomed ends

When you've scallomed the ends of all the stakes, soak the piece for about an hour (if you're using peeled willow). Then place the platter on your knees so that the unattached ends point away from you. (If they point toward you, they could easily get broken.) The scallomed surfaces should be facing down, and the top side of the platter facing upward. Attach the scalloms, from the

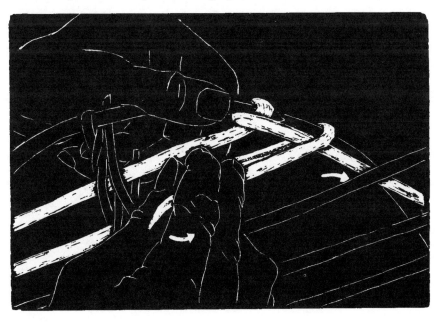

297

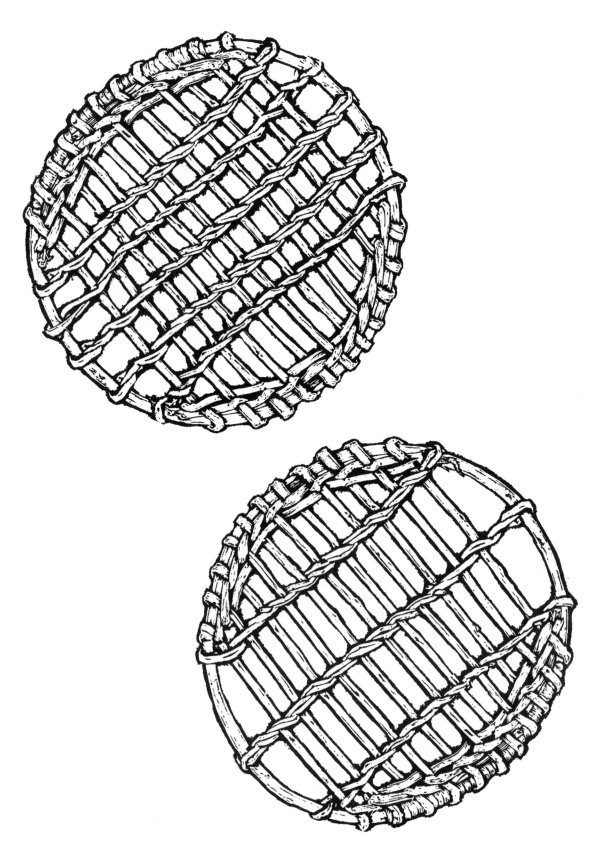

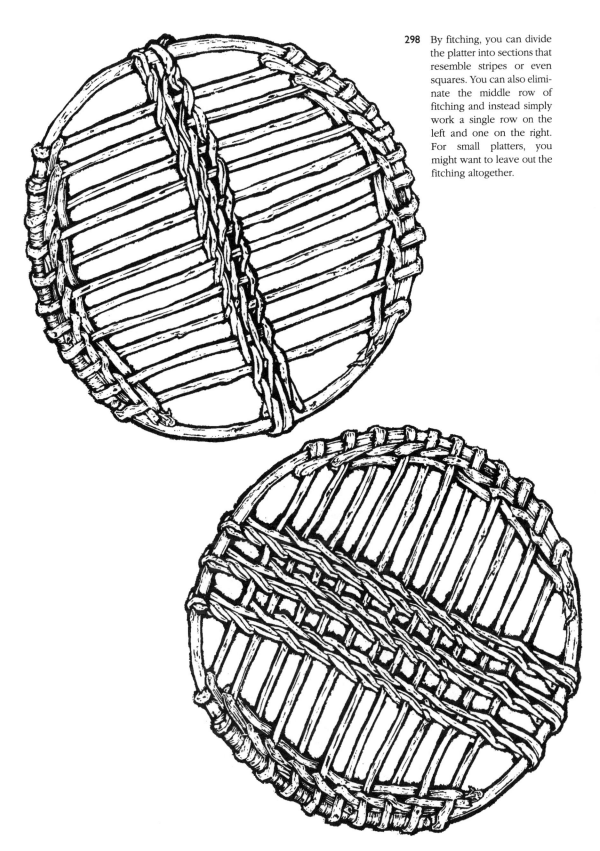

298 By fitching, you can divide the platter into sections that resemble stripes or even squares. You can also eliminate the middle row of fitching and instead simply work a single row on the left and one on the right. For small platters, you might want to leave out the fitching altogether.

left side, and work as you did at the start (pp. 234-235). Wrap each scallomed end around the ring, to the left side of the rod, over, and to the right, parallel to the inside curve of the ring. The last scallomed end is worked over and under in the opposite direction.

Picking off   Pick off any ends protruding from the platter.

Note   This technique is also used on other types of baskets, and the base may not be openwork. The ring itself, for example, may be the outer edge of the base. The scalloms are then positioned at a right angle to the base so the stakes can be woven as the basket wall.

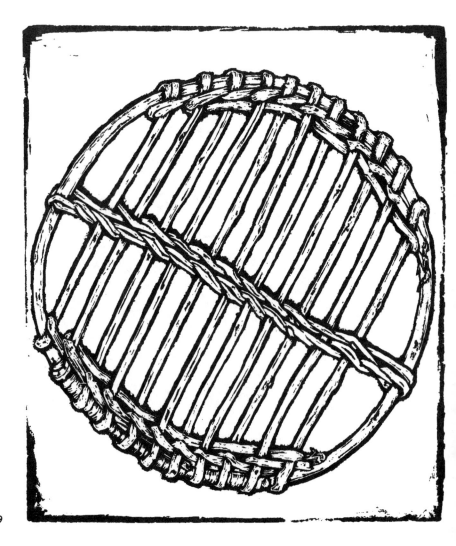

299

Oval Baskets

Although it has structural variations, the basic oval is the second most common form in basketry. The oval is often not, as the name indicates, an elliptical or egg shape. For example, the skeined basket on p. 256 and the openwork basket on p. 286 can be drawn as two semicircles connected by parallel lines.

The easiest way to construct a basket in the shape of an ellipse is by following the instructions for the ribbed, or frame basket, with it's long, convex sides as described here.

An oval basket whose long sides are parallel can be worked with several kinds of weave, including French randing, a chase weave, openwork, or coiled work.

Naturally it is possible to construct elliptical bases with these weave structures. The straight sides of the base could be rounded by adding on, but structural, aesthetic, and functional considerations often rule this out.

On the other hand, if the base is straight-sided and the wall is worked into the elliptical shape, the finished basket will look quite natural and attractive.

300

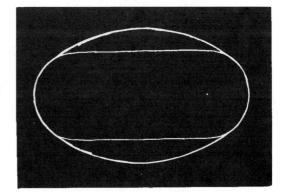

302

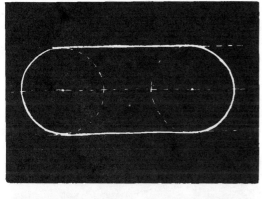

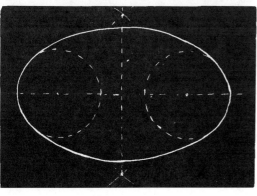

301

The Ribbed Basket

This ribbed, or frame, basket could also be constructed in a circular shape as a dish, bowl, tub, or anything else you wish. The oval form, however, is the natural result of its structure.

The outer frame is related to that of the platter presented on p. 230. A thick, scallomed rod is attached across the center of the ring. When the rod is in place, the ring appears to be one half of an ellipse. Additional stakes, or ribs, are added to this first one as the weave is being worked.

Because of its straightforward construction, this basket, when properly done, has a strong form and compelling presence.

The ribbed basket, often constructed with rods that still have bark (particularly willow, chestnut, and hazelnut), is used mainly to carry unbreakable objects. A "Moses basket," made the same way but with more delicate material, has a very different appearance.

A basket representing the middle between these two extremes is the rectangular "Tosca basket," which has rounded corners. The basket has one handle and is frequently lined because of the many protruding ends. Its form makes it convenient for shopping.

Material   The oval ring shown in the drawing below is made from a long stick about as thick as your thumb. It can be willow, hazelnut, or chestnut. It must be thoroughly soaked or cut fresh from the tree.

Weaving rods: The best material to use for the ribbed basket is brown willow, because it's less sensitive to strain. You'll see why in the next few pages. You'll need about 300 gm of rods, 3 to 6 mm thick and 1.2 m long. You'll also need eight to ten thicker rods, 1.6 m long, for the ribs.

The ring   For the most part, the shape of the ring determines the shape of the finished basket. You can use your thigh as a form around which to bend the ring to its desired size and shape.

Bending: Bend the ring (see p. 121), and scallom the ends straight (see p. 131) along a length of 15 cm. Then fasten the ends together by pushing through a nail and bending over its point with pliers.

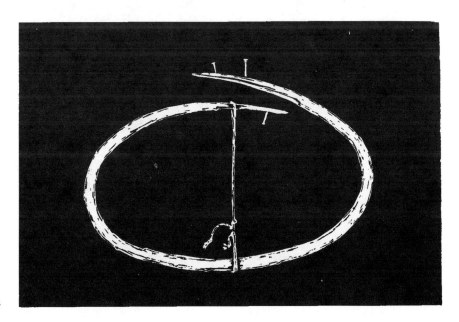

304

The two ends should join evenly on what will be the long side of the basket. To check this, place the ring on the floor and, if necessary, twist and turn it until it lies flat all around. Then after you have nailed the two ends, reinforce the ring by tying a string across its width, as shown in drawing 304 on p. 245.

The Ribbed Basket Weave

Ribs When making a ribbed basket, we call the stakes "ribs." There are an odd number of them. Along the width of the oval, there should be a rib every 3 cm. The one in the middle, scallomed straight for 50 cm, is placed on the ring before weaving begins. None of the ribs is cut to final size until the basket is almost finished.

Designing the form It's possible to make the shape deeper or shallower while you are working, but if you want a basket with steep sides, you must establish this in the first strokes of the weaving. When you have worked to the middle, not much can be modified.

  The shape must be as symmetrical as possible when viewed from the side, unless you have specifically planned another design.

305

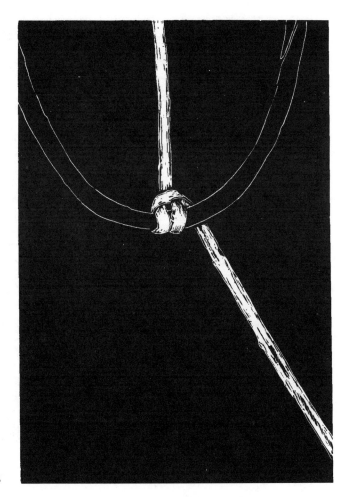

306

Attaching the scallom

Keep the work on your knees, with the narrow end of the ring and the scallom of the middle rib facing you. Wrap the scallom (cut surface upward) under the ring, over the ring, and turn it down inside the ring on the right so that it falls behind the rib to the left, and wrap it over the ring again. Now wrap it up around the ring again and over the middle rib to the right and then back down inside the ring. Continue this series of steps, as shown in drawings 305 and 306, until the scallom has been completely worked. Continue the pattern with the first weaving rod.

Bistaking

Before the first rod has been entirely worked, add two wet ribs to the work. Slype the rods twice, as described on p. 128, and insert them a short way into the weave, as shown in drawing 307 on p. 248. The next rods woven will integrate these new ribs into the basket.

247

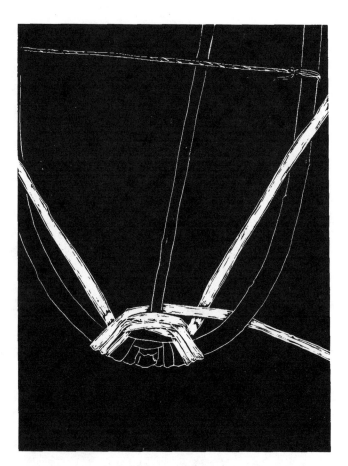

307

Additional ribs: After weaving several rounds, insert slyped rods on each side of the middle rib and beside the ring, for a total of seven ribs (including the middle rib), as shown in drawing 309.

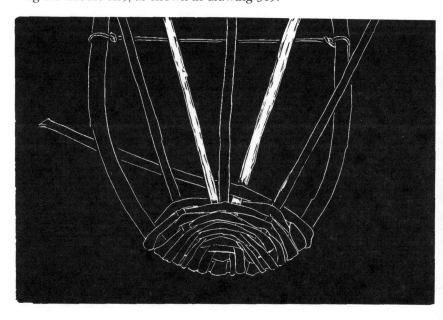

308

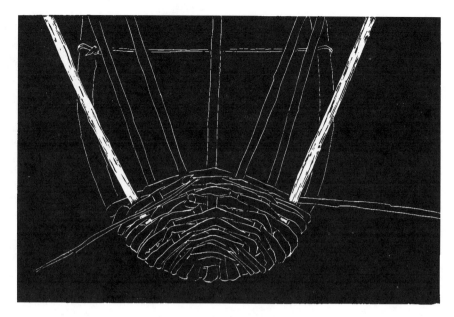

309

Full wraps   Occasionally, you'll have to weave completely around the ring to straighten the top edge of the weaving line. Each time you bring a weaving rod around the ring, position it flush against the previous wrap. Keep the material taut.

Inserting   If a rod has been worked almost to its tip, insert the butt end of a new rod. Leave the thickest part in front of the weave, and work the old and new rods together for several strokes. Unless the basket's intended purpose won't allow it, let the ends protrude.

Turning the work: To make the work a little easier, turn the piece over so that the convex shape faces upward. It will also be easier to see how the shape of the basket is developing.

Form: As mentioned earlier, you can modify the shape of the basket some-what while you are working. The ribs determine the form. For a flatter shape on the basket, for example, you would work the ribs almost level to the ring.

The middle   When you have woven to the middle, remove the string, which had been holding the ring's shape. Be sure now that the oval does not get any wider than you planned. The ribs should cross from one end to the other in straight lines and not be wavy. It's not advisable to use weaving rods that are too thick.

Second half   As soon as you have worked to within 7 cm of the end, reduce the number of ribs at the same rate at which you added them.

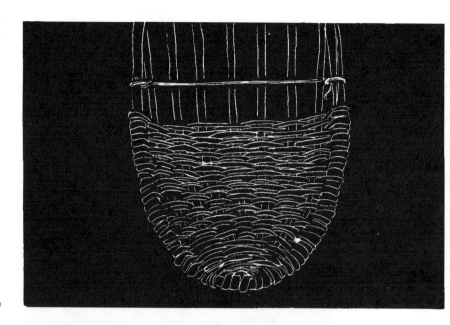

310

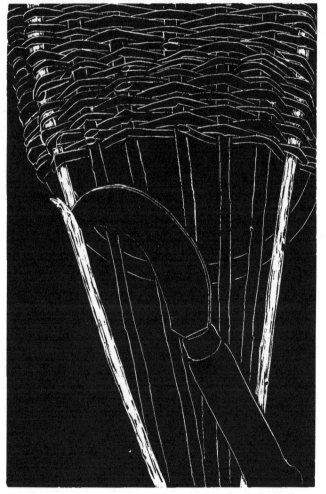

311

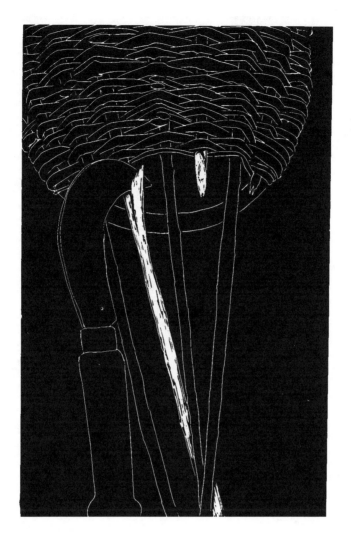

312

Cutting the ribs Now slype the ribs next to the ring, and then those ribs to the immediate left and right of the middle rib, as shown in drawing 311. Continue working the weave and, as you approach the inner edge of the ring, slype the remaining ribs, as shown in drawing 312. Just before finishing, scallom the end of the middle rib and weave it in place, in the same way you did at the start.

Finishing the weaving The long scallomed end will fill in any remaining gaps as you work from the rim inward. This last bit of work takes time. Pull the inserted loop with your index finger so it won't break off. As the weave structure gets tighter, you may need to open it with an awl.

313

Another way of finishing

An easier, but less exciting, method is finishing the weave in the middle. With whole willow, we think the first method is best. When you work toward the middle, the structure often loosens, detracting from the basket's appearance and reducing its useful life.

Also, you need to predetermine the form of the basket and cut all the ribs exactly to length in advance. For example, the middle rib must be calculated to include scallomed ends, plus the length of the basket, plus its depth.

Working the weave: Work the second half exactly as you did the first half. The closer you get to the middle, however, the more difficult it becomes to weave the rods. They should be damp and twisted slightly before you insert them, in order to prevent them from breaking repeatedly.

Skeins

If you decide to make a frame basket with skeins, use the second method, as it will be easier to control the thin, flat material. Experience teaches the limits of the techniques and materials.

252

Picking off   Pick off any protruding ends close to the surface of the weave, as described on pp. 126 and 127.

Drying   If you have made the basket of brown willow, be sure to give it enough time to dry thoroughly before using it. Do not dry it in the sun or near a radiator.

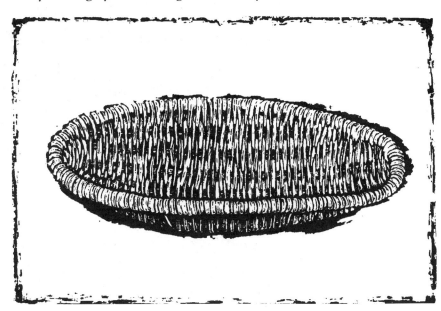

314

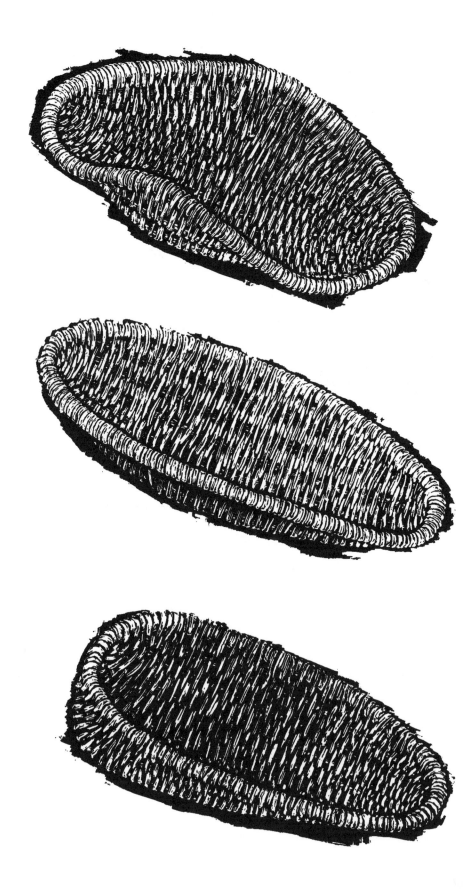

315 The oval basket form allows for a rich variety of shapes and designs—asymmetrical or symmetrical, shallow or deep, convex or straight. The three ribbed baskets shown on this page have the middle ribs fastened across their widths, which creates a different effect in the shape and woven surface.

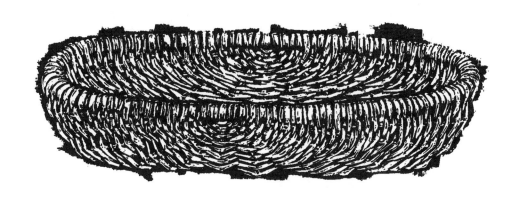

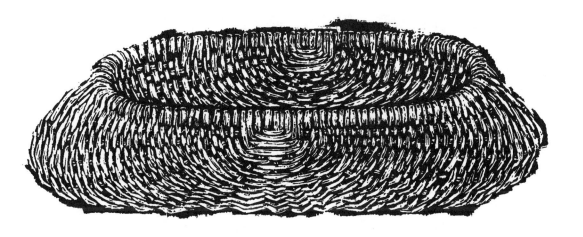

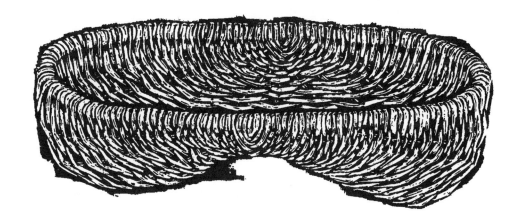

Oval Skeined Basket

We make this skeined basket with a base worked in whole willow rods. The stakes and braided border are also made with whole willow. The walls are not randed as were the first two round basket projects we presented. Instead, they are worked in a chase weave. This style of basket is often used as a bread basket.

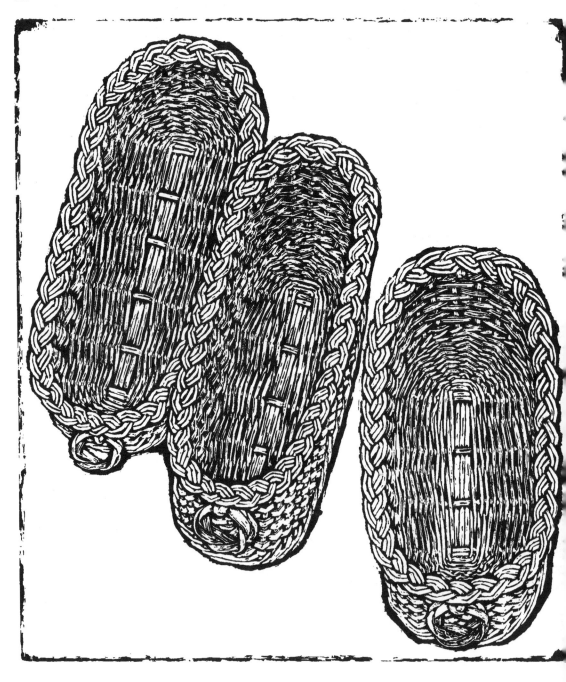

A detailed explanation of how to produce skeins using the three-way cleave can be found on p. 113.

It's a good idea to practice cleaving until you have more than enough clefts to finish a whole basket. The triangular cross sections of the clefts must be shaved flat to make skeins. If you don't have a shave, you can use the blade of a knife. Be certain to hold the blade at a very low angle to the cleft (see p. 116).

Material

To make the base sticks, you'll need about 15 thick rods, 1.2 m long. The base weave can be worked with a handful of 1 m long rods; you'll need another two handfuls for the stakes and the upsett. For the skeins, you'll need a little more than a handful of 2 m long rods; the exact amount depends on how much comes off the rods as waste. Don't forget to soak all your material properly.

French Randing the Base

There are various types of weave structures used for oval bases. For this basket, we work the slath in a French rand pattern with whole willow rods (see p. 160).

This base gets its oval shape from the way the slath is constructed.

The slath

The slath is made up of short and long sticks. It's similar to the slath shown on p. 177, but is instead made up of three long sticks threaded through six shorter, split sticks, and evenly spaced. The six are separated—three on one side and three on the other—to form two crosses with legs of equal length at each end. Then, to evenly fill the space between them, one stick from each cross is moved toward the center. The basket's finished length determines the interval and the number of sticks (see pp. 262-264).

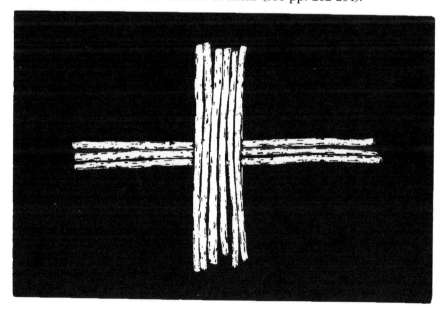

317

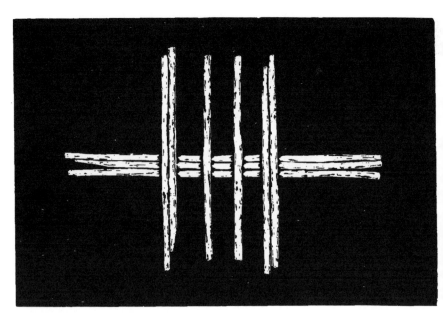

Spacing the base sticks: For this project, leave at least a finger's width of space between the sticks.

Length: The rods for the base sticks must be 10 cm longer in all directions than the size of the finished base.

Quantity: You'll need six short and three long sticks.

Note: The protruding legs of the short and long sticks must be the same length. The slath should lie on your knees, dome side up. The first strokes will be nerve-wracking for the beginner. The slath often loses its shape and twists as you work.

Inserting the rods

Cut the butt ends of eight thin, wet rods. Insert the butt ends of four of the rods, from right to left as for French randing, in the intervals between the short sticks, as shown in drawing 319. Because you insert the rods from the right, the first rod is the one farthest to the right, under the double sticks. To hold the weaving rods in place, move the third rod behind the right-hand pair of sticks and work the fourth rod behind the second stick, as shown in drawing 320.

Tying in

As shown in drawing 321, move the second rod over the double sticks and behind the long sticks. Weave the first rod over the second rod and the long sticks. Move the second rod over the first rod and the double sticks, and leave it behind the second short stick.

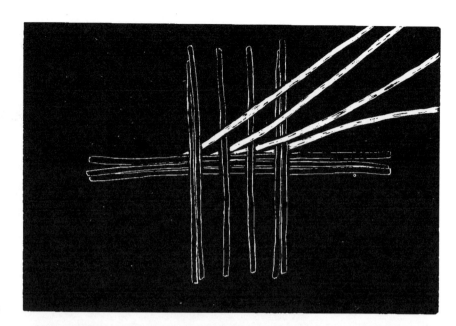

319

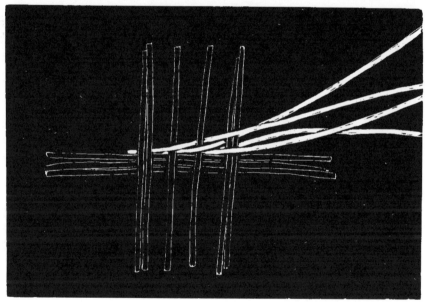

320

Turning the work   The dome of the base sticks should always be facing up. Turn the work 180° and repeat the process. Insert the butt ends of the second set of weaving rods, from right to left, in the intervals between the short sticks. Lock in the third and fourth rods with one stroke. Work the first and second rods around the long sticks, as described on p. 258. (In drawing 322 the base has not been turned; the second set has been inserted, but not worked.)

259

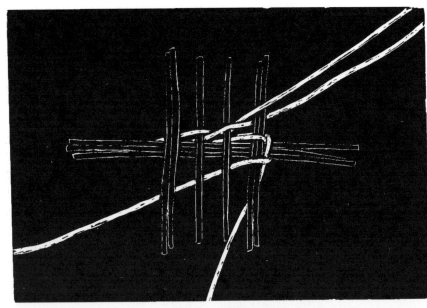

321

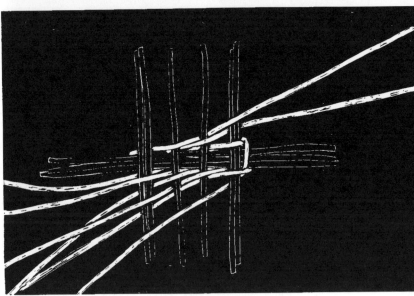

322

Working with eight rods

Now turn the work 180° again. (The first side you worked is again away from you.) The second rod from the second side you worked is now over the left-hand pair of sticks and rests behind the next single stick. Weave this rod in front of the next stick and behind the right-hand pair of sticks. Weave the first rod (which is behind the left-hand pair) in front of one stick, behind one, and over the right-hand pair. Repeat these steps with the second and first rods of the remaining set.

Now you'll work three rounds with all the rods. The long sides are randed and the narrow ends are reverse-paired. The reverse pairing occurs in the large corner intervals.

Opening up   Open up the double sticks by spreading the two outermost sticks to span the gaps in the corner intervals. Next, spread the two outer legs of the long sticks, but leave the middle leg straight.

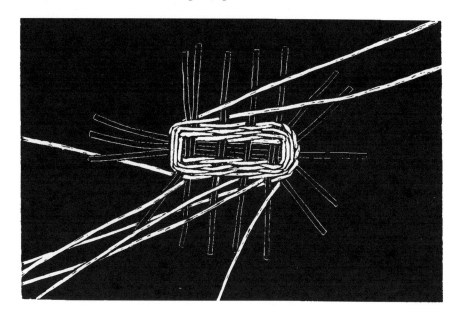

323

Narrow ends   When you work the pair of rods around the narrow ends, you twist them together in each interval. (This is the same reverse pairing used in the base of the shopping basket.) Be sure the sticks are equally spaced and that the weave gradually forms an evenly shaped curve.

Long sides   Work the long sides of the base with two-strand randing (1/1). The rods are not twisted, but rather worked side by side.

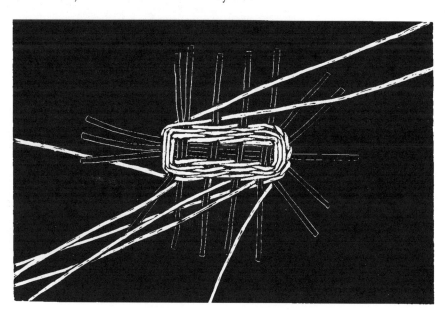

324

Complete round: The reverse pairing on the narrow end fills in the intervals and allows you to work an attractive, full curve.

If you've skipped a weaving rod, the next rod will fall into its path automatically, and you'll see the mistake immediately.

When a entire round is finished, there should be two pairs (four rods) remaining on each long side. (If there are two rods on one side and six on the other, however, it may be that you are looking at an unfinished round and not at a mistake.)

Tight weaving: The soaked weaving rods must be pulled tight again and again to prevent gaps in the weave structure, both along the long sides or in the curves of the narrow ends. A solid weave structure makes the basket strong.

Ending the randing

As you get near the tips of the weaving rods, be sure the four rods are positioned on each long side. The join is made by adding the butt ends of another eight rods, as similar in thickness as possible to the first rods. By starting with the butt ends, you can finish the base weave with tips, guaranteeing a nice edge.

Pairing

Start two rods after you have finished randing, inserting tip ends first. Twine the pair until they are used up, rapping down as needed. Join a second pair, butt ends first, so you can finish the edge with tips. Lock in the tips, and the oval base is finished.

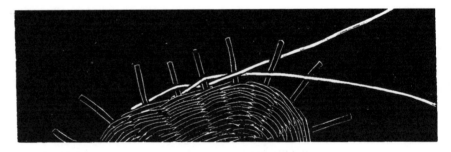

325

Planning the slath

If you want to know exactly how many stakes are needed for a basket, you must first calculate the dimensions of the slath.

Example:
   Top border (large oval)
   45 x 60 cm

   Base (small oval)
   30 x 40 cm

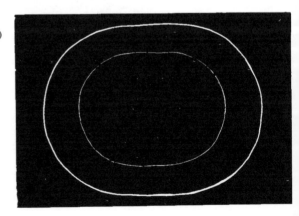

326

Stake intervals along top border: about 3 cm

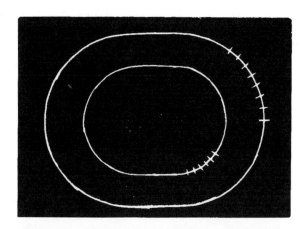

327

Border circumference: Subtract the diameter from the total basket length to determine the length of the straight sides. Multiply the diameter by *pi* (3.14) to determine the measurement of the narrow ends.

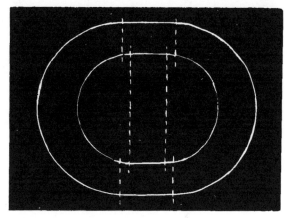

328

Two straight sides + Two semicircles = Circumference
    60 cm - 45 cm = 15 cm x 2 =   30 cm
        45 cm diameter x 3.14 = <u>141 cm</u>
    Top border circumference = 171 cm

Number of stakes:
Top circumference ÷ Interval = Number of stakes
    171 cm ÷ 3 cm = 57 stakes, rounded down to 56

Number of sticks in slath:
Number of bistaked stakes ÷ 4 = Number of slath sticks
    56 stakes ÷ 4 = 14 slath sticks

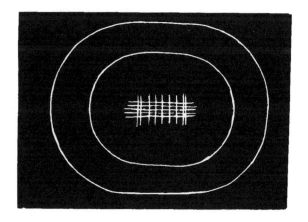

329

Distribution of short and long sticks:
$$40 \text{ cm} - 30 \text{ cm} = 10 \text{ cm} \times 2 = \ 20 \text{ cm}$$
$$30 \text{ cm diameter} \times 3.14 = \ \underline{94 \text{ cm}}$$
$$\text{Base circumference} = 114 \text{ cm}$$

Base circumference ÷ Number of stakes = Interval of slath sticks
   114 cm ÷ 56 stakes = about 2 cm interval

Straight side ÷ Stick interval = Number of short sticks
   10 cm ÷ 2 cm = 5 + 4 (the 4 additional sticks are the double short sticks at the ends)

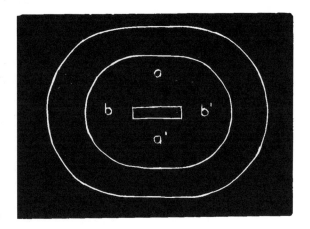

330

Length and width of the base: Of the 14 slath sticks, 5 are the long sticks, 9 are the short sticks. The five long sticks are placed directly beside each other and together are about 3 cm wide.

Base diameter - Width of the long sticks = a + a′ (see drawing 330)
   30 cm - 3 cm = 27 cm

The slath should be long enough so that b + b' is equal to (a + a′):
Base length - (a + a′) = Slath length
   40 cm - 27 cm = 13 cm
The short sticks are distributed along 13 cm of the long sticks.

Using these formulas, you can precisely calculate the proper dimensions for a correctly worked base. Even for an experienced basketmaker, this is a must when making any oval basket, not only when a customer has requested a specific size.

Picking off   It's usually advantageous, aesthetically and practically, to pick off the ends in the base so that they are underneath. With shears, pick off the slath sticks flush to the surface. To make a platter, you can add a border onto an oval base, as was done for the lid on p. 223. This particular basket doesn't require a border, however.

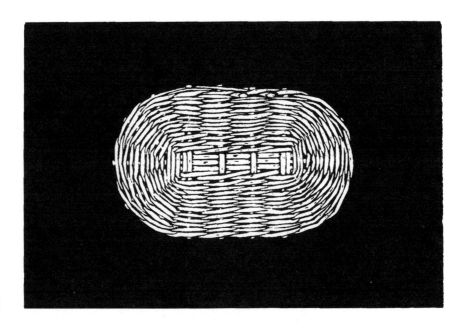

331

The Bottom Waling

The bottom waling, or foot wale, is also referred to as the false foot. It covers up the ends of the slath sticks, as on p. 184 for the shopping basket, making it unnecessary to add a genuine foot.

In fact, the false foot raises the base of the basket slightly off the floor. This bottom waling also gives the bottom edge an even and flowing appearance.

Inserting the stakes

First, you'll set up the framework for the waling and the wall.

Determine the number of stakes you need by counting all the ends of the base sticks and multiplying the results by two. (Remember, you are bistaking.)

Depending on the form and height of the basket body, it may be necessary to use slightly fewer or slightly more.

Anchor the stakes in the base as you did when bistaking the shopping basket (dome side up). Keep everything damp.

Waling

For a basket of a size suitable for a beginner's project, you'll need two groups of rods, as described on p. 187.

The false foot is worked with two groups of five rods. They are worked in front of four, behind one (4/1), which results in a broad pattern of strokes across the front of the weave.

Insert the two groups of five along the left half of each long side, one rod to the right of each stake.

With an awl, prick up the rods at right angles (see p. 134).

265

Move the rod farthest to the left over the four waling rods and in front of four stakes, behind one stake, and out again (4/1). Work the remaining four rods in the same way, each time advancing by one stake. The stroke is always in front of four, behind one.

332

Joining the first and the second groups: When the first group has been worked around to meet the second, continue the stroke another four stakes, so that you have overlapped the second group of rods, as shown in the drawing below. Continue weaving with the second group of rods. When you reach the first group again, insert the tips of the rods so that the whole weave appears to merge together smoothly, as shown in drawing 334.

333

Tie the stakes upright with a cord or skein around their centers.
Secure the work: Secure the base to the work surface with an awl.

Chase Weave with Skeins

For this basket, you'll work a chase weave with skeins and whole willow stakes.
Making skeins: Refer to the detailed description of cleaving and shaving rods to produce skeins, pp. 113-116.

The weaving pattern   If there is are even number of stakes, which is the usual situation, you work the pattern with two skeins. (If there are an odd number of stakes, one skein is worked continuously at a time.)
Starting the weave: Taper the end of one wet skein, and insert it to the left of a stake in a narrow end of the basket, as shown in drawing 335 on p. 268. Work the skein in front of one and behind one (1/1) around half the basket. Insert another tapered skein and; work the second half. The bark side must always face out; otherwise the skein breaks easily.
Continue in 1/1 so that one skein "chases" the other, and catches up to but does not overtake it. When the two skeins meet, drop the working skein and pick up the skein that is now in front to continue.
Inserting a new skein: Overlap the end of a new skein with the end of the used skein. Work both together for several stakes, as shown in drawing 336 on p. 268.

335

336

Form   Because skeins produce a less rigid surface than whole willow, you should check the shape of the basket often.

    If the weave structure has opened up too much, it can't simply be pushed together! There's no other way to correct the problem than by taking apart the wall. The used skeins can't be used again because they have kinks where they've passed around stakes.

Height   The height is determined by the basket's intended function. Skeined baskets are mainly suitable for holding or carrying lightweight contents. For example, for a bread basket, you only need to weave a few rounds.

Note: While working the weave, you must continuously watch that the stakes remain evenly spaced. As when working whole willow, you move the skeins around the stakes—not the reverse.

Finishing: Pick off the skeins as you work them to their ends for an even edge on the border. Rap down the weave structure and tap down high spots with a lightweight rapping iron.

Wrapped Waling

For the top, waled border, we have chosen a lighter technique than was used for the bottom waling. Wrapped or lashed work is popularly used with finer weave structures.

Material   One thick rod, about 1.2 m long, split with a knife along its whole length, is the core around which the wrap is made. Shave the two halves along their

337

lengths. They must be 20 cm longer than the outer circumference of the basket, and each half rod must have 10 cm of its convex side shaved flat at one end.

Beginning: With a clothespin, attach the two halves (flat surfaces facing each other) on either side of the stakes in the middle of the straight sides of the basket. Position them on top of and parallel to the last row of weaving.

Use another thin skein as a wrapper. If you pull the skein between your thumb and the awl or the handle of a hammer a couple of times, it will be easier to manipulate (this technique is similar to curling a ribbon for a gift package). Trim the end and, with its bark side facing outward, insert it to the left of one stake, as shown in the drawing on p. 269.

Wrapping

Sew, or lash, over the halved rod in front of the basket and between two stakes. Now pass diagonally behind one stake to the right, under the halved rods, and back out to the front. Repeat. Pull the skein tightly as you work. The stakes are clamped between the halved rods, which are securely bound by the wrapping skein.

338

Joining the ends

The flat inside surfaces of the halved rods are tapered so that all four ends overlap evenly and neatly. Lash around to the start of the stitching. Hold the skein taut and in place with a clothespin.

339

Securing the end: Weave away the skein end with two strokes of 1/1 under the wrapped rods, as shown in the drawing below.

340

Rapping down   Carefully press the lashing down onto the last row of weaving.

Soaking   Before shaping the stakes into a border, soak the upper portion of the basket and the unworked stakes for at least half an hour.

Adding on   If the wrapping skein is too short to finish the round, insert its end into the weave and begin a second one as you did the first.

The Braided Border

Braided borders can be made in a wide variety of patterns. This basket has a three-rod, French braided border.

As a rule, you start the border where the crossover or side handle will be attached. If you don't intend to make one of these, you can start the border on the curve. People are less likely to spot any unevenness in the rounded sections of the basket.

Beginning the braided border   Drawing 341, p. 272: You'll work with three pairs of equally thin rods. Insert the first pair in an interval on the narrow end of the basket, butt ends inside the basket and angled to the left. Insert the second pair in the interval to the right, crossing the first pair, with butt ends outside. Insert the third pair in the same interval with the second, on top of the second pair, and parallel to the first.

Drawing 342: Move the first pair in front of two stakes and the third pair.

Drawing 343: With your left thumb, turn down the leftmost stake in the interval that the first pair has just passed through.

Drawing 344: With the right hand, move the second pair out beside the turned-down stake. Hold them down with the left thumb.

Drawing 345: Move the third pair in front of the second pair, turned-down stake, and upright stake, and into the next interval.

Drawing 346: Kink this last stake, and move it, together with the pair of rods behind it, to the front of the basket.

341

342

343

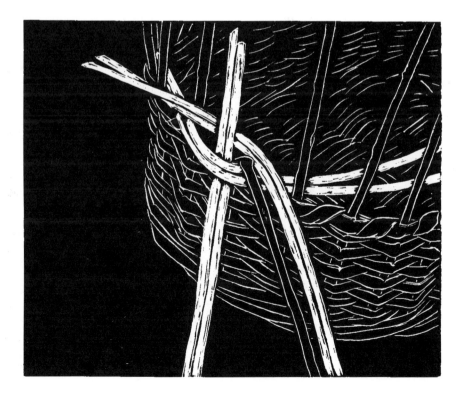

344

345

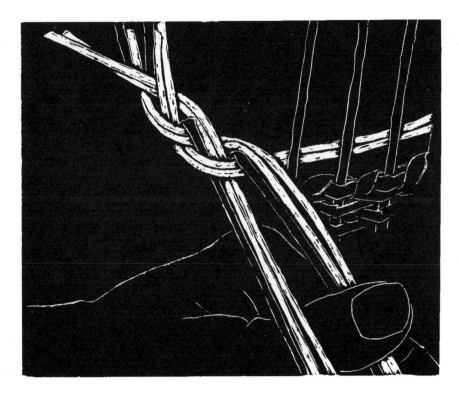

346

274

347

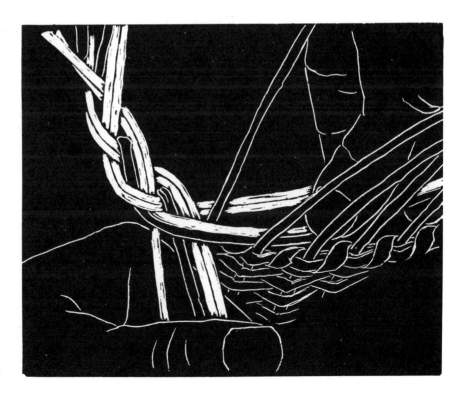

348

275

Drawing 347: With your right hand, move the first turned-down stake and the adjacent rod in front of two stakes (one is turned down; the other is still standing). Leave them inside the basket.

Note: Starting with this stroke, the rightmost rod of each pair is left in front of the basket (as the single rod shown here at far left under the thumb). Later these remaining rods will be picked off.

Drawing 348: Turn down the next standing stake and move the inside pair out of the basket with it. Work a pair again in front of two stakes.

Continue in the same way around the basket. Keep the material damp enough that it is pliable.

Be sure the outer edge of the braid contains only two rods.

Completing the border   If necessary, loosen up the butt ends of the first and third pairs at the beginning of the braid to make room for the final stroke. Move two rods in front of the last standing stake.

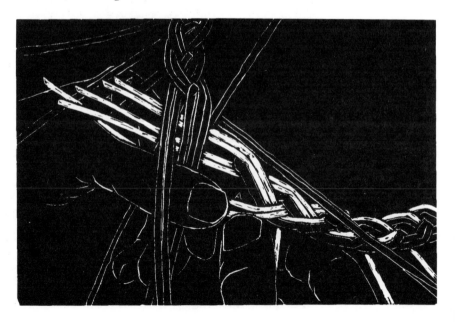

349

Turn this stake down and bring the two rods with it out of the basket (in drawing 349, the two rods are shown crossing over the braid at far right). Now insert two rods under the stakes at the beginning of the braid (see the arrows in the drawing below).

350

Do the same with the next turned-down stake and accompanying rod. Use the awl to make an opening, as shown below. First insert the rod, then the stake beside it. The rightmost rod is not used.

351

Drawing 352: Now the butt ends of all three beginning pairs are outside the basket (one of each is labelled A in the drawings). The tips of the three pairs just woven are inside the basket. You'll remove the A rods, one at a time, replacing them with tips.

Drawing 353: Work with the rightmost tip of each pair inside the basket. Remove the A rod. Twist each tip as you insert it to the front, through the space where the A rod had been located.

Drawing 354: When you've finished, three butt ends remain outside the basket; three tips remain inside. Pick off all the protruding rods.

Note: These braided borders are also frequently worked vertically around the wall, as shown in drawing 133 on p. 119.

352

353

354

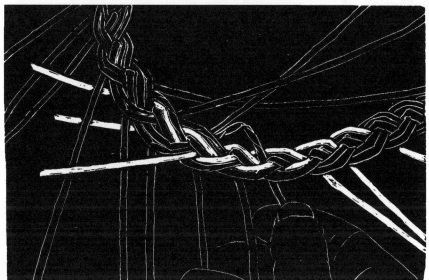

355

Rings Woven from One Skein

When you've finished, you should have a few long skeins left over. Rings for this basket could be made in other ways, for example, by bending (see drawing 135, p. 122). The rings described here, however, can only be made with skeins. They harmonize visually with the weave structure and the braided border, also made with skeins.

Starting

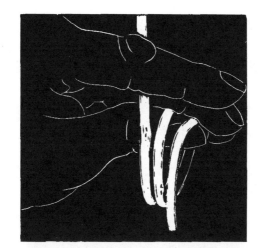

356

Hold about half the length of the skein vertically between your left index finger and middle finger. You will now wrap the skein into two loops about 4 cm in diameter, with shaved side in. Wrap twice around your thumb from back to front, working from left to right to make the two loops.

Braiding

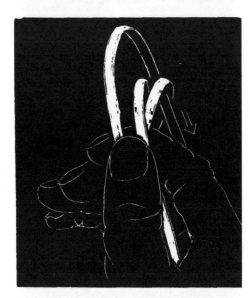

357

Transfer the skein to your right hand, holding the loops and the end that is pointing downward securely under your thumb. (This end is inactive; the end held vertically is the weaving end.) Cross the right loop over the left loop. Insert the weaving end under the right loop, passing over the left loop, as shown in the drawing.

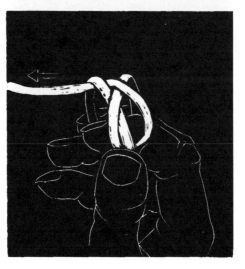

358

Now cross the left loop over the right loop. Weave the end over the right loop and under the left loop. As needed, turn the ring slightly as you work.

Cross the right loop over the left loop. Now weave the end over the left loop and then under the right, as shown.

359

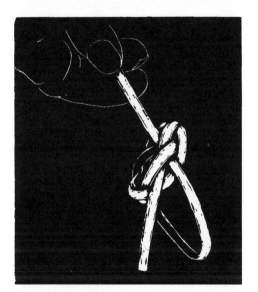

Continue to work, alternately crossing loops and inserting the weaving end. When the ends meet on the same path, over-lap them and work them just enough in pattern to secure them.

Do not cut either end of the fin-ished ring too short.

360

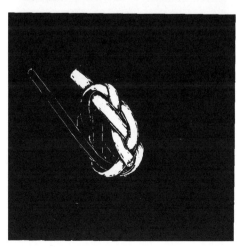

With this technique, you can make rings as large as the length of the skein allows. Materials other than willow can also be woven into rings to be used in many ways: for example, as napkin rings, garlands, and rings to play catch or other games with.

361

362

Fastening rings to the basket

The rings are tied firmly to the lashing under the border. Lock the tied ends securely into the weave.

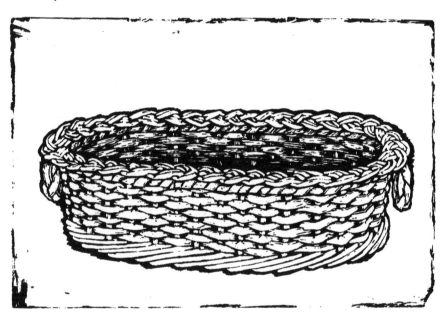

363

If you want to decorate the basket with a chain of rings, weave the wall of the basket in as simple a pattern as possible, for example, a 1/1 pattern.

Remember, this fanciful decoration must not get in the way of the basket's intended use. Carefully consider how elaborate, how long, and how conspicuous you want the chain to be. Plan the ring sizes and the skein widths. Make several rings of various sizes in advance. The rings for the chain must be interlinked as they're made. In other words, before you make the second ring, draw the skein you'll use through the first ring twice. Do the same for each ring you add.

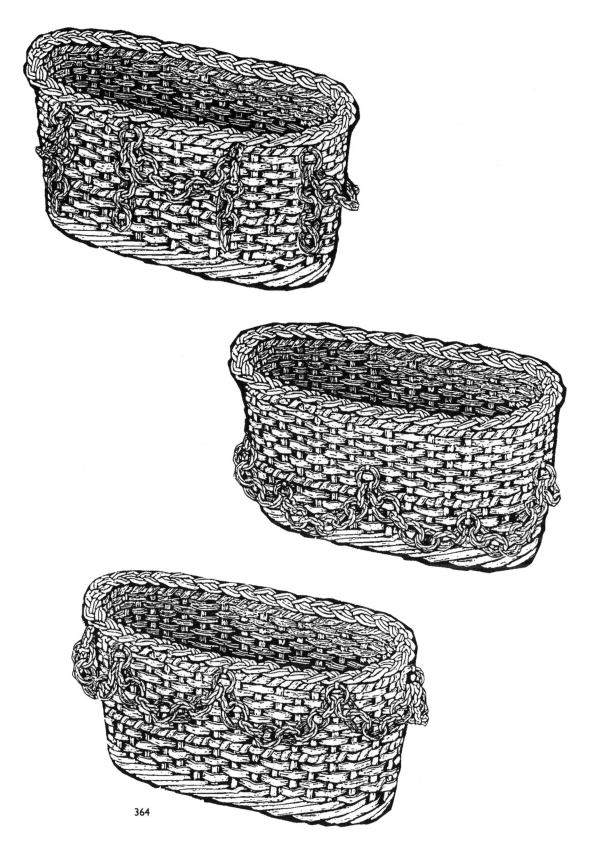

364

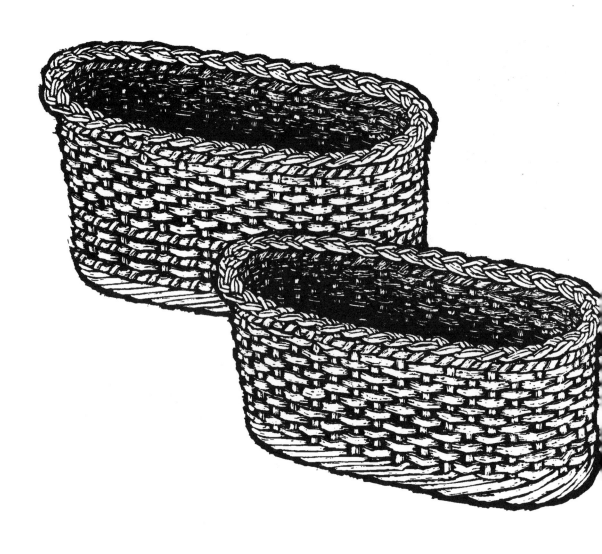

365 Baskets with high walls provide you with an opportunity to vary the surface-pattern designs. The weaving on the baskets here is done in bands of varied heights, interrupted or framed by single or multiple bands of wrapping. (Avoid placing bands in the exact center of the basket's height; they cut the basket in half visually and detract from the overall appearance.)

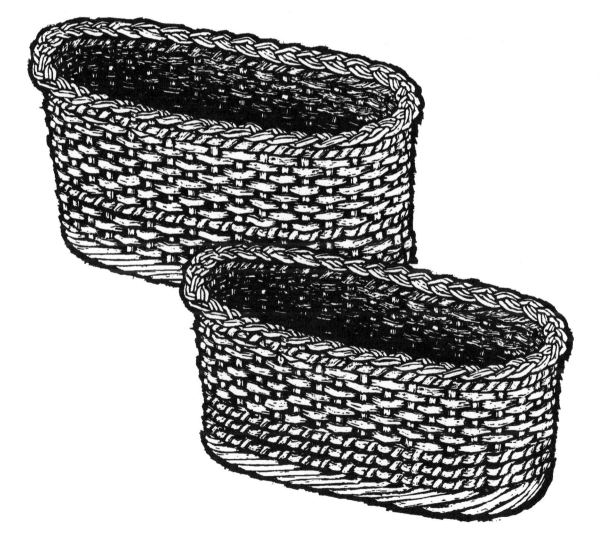

Openwork Basket

You frequently see openwork baskets in the paintings of the sixteenth and seventeenth centuries. These studies of still life and home interiors illustrate the basket's innumerable functions in everyday life.

366

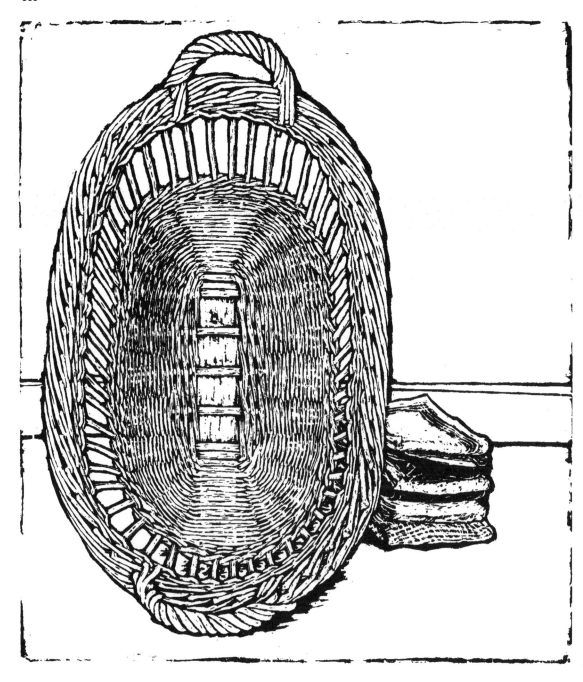

In a painting by Jan van Balen (1611-1654), you can find a lovely rectangular, openwork basket filled with dishes. In a painting by Gerrit Dou (1613-1675), you can admire a portable chicken cage made of whole willow.

Despite this long tradition, openwork baskets have been overlooked for some time. The most common place to find them now is in the small bakeries in the French countryside. There, long baguettes of bread are displayed in tall, rectangular, openwork baskets and breakfast rolls in short ones.

At one time, it was common to keep cheese, eggs, plants, and other farm products in openwork baskets and containers for display, transport, or storage. Wastepaper, sewing, and laundry baskets, as well as armchairs, cradles, and small tables, were often constructed using openwork techniques.

The light and simple appearance of openwork makes it suitable for use with any sort of natural, organic object. These baskets also have many practical advantages. They are lightweight, sturdy (everyday use proves it), and easy to keep clean, and their contents are clearly visible. For experienced basketmakers, openwork is a fast way to make a basket. The beginner may have difficulty maintaining the basket's shape.

Material For a base of about 20 x 30 cm, you'll need 15 to 20 thick rods, 1.4 m long, as short sticks; instead of long sticks, you'll need a wood slat about 4 cm wide and 6 mm thick. The best sort of wood is hand-finished, of the same color as the rods (the wood is not soaked). The base weave, stakes, and waling require three handfuls of thin rods, 1.2 m long. For the fitching and handles, you need 12 to 15 of the best quality, thin rods, 1.6 m long. For handle cores, you'll need a stick about 12 mm thick.

Base with Slat

The wood slat, which is worked into the weave, gives the base stability and is especially suitable for very long baskets. It also helps the beginner to start more easily and to make a level base.

The slat takes the place of the long sticks in the slath. The short sticks, split in the middle, are threaded onto the board. For a larger project, you can calculate the number of short sticks you'll need with the method described on pp. 262-264. To work this base to the size already mentioned, you'll need seven sticks—a pair at each end and three sticks arranged between them at regular intervals. Don't forget to cut the stakes 10 cm longer than the finished width of the base!

Starting the weaving With three short sticks in the middle, you'll have four intervals, so start the weaving with four rods on each side. As usual, insert the butt ends into the intervals, from right to left. The first rod crosses over the double sticks, and

287

the tip is pulled under the slat to the right (clockwise). Move the second rod in front of the first single base stick, behind the double sticks, and through, so that the tip is on top of the slat. Continue, working three rounds, the same way as you did the skeined basket (pp. 260-262). Dampen the materials as needed.

Staking up   At the beginning of the fourth round, insert one slyped, soaked rod of the same diameter as the neighboring sticks at each corner, directly beside the slat.

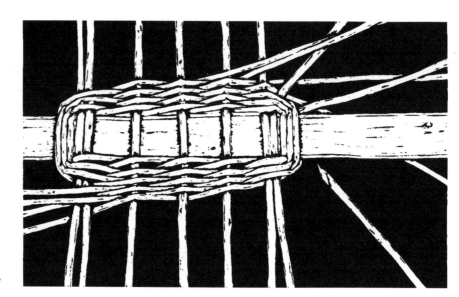

367

Opening up   At the same time, open up the outer stick of each pair of sticks, that is, spread them in the direction of the newly inserted rods. Remember, for this oval base, the short, curved sides of the oval base are worked as reverse pairing. The straight sides are usually randed over and under. Work the weaving rods to their tip ends and join eight new butt ends to continue weaving.

Finishing   As was the base of the skeined basket, this base is also finished with pairing. Joins are made with butt ends of new rods to tips of old rods, and the work is finished with tips. Keep the paired rods taut, especially when you are working the curves. Repeatedly rap down the straight sides with a rapping iron. Pick off the base sticks when you've finished weaving.

Important: If the base has gone out of shape or is unbalanced to one side, it will affect the look of the whole basket. The base provides the foundation for the entire basket's shape. If the base does lose its shape, you must either start over again or replace a section of the weave before proceeding.

Plain Openwork

The smaller the intervals between stakes, the more difficult your work will be. Weaving through closely spaced stakes demands more skill than weaving through widely spaced ones. The results will be more solid, however, and, you could say, more attractive as well.

Stakes
With dome side up, bistake by inserting one stake to the left and one to the right of each base stick. Insert one stake on each side of the slat ends and two on top of each end. You began with seven short sticks and the slat; now you should have a total of 52 stakes. Prick up the stakes, as shown on p. 184, and tie them together near their tips to hold the oval form of the basket.

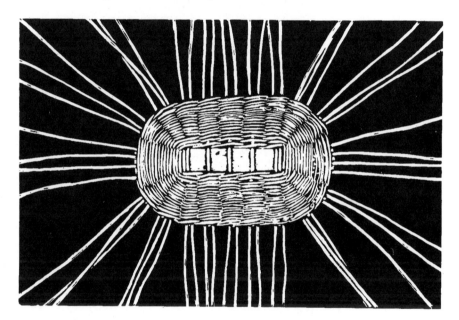

368

Bottom waling
Work the waling with two groups of five rods. The wale is worked in the same way as for the shopping basket, pp. 184-188, but the stroke is worked in front of three, behind two (3/2). This stroke creates a lovely pattern on the inside and a long pattern on the outside of the basket that covers the ends of the base sticks.

Inserting: Insert a butt end in each of the five intervals, from left to right, on both sides of the basket, as shown in drawing 369, p. 290.

Waling: Move the leftmost rod over the others, in front of three stakes, behind two, and out (drawing 370). Work each of the five rods the same way until you reach the second group of five. Work the second group around to the first in 3/2. When a rod from the second group rests in the same interval with the butt end of the first rod of the first group, work the remaining four rods of the second group in 3/2. If the waling has been worked well, neither its beginning nor end will be visible. Pull the rods tightly. Rap down if necessary and pick off the protruding ends.

369

370

Holding the work   Up until now, you have been holding the work on your knees. Now secure it to the work surface with a thin awl, a bit to one side of the middle.

Waling   Drawing 371: After you have made the waled false foot, you'll begin the waling that holds the stakes at the proper angle and keeps them evenly spaced. Insert a group of four rods, tips first, on each side of the basket.

Work them in front of two, behind two (2/2). While you're working, frequently rap down the weave structure so that it is solid. Drawing 372: End the round of waling with butt ends. Stick these ends into the previous round, and make the join by inserting new butt ends.

371

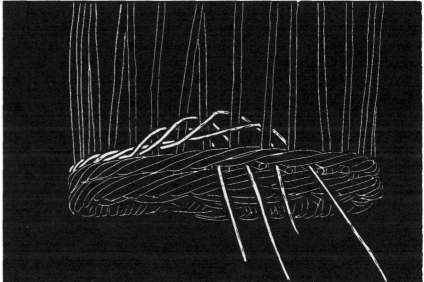

372

Checking the base If the base does not lie flat on the work surface, press it flat before you continue working. You can correct any deformity by pressing the woven surface against a corner of a table. This will force the stakes to point straight upward so they're symmetrical.

Fitching   The stakes in this openwork basket are held in place only by the bottom waling and the upper border, so we added a round of fitching. It's worked in the same way as for the platter on p. 236.

Marking: Mark the desired height of the fitching (basket height less about 2 cm) on every third or fourth stake with a pencil.

Starting: On the straight basket side, a little to the left of the middle, fold the plied ends around the first stake at the desired height, and begin fitching (see drawings 291 and 292). Twist the rods once counterclockwise in the interval to the right. The rod that was in front of the first stake is now behind the next; the rod that was behind the first stake is now in front of the next.

Hand position: If you want the work to appear uniform, it's important both to work the fitch at the proper height and to position your hands correctly. See the instructions on p. 237.

373

A general rule   On openwork oval baskets, the walls along the straight sides are almost vertical, but the curved ends flare somewhat toward the top. This widening at the top makes the basket appear lighter and somewhat more delicate than it would with straight walls, and the slightly conical form has functional advantages.

To obtain this shape, you have to fitch the stakes properly. The stakes in the curved walls must not be pressed tightly against the twist in the fitching. The fitching determines the final shape of the walls, and they cannot be changed afterward.

Inserting   Continue fitching until you have worked the rods about one hand's length away from their ends. To continue around the circumference of the basket, you will have to make a join, butt end to butt end.

You will again need two, top-quality, soaked rods of the same length and width. Prick them up about one hand's length from their ends with round-nosed pliers. The first rod to be replaced is the one emerging from behind the last stake. Position the kink in the new rod behind this stake; the old end should be pointing out. Lock in the old end by twisting the replacement rod and the second old rod together. Continue fitching for several stakes, and replace the second rod in the same way, as shown in the drawing below.

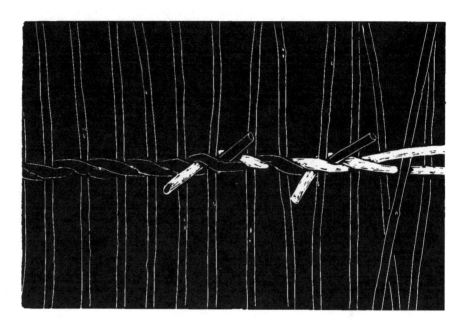

374

Finishing the fitching

Once you've fitched all around, the second pair of rods will also be close to their tips. Continue to work the weave a little beyond the start, so that there are seven or eight stakes with a double layer of fitching. Now you can simply pick off the two rods on the outside; there is no need to fasten them. The butt ends sticking out at the join should also be picked off, but don't cut them too short or they'll slip through the weave.

Variations

You can work rounds of fitching below the border, halfway up the walls, or at a distance of one-third or one-quarter the total height from the bottom. This way, you would also have several rounds of fitching holding the stakes in place. If you decide to add rounds of fitching, don't cut the rods at the end of one round. Instead, spiral the fitching up to the next level so that it is continuous and proceed to work the next round. (See pp. 167-168 for more information on variations in openwork.)

Note: If the stake intervals become irregular or the basket loses its shape while you're working, remove the whole round and start again. Check the basket shape often, as well as the vertical line and spacing of the stakes.

Be sure your weaving rods are of equal diameter. If they are, they will then wrap like yarn uniformly around the stakes, and strengthen the basket wall.

Top waling   This four-rod wale is worked immediately above the fitching. The stroke is in front of two, behind two (2/2). The pattern is worked with one group until the rods run out. Four new butt ends are joined and the weaving continues, as described on pp. 193-194.

Inserting: The join is made by inserting a new butt end beside the old tip in each interval, working left to right. Press the old tip to the left to make it easier to insert the new butt end.

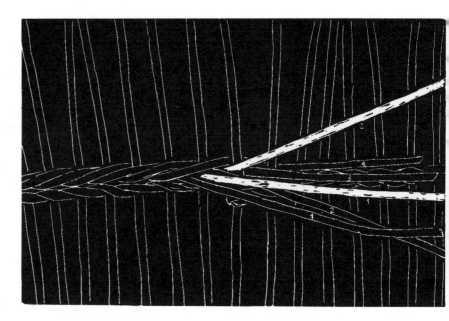

375

As you can see in drawing 376, the butt end of a new rod has been inserted in each of four intervals and worked one stroke. Five strokes are shown because the first rod has been worked twice.

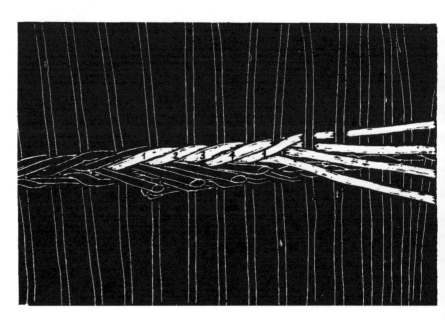

376

The Border with Six Behind Two

This weave pattern will give you a lovely, wide border. Starting at the curve of the basket, turn down each of six stakes behind two stakes. Leave the tips outside the basket.

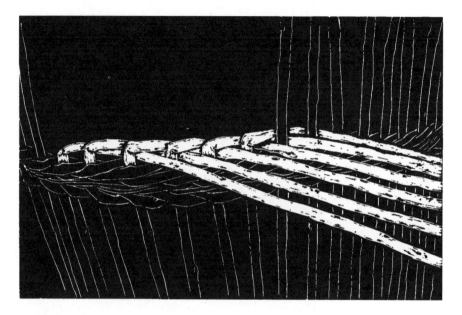

377

Move the leftmost turned-down stake in front of five and behind one (5/1) and leave it in front of the basket, allowing a bit of slack. Now turn down the first upright stake behind two so that it rests in the interval with the previously worked rod and to the right of it, as shown in the drawing below. Continue the pattern.

378

Finishing the border: The longer the strokes, the more difficult it is to finish this sort of border. You continue in 5/1 so the ends are worked in pattern. Twist the rods slightly to make it easier to insert them into the tight weave as you finish.

379

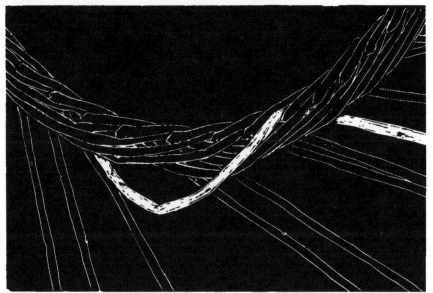

380

The Side Handle

Keep the project secured to the work surface while you're putting on the side handles. Each handle requires one stick for the core and two rods. You can use woods other than willow.

The handle core　Soak the core stick well and make three slypes at each end. On one end of the basket, locate the stake two stakes to the left of the center stake. Insert one end of the stick as deeply as possible into the weave on the left side of this stake (open the weave with an awl). Now, find the stake two stakes to the right of the center stake, and insert the other stick end to the left of that stake.

The arch of the stick should be two to three fingers' width high. Remember, the space in the handle will be smaller after you've wrapped the core. Be sure there is ample room for fingers. Handles that are too large will dominate the overall appearance.

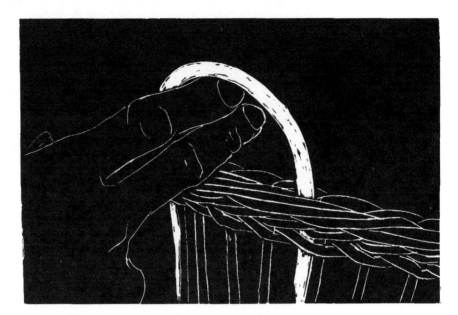

381

Wrapping the handle　Insert the butt end of a thin, slyped rod to the left of the left leg of the handle. Twist it, as described on p. 138, to make the rod into a rigid cord. Leave a 20 cm length untwisted at the tip.

First wrap: Wrap the twisted rod around the core, without losing the twist, alternately in front of and behind it, as shown in drawing 382 on p. 298. End on the right side of the right leg of the handle. From the outside of the basket, insert the tip (having made a path with the awl) under the border and the first round of waling to the inside, as shown in drawing 383.

Second wrap: Twist the rod again and bring it from inside the basket, under the core (to the left of the right leg), and over and under twice again. End on the right side of the left leg of the core. Insert the tip again through the weave from outside of the basket so that it emerges on the left side of the right leg of the core, as shown in drawing 384.

Third wrap: Without losing the cord's twist, make a third wrap parallel to the first, along its right side, from left to right. All the wraps fit tightly together, even at the base.

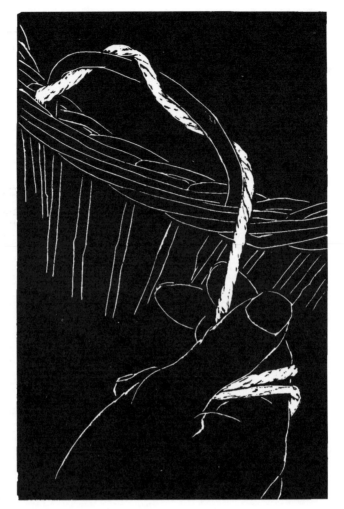

382

383

384

385

386

Fourth wrap: Work the fourth wrap back from right to left.

The second rod: The first rod is now too short to work. Insert a second slyped rod to the right of the right leg of the handle, as shown in drawing 385. Twist it as you did the first rod, and wrap it under and around the handle, from right to left, tightly against the previous wrap. Work it back to the right and lock it into the weave. The finished handle is shown in drawing 386.

Visible core: If you don't want the core completely covered, work the second rod only once to the left and end there.

Securing the rod With in and out strokes between the rounds of waling, weave the end away to secure it. Twist the rod slightly but often as you work. Pick off the protruding end.

Twisting: To be sure the wrapping rod is tight and flat against the core, keep it twisted and damp enough to be pliable as you work it.

Second handle Make the second handle the same way you made the first. Many people often have more difficulty making the second handle because they become overconfident—and it's a challenge to make both match!

Picking off Trim off all the ends that are protruding from the basket with the picking knife.

A finished basket with two handles is shown on pp. 302-303.

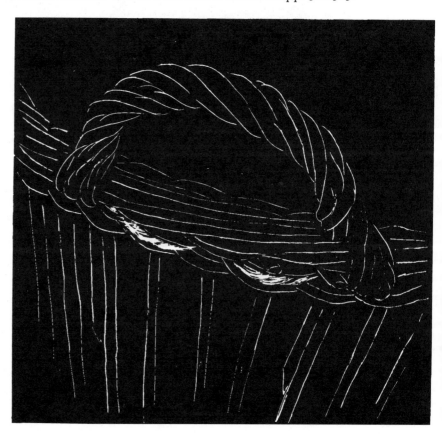

387

388 The movable handles on the top basket are made of single, curved scalloms (pp. 131-132) that have been fastened to small willow loops. This shape is reminiscent of a doll's crib. The openwork basket can also be made without any handles.

389 With thick wire hooks, you can hang an openwork basket on a bicycle frame. Movable handles can be fastened with willow loops, as for the doll's crib shown on p. 301. With a fixed crossover handle (pp. 198-204), an openwork basket makes an ideal shopping basket.

Squarework

Squarework refers to baskets of many shapes that have right-angled corners. These baskets are constructed most commonly on a frame. Making a four-sided base requires precision work and a good feel for the material.

Squarework bases can be woven as openwork, with skein-work techniques, with randing (as for ribbed baskets), or with a wooden frame, as for the stool on p. 326. For the tray you'll be making in this chapter, you start with a wide, flat, rectangular shape.

You'll need thick sticks as the warp for the base, and for the lid, if you intend to have one. The stakes for the wall are fastened to these base sticks. Sticks or dowels are used as corner posts. Two cross strips are nailed onto the top of the posts in order to keep the work square while you're weaving (particularly important if you are making large or heavy frames).

This project is simple in construction and lightweight because of its size and function. For those without a lot of experience, it will be challenging enough. You can also weave panels for ceilings, walls, or furniture using the techniques for the tray base.

Tray

No doubt, you often see these shallow baskets in grocery stores and bakeries. They are used to display fruits, vegetables, small baked goods, or sweets. Appealing containers such as these attract the eyes of potential customers. But rectangular, flat baskets are also useful on desks, in workshops, and in the kitchen.

Material For the long sides of the base, you'll need two rods, about as thick as your little finger and cut about 10 cm longer than the desired length of the tray. Cut six thinner rods to the same length. You'll also need two thick end sticks, 1.8 to 2 m long, a handful of 1.2 m long rods for the stakes, and another 20 to 25, the same length, for the waling. Soak all thoroughly.

390

The Base

As you make the base of the tray, you need to hold the sticks in place. Here are two ways to do it.

The first option In France, basketmakers use a special board and cross pieces to clamp the warp securely in place. This method is practical, particularly for very large pieces. With a board, you can easily construct a similar device. (The drawing on p. 306 shows the arrangement using the work surface we've described on p. 91. Also see drawing 103, p. 89). Insert the stakes you'll be working

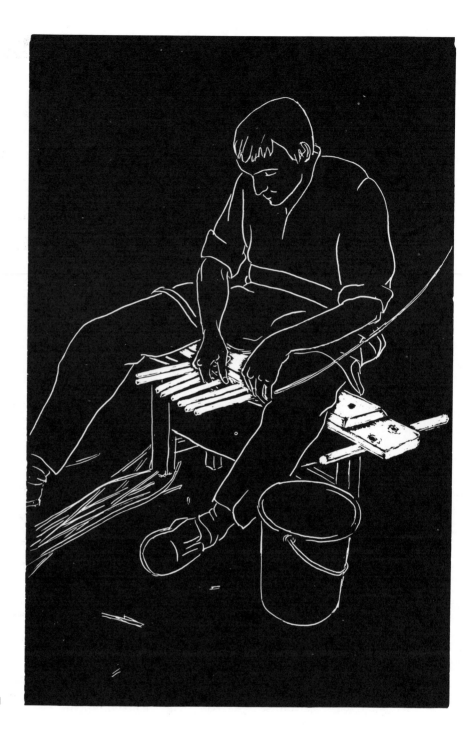

391

between the board and the bench. When you sit on the board, they are securely clamped. You can keep the unworked stakes directly in front of you simply by lifting the board and pushing the finished rows back underneath it. The weave pattern is worked horizontally.

Nail two strips of wood across the underside of the board, parallel to the stakes (these are not visible in the drawing).

The interval between them can be adjusted, but the maximum width of the work is determined by how far apart you can spread your legs. If you're working a wide piece, use this next method.

The second option   Basketmakers also use a screwblock, which consists of two straight boards, usually as wide as the work surface, and fitted with bolts and wing nuts, as shown in the drawing below. The stakes are held vertically, and the weaving progresses from bottom to top. The advantages to this system are that you can make woven surfaces of almost any width and you need not use your own weight to hold the stakes in place. Although this technique limits the height of the woven structure, it is easier on your back.

392

Starting   With a knife, cut two equally thick, well-soaked sticks so that you create flat surfaces that can be clamped tightly together. Make sure to remove an equal amount of wood from each. Depending on the method you've chosen, distribute the stakes for the intended width of the weave under the board or in the screwblock. The intervals should be about two and a half times as wide as the stakes are thick. Place the two cut sticks beside each other in the center for added strength. Be sure that butts and tips alternate.

Weaving   Fold one soaked rod in half. Position the fold on the left stake, and move the butt end through the first interval. Leave it in front of the second stake. The other half crosses the first half as it's worked behind one and through the second interval, as shown in drawing 393. Work these two halves as

393

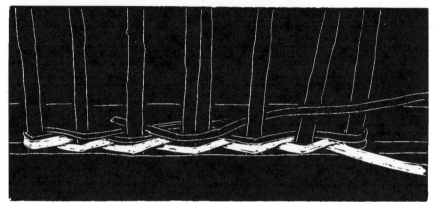

394

twining, or pairing, across the stakes to the other end. Starting at the right end stake, continue randing with the tip only. (The white rod in drawing 394 is the butt end; it is no longer worked.)

Complete wrap Because of the nature of the weave structure and the differences in diameter along the rods, the line of weaving will be lower at the ends than it is across the middle. To compensate for this, wrap the rod completely around the end stakes every two rows as needed.

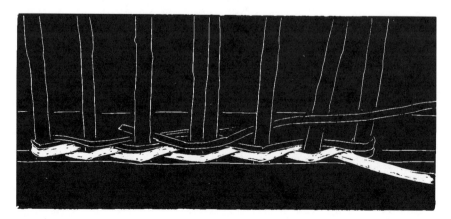

395

Inserting: When you've worked the first rod to the butt end, join a new butt end. Beginning with the third rod, continue joining butt ends to tips. The ends should protrude behind the work.

396

Rapping: Rap down hard enough so that the end stakes are completely covered by the rods. This will give you more attractive edges and a stronger weave structure.

Checking your work

While working, check that the stake intervals are even, especially those at the ends. The stakes should all be in the same plane, so that when the base is finished, it will lie flat upon the floor.

Don't allow the width of the woven surface to narrow at all. The tension of the woven rods is great enough to pull the sticks closer together. Then you must cut all the rods between two stakes as far back as necessary to correct the problem. Measure the width after each row—this problem is not immediately visible.

Be careful not to oversoak the rods, or they can easily snap.

Finishing

To cover the last 5 cm, work another row of pairing (see drawings 397 and 398 on p. 310). This will keep the woven rods from sliding off the ends. Fold the rod so that the thicker end is a little longer than the full width of the weaving. Work the butt end and leave it between the sixth and the seventh stake, as shown in drawing 399. Work the tip behind the seventh stake, to the front, around the end stake, and back to the front. Now insert the tip to the left of the seventh stake and under the top row of weaving. (Twist it first to keep it from breaking.) Thread it through and weave it away to its end. Use a rapping iron to ensure that the top edge is straight.

397

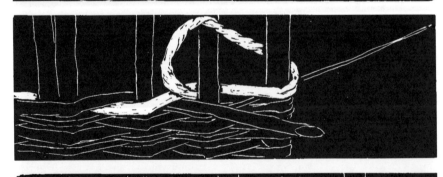

398

399

400

Cutting away the pairing

Now remove the work from the clamping device. Cut away the pairing that you made when you started to weave. This pairing was simply to hold the stakes in place. Also cut away all the loose ends.

Additional rows: Before you can proceed, you have to finish weaving the stakes. Mark the desired finished length on the unwoven ends of the end stakes. Weave until you are 1 cm away from the marks, and finish with a row of pairing.

Checking: Now measure the base—corner to corner, end to end, side to side. If it's misshapen, push and pull it right. Then cut both ends of the stakes almost flush to the woven edges.

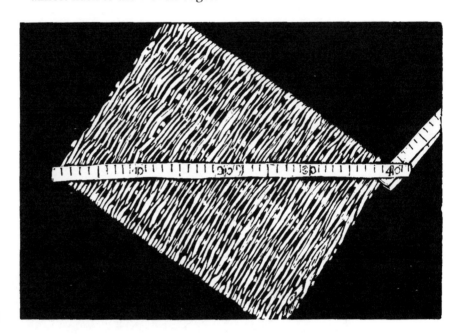

401

The finished base

On most baskets, the picked-off ends are underneath the base. First decide how you intend to use this piece and then consider carefully where the ends might be more troublesome. This base can certainly be used very well as it is, and in any number of ways. But if you decide to use it this way, don't cut the ends too short.

Waling the Walls

There are various ways to connect the stakes to the base. We have chosen to attach them by scalloming.

Scalloming the stakes

Scallom the rods to a curved shape at their butt ends. The scalloms should be 15 cm long. You can only fasten scallomed ends to the bases of basket that will not be used to carry heavy loads. For laundry baskets and other large, squarework baskets, you have to insert stakes and corner stakes that are as thick as your thumb.

| Stake intervals | Make a pencil mark about every 3 cm on all four sides of the base to indicate where each stake will be attached. Be sure to space the intervals evenly, while allowing room for a stake at each corner. |

| Holding the piece | Hold the base between your knees, lengthwise, in a vertical position. If you want the picked-off ends to be outside the basket, they should be on the right side of the base. |

| Fastening the stakes | At one of the pencil marks on the center of a long side, use the awl to open the weave structure beside the end stake. Insert a scallomed end from right to left through the weave. Hold the scallom with your left hand, and fold the other end of the rod over the end stake with your right, as shown in drawing 402. Keep the scallomed end taut, and wrap it around the rod close to the end stake. Insert the next scallom at the next mark; fold and wrap the rod the same way, gripping the first scallomed end in the process. Continue to work, with the lower half of the base toward you. |

Drawing 404: Fold the scallomed end around the corner stake. If all the scalloms were cut to the same length, the ends will automatically be woven into the work.

Note: Once you've worked around, there shouldn't be any ends to pick off. If some ends have not been secured, you'll have to pull them through afterward, which is quite difficult. If you are called away from your work, clamp the scallom with a clothespin.

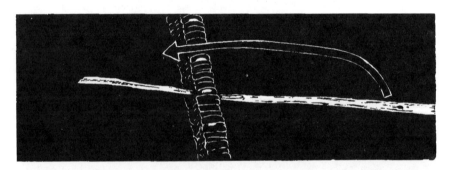

402

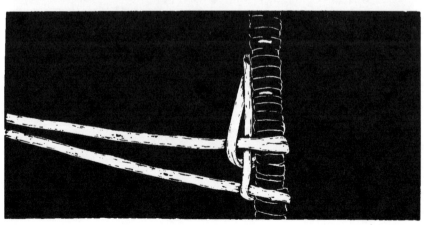

403

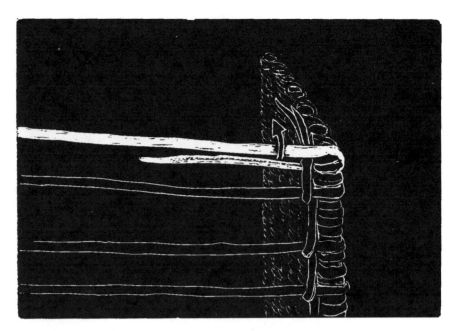

404

Along the short sides, insert the scalloms into the weave about 1 to 2 cm away from the edge so they hold firmly.

Drawings 405 and 406: The tips of the last few scalloms are inserted through the first scalloms, which must be opened up gently with an awl. (If you were making a tall basket, you would now square up the corner stakes with a crosspiece, as shown in drawing 429 on p. 330.)

Waling Secure the base to the work surface with an awl. Bind the stakes together toward their tips, as shown on p. 91. First and second group: Start the walls with two groups of four rods. Each rod is inserted in its own interval, tip first. Insert one group on each long side of the base.

Work the four rods in a 2/2 pattern, starting with the rod farthest to the left. Work the first group until it meets the second; then the second until it meets the first. Continue working the first and second groups alternately until the ends run out.

405

406

407

408

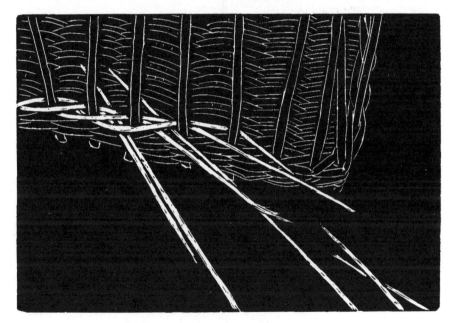

409

Inserting: When the rods have almost been completely woven to their ends, add new rods, joining butt ends to butt ends, and tips to tips. It's best to make the first joins on the long sides of the basket.

Continuing the weave: Weave the entire wall in 2/2. This pattern creates a firm, durable, and heavy weave structure. As you work, check often to see if the stakes are still vertical. To ensure straight walls, pull the stakes outward slightly while working. Pulling the corner stakes is especially important; if you don't, the quadrangle will look slightly squeezed.

Soaking   If you're using peeled willow, place the part of the basket and the stakes you will be working next in water for about one half hour.

410

The Squared Border

Begin turning down the stakes on the long side of the basket, where it's easier to keep track of your work. With the round-nosed pliers, turn down four stakes behind two, working from left to right, as shown in the drawing below. Don't pull them tight; leave space for the remaining border strokes. Work the turned-down stake farthest to the left in front of three and behind one (3/1). Now turn down the first upright stake behind two, so that it lies in the same interval with the stake just worked, as shown in drawing 412. This is the first pair. Continue working to the corner stake.

411

412

The corners Pay close attention to the following drawings and directions concerning how to work the corners. Otherwise, you run the risk of getting lost. When you've woven to the point where the first pair is in the interval before the corner stake, the right rod of the pair farthest to the left is worked next.

413

Important: In the above drawing and elsewhere, each time the first corner is worked, the rod to be worked is not yet paired.

Move this single rod in front of two and behind the corner stake, leaving it in front of the basket, as shown by the arrow in the drawing. The single rod is worked 2/1.

Drawing 414: Turn down the next to the last stake before the corner stake so that it shares the interval with the rod just worked. (In the drawing, it's in place.) Turn down the next stake behind the corner stake and through the next interval, as shown by the arrow. There are now three rods in the interval; two of them form a pair.

414

Next step: Take the rod (marked X in the drawing) under the pair and turn it up into a vertical position, parallel to the stakes. With the left hand, take the leftmost, single rod labelled 1 in drawing 415 firmly across the corner, as shown by the arrow.

415

Now take the rod labelled 2 in your left hand and move it across so that it is beside rod 1 and closest to you, as shown below.

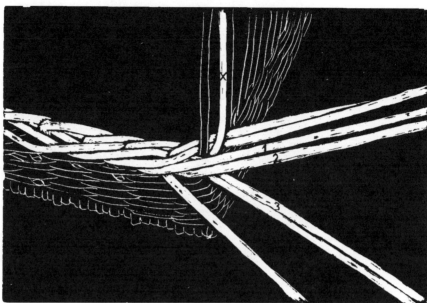

416

Move rod 3 in front of the corner stake, over rods 1 and 2, over the other pair, and behind the first stake beyond the corner stake. Bring it out the next interval, making a nice right angle.

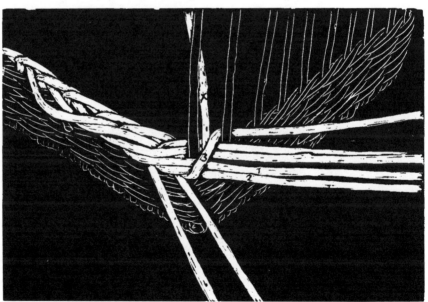

417

Next step: Drawing 418: Move rod 2 in front of one stake, over rod 1 and the other three rods, behind one, and into the next interval. Turn down the upright rod marked X in the drawing behind two so that it lies in the same interval with rod 2, making a pair.

Next step: Work rod 1 over the three rods and in front of two stakes, behind one stake, and into the interval. Turn down the first stake after the corner stake to make a pair.

418

Next step: Work the right rod of the next pair in front of three, behind one (3/1), as you did along the long side. Turn down the second stake after the corner to make a pair. Drawing 420: Move the next single rod (the second one after the corner) in front of three, behind one (3/1), as shown by the arrow. Turn down the next stake to make a pair.

Work in pattern until you come to the challenge of the next corner. Be certain the stakes don't dry out while you're working.

When you've finished, you'll pick off the corner stake and the two remaining rods.

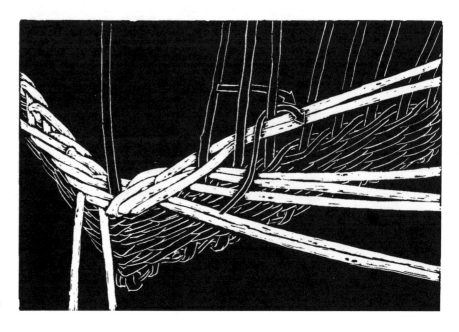

419

420

Finishing the border

To finish, continue working in front of three, behind one (3/1) along the long side. The next to the last upright stake is the first, together with its partner, to be incorporated into the beginning border strokes, under the turned-down stakes. (In drawing 421, this step has been completed.) Now work the right rod of the leftmost pair with the last upright stake, as shown by the arrow.

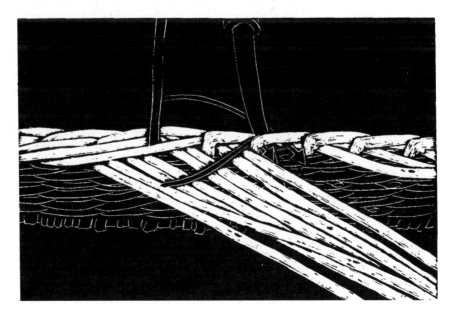

421

422

Work the right rods of the last three pairs, and your work is finished. Scrutinize it again from every side. Pick off the remaining corner stakes and rods flush to the weave, along with any other protruding ends. Rap the border if needed to make it level.

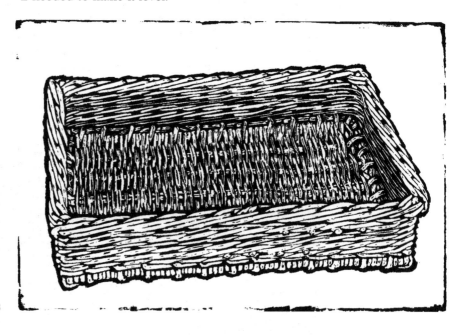

423

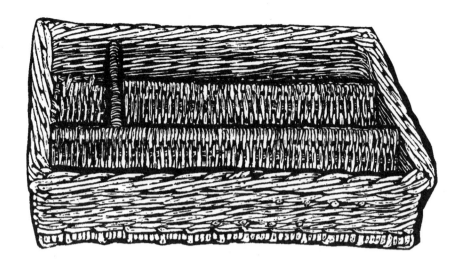

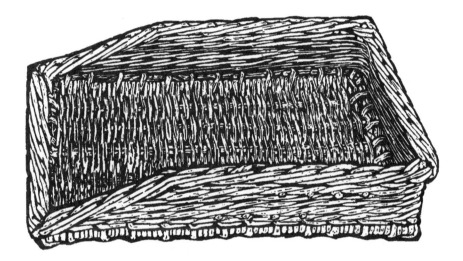

424
You can add a partition to the interior of the tray. It's a good place to keep all kinds of odds and ends in a home or office.

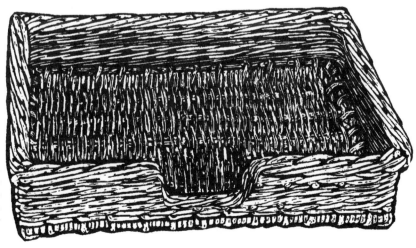

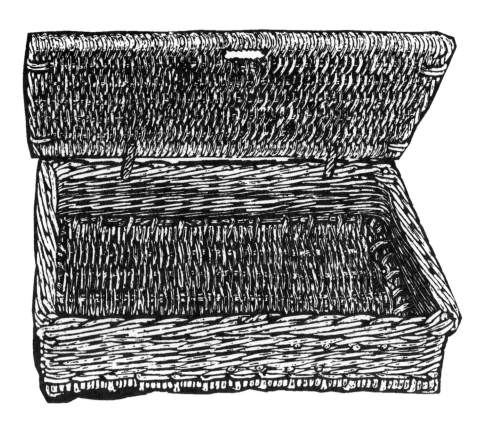

425 If the little basket has turned out well, you might want to transform it into a small lidded case, to use for storage or perhaps as a doll's suitcase. The locks shown in the bottom drawing at right consist of loops and short pegs cut from willow sticks.

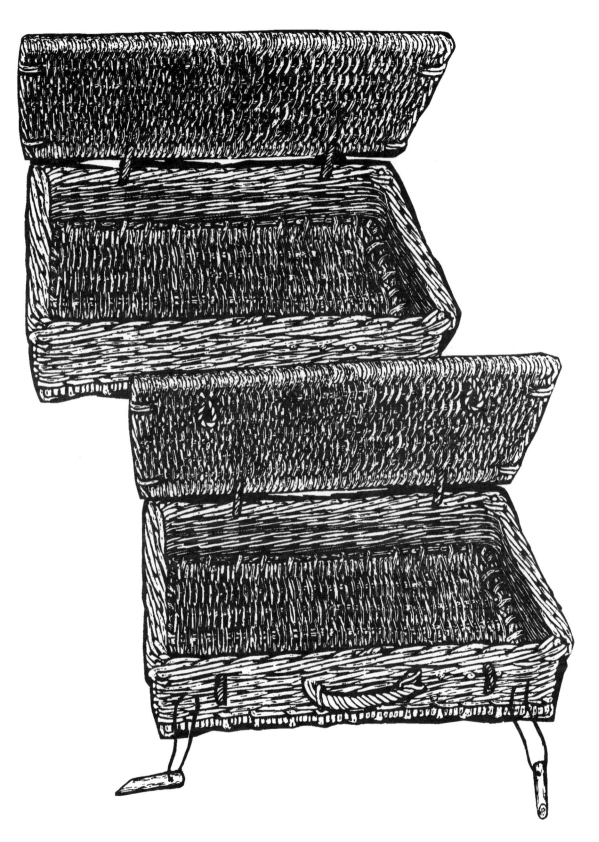

The Stool

Furniture as lightweight and portable as baskets were made from willow as far back as ancient times. Probably the oldest known example is a wicker armchair depicted in stone in about 200 A.D., and on view in the Roman-German Central Museum in Trier.

426

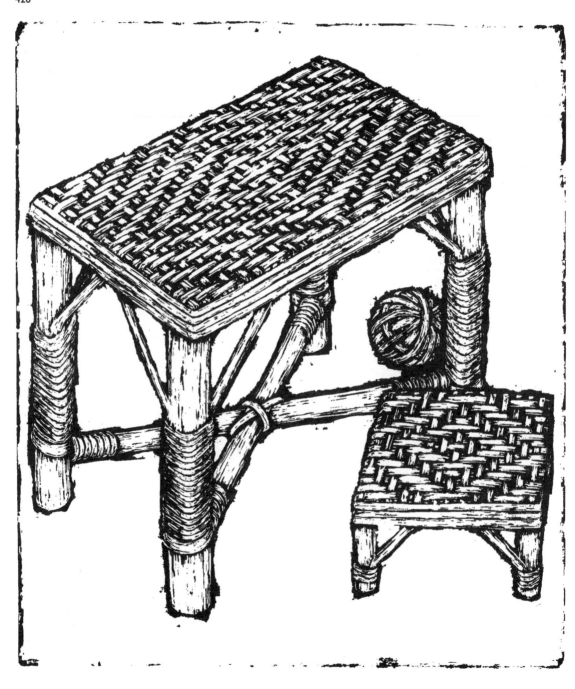

There repeatedly have been periods when wicker furniture, made from willow or other round reed materials, has been more widespread than in others—for example, after wars, when wood was scarce. The characteristic rigid, supporting frames can be constructed from one- to two-year-old wood, and the wood source can be quickly replenished. Today, people use wicker furniture primarily because they enjoy its casual appearance and form.

In the course of making this footstool, you'll learn the basics of how wicker furniture is traditionally constructed and woven. The work process can be divided into two main parts:

- assembling the supporting frame
- weaving the seat

The seat is woven onto the supporting frame, and both elements have a great number of other potential uses.

You need not adhere to the specified proportions in these directions. What is presented here is simply a basic design whose dimensions can be changed to create a variety of new results.

Material
For the supporting frame, you'll need straight sticks, 10 to 25 mm thick, which have been thoroughly dried and usually stripped of their bark. The bark on dry sticks can be cut away with a knife. Soak the following:

- a few fairly thick willow rods, 1.8 to 2 m long, for the corner sticks of the frame;
- two handfuls of thick rods, 2 to 2.2 m long, for the skeins;
- finishing nails, in lengths of 40, 35, 20, and 10 mm.

Frame Construction

An accurate eye and precision help make this work easier.

The seat frame
The frame could be constructed as a rectangular shape with the proportions 2 to 3, that is, with the short sides two-thirds the length of the long sides. If the sticks are not straight, straighten them with pincers (p. 98) or a commander (p. 100).

Proportions
It's a good idea to construct some paper models of the overall frame before you start, on a scale of 1 to 10, for example. The whole construction entails quite a bit of effort, and it would be a shame to carefully build a stool only to find it is too narrow or its legs are too long or too short. A knowledge of mathematics can be helpful in determining the best proportions (p. 172), but a well-trained eye is invaluable.

Cutting to size
Cut all four sticks for the seat to the outer dimensions. To join them together, cut each end, as shown in the drawing on p. 328.

Make flat cuts to create tongues that are the same length as the stick's diameter. Make a tongue on the bottom half of the stick at one end, and on the upper half on the other. This way, the sticks will overlap each other when assembled.

Note: Use a pencil to mark which half you will cut on each stick end. This way, you'll be sure they fit together to make a frame. Also, be sure the cuts are level or the frame will not lie flat.

If the four sticks fit together well, number them. Be sure all the corners are 90° angles, or the next steps will be very difficult.

The supporting frame could be constructed just as well with dowels of equal thickness, but it would be a waste not to make use of the natural shape of the willow. We are not simply trying to produce a functional stool in the same way a carpenter would.

Crosspiece Mark the center of the long sides of the frame. Then cut, or saw, a stick of the same thickness as the others to the length of the interval between the long sides. This crosspiece braces the frame, providing additional stability and ensuring that it does not go out of shape as you are working the skeins.

Legs From the same stick, cut four legs to perhaps half the length of the frame, and at exact right angles. They'll be slightly tapered, so mark the thick ends. The thin ends are nailed to the frame.

Assembling the frame First, assemble the frame. Then fasten the pieces together with 40 mm nails. The surest way to get this right is to work on a flat surface, keeping the pieces flat and at right angles to each other with clamps.

Nails   Blunt the tips of the nails a bit with a hammer so the willow does not split. To be on the safe side, also bore a small hole with an awl to start the nail. Tap the nails in until you can see their tips on the back side. Fasten the cross-piece as well.

428

Adding the legs   When all the corners are fastened, use more nails to attach the legs. (Be careful that you do not nail into the pith.) Position the legs so that they are flush with the outer edges of the seat frame. The stool is beginning to take shape. Turn it so it's standing upright on the legs. If everything looks square and level, fasten each leg with an additional nail. If you split a leg as you nail, replace it with a new one. At this rough stage of construction, the stool is not yet strong enough to bear any weight.

The brackets   Each bracket forms a triangle beneath the seat frame, and gives the overall frame the stability it requires.

Marking the position: Working in each corner, mark four points to indicate the position of the brackets. The marks should be equidistant from the corner along the long side of the frame and on the legs; on the short sides, the marks should probably be somewhat closer to the corners. Before marking, hold a rod in the intended location to judge which angle seems most suitable. Between the two brackets on the short side, there should be at least 2 cm of clearance. Drawing 430 on p. 330 shows the brackets in place on the long sides.

The brackets on each side should form equal-angle triangles. On the short sides, consider whether it will look better to have large triangles or, because of the bracket lengths, to have smaller, equal-angle triangles.

Temporary braces   Crosspieces are nailed to the bottom of the stool to hold the legs parallel to each other. Turn the stool upside down and nail two diagonal strips, of equal length, to the ends of the legs so that they cross exactly at the center of the stool. Nail the strips together at the point where they cross (this method is also used when making tall squarework baskets).

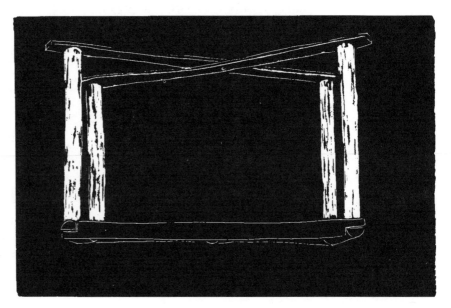

429

Fastening the brackets   You'll need two soaked, top-quality rods, 1.8 to 2 m long. With these two rods, you'll make the four sets of brackets. Cut a few centimeters off the butt ends.

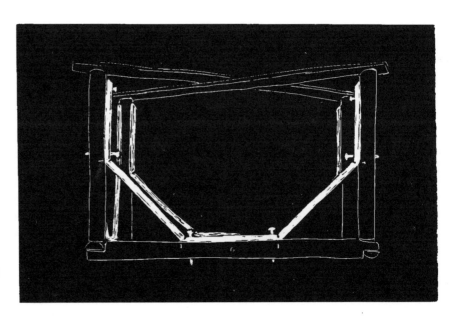

430

Work on the long side of the upside-down stool, as shown in drawing 430. Add the distance from the end of the leg to the mark on the leg to the distance from the mark on the leg to the lefthand mark on the frame. Use the pincers to pinch the rod this same distance from its thick end. Position this first kink on the lefthand mark on the frame. Now measure the distance to the righthand mark on the frame and pinch the rod at that point to make a second kink. Bend the rod only as much as necessary!

Insert a nail into the frame 1 cm from each kink. Before you attach the bracket to the legs, double-check the distances between marks: both the distance from the mark on the frame to the mark on the leg and from the mark on the leg to the end of the leg. Hold the free ends of the rods against the leg marks; mark the rods, pinch them and nail them, as you did before. Once you're certain of their position, tap a 20 mm nail a few centimeters from the first ones. (A nail of the same diameter as the first might split the rod, and then the whole bracket would have to be replaced.)

The remaining brackets: Fasten the rest of the brackets in the same way.

You'll need a second rod because the willow tapers and will become too thin to make these last brackets.

If the tips of the nails protrude, bend them over with a hammer. Pick off the bracket ends at an angle just above the leg ends.

Wrapping the legs
The beginning of the wrapping skein is inserted into the space between the bracket and the leg, where it's tightly clamped. Wrap it once around the bracket before starting to wrap the leg.

Wrap the wet skein tightly around the leg and the two bracket ends until the nails are covered.

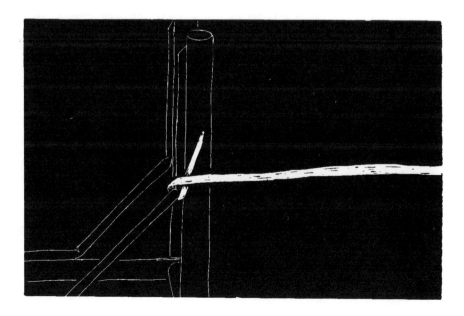

431

To secure the end of the skein, thread it back up into the wrapping on the inside of the leg. Pull the end taut as you fasten it with a 10 mm nail.

Before you wrap the other legs, observe your work from a distance. Decide whether or not it would look nicer to have one or two more rounds of wrapping, or whether one less might look more attractive. These details have a subtle influence on the overall appearance. Wrap all the legs, and remove the temporary braces.

432

Rounding
the corners

With a knife and sandpaper, round the frame's corners a bit to prevent the woven seat from wearing out too quickly in those spots.

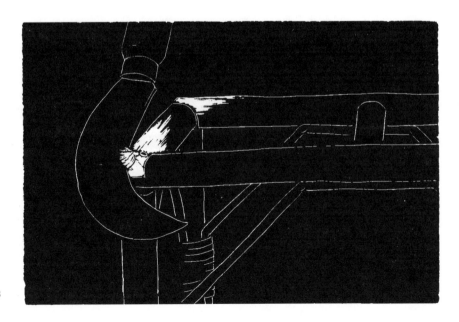

433

Weaving the Skeins

There are many names for a weave structure in which skeins are interlaced with skeins. The crossed weave pattern presented here is a variation on twill or plaiting.

The warp   For the warp, you need 30 skeins of the same length, fastened across the short dimension of the stool. Soak the skeins for an hour and shave them until they are somewhat thinner. To begin, position the first skein at the center of the frame. As shown in drawing 434, fasten the skeins to the edges of the long sides with 10 mm finishing nails, about 1 cm from the end of the

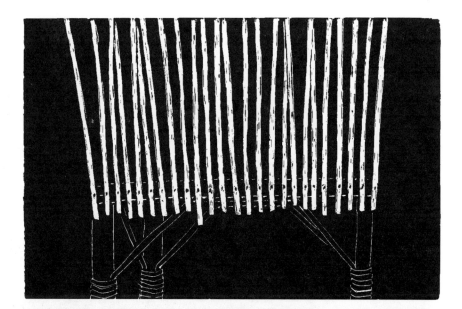

434

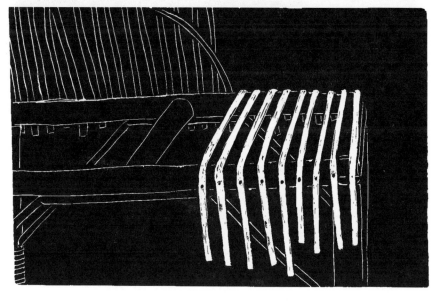

435

skein. The interval between the skeins should be about one and one half times the skein width.

The work is easier if you nail all the skeins to one side of the frame first and then to the other. Continue until you've nailed skeins along both edges of the frame for the length of the stool. Be sure they are all parallel. (You can use a piece of cardboard cut to the desired width of the interval to use as a template.)

Note: Don't pull the warp skeins too tightly or it will be difficult to work the weft skeins.

The weft   Begin with skeins of the same size and length as those that were used for the warp.

Determine the number of skeins needed (frame width ÷ skein width = quantity). Now cut them to the length of the stool plus 6 cm. For the twill pattern shown in the drawings, you weave each row from the middle of the warp out to the ends.

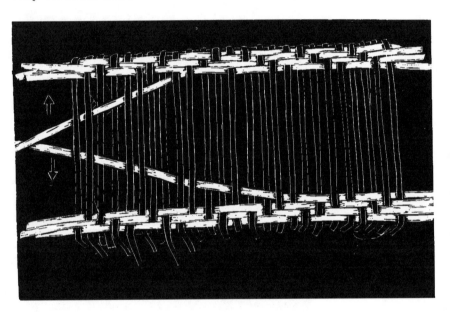

436

First row: Work two skeins under the three center warp skeins, then over two and under two (2/2) to one end of the warp. Work the other half of the skeins the same way (2/2) to the opposite end of the warp, as shown in the drawing. The skeins are woven as one across the warp. Now separate them by moving one skein to one long side of the frame and the other to the opposite side. This is a convenient way to weave a symmetrical pattern.

Second row: For the moment, ignore the center warp skein. Starting with the skein to the left of it and working to the left, weave two new weft skeins under two and over two (2/2) to one end. To work the second half, float the weft skeins over the center warp skein, and then work 2/2 to the other end.

Third row: Float the weft skeins over three center warp skeins, then work 2/2 to both ends.

Fourth row: Float the weft under the center warp skein. Weave 2/2.

Fifth row: This row begins the four-row repeat sequence. In fabric, this pattern is called extended diamond or goose-eye twill. Add the last few skeins at center, making sure you have left enough room to work them in pattern.

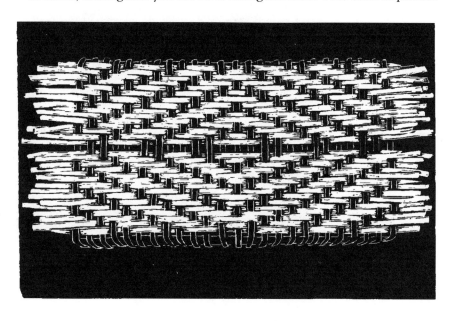

437

Checking your work
Any mistakes you find at the end cannot be corrected very easily. Check for them as you work. You can see them immediately when you raise the surface to eye level and look across it.

Fastening
You must wet all the ends of the weft skeins, wrap them around the end stakes, and nail them securely, as you did the warp skeins. Fasten one skein at a time, keeping them as taut as possible. In production shops, the workers use staple guns for this.

Picking off
With the picking knife, trim all the skeins uniformly about 1 cm or less from the nails.

Border skeins
Now you'll cover the edges of the frame. These border skeins will enclose the weave structure visually as well as prevent the ends from catching on somebody's clothing.

You'll fasten three skeins along the edges of the frame with 20 mm, round-headed nails. Don't use bright or brassy nails, as they'll draw attention to themselves and away from the weaving. The three skeins should be as long as the perimeter of the stool, and fastened flush to each other. Start on a short side and offset the ends as shown in drawing 438 on p. 336. Fasten each separately. The nails should be evenly spaced and not too far apart.

When you wrap the skeins around the corners, be sure all the ends are covered. Tap a nail in about 1 cm to the left and the right of each corner.

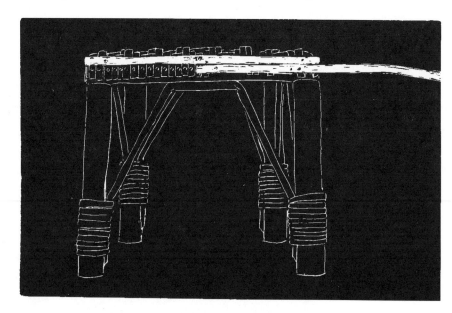

438

Trimming the feet Round the ends of the legs somewhat with a sharp knife. This will prevent them from splitting or splintering.

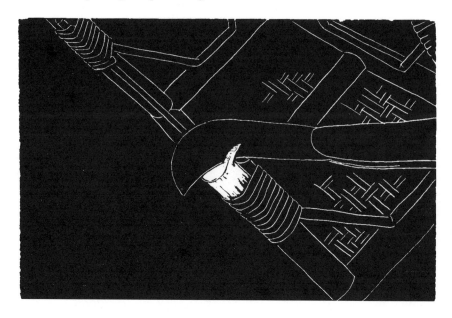

439

Trying it out It would be nice to try out the stool immediately to see if it will really do what it was made to do. But you will have to be patient for one day. After 24 hours, you can stand on it, sit on it, or even lie down on it (although it's a bit short for that).

440

441 The woven surfaces shown here have all been worked in 2/2, using skeins of the same width for both warp and weft. As you can see, this simple weave structure still allows room for creativity. For example, if you want to create a check pattern, fasten the skeins in equal intervals on two sides of the frame and alternately interlace the warp and weft in both directions.

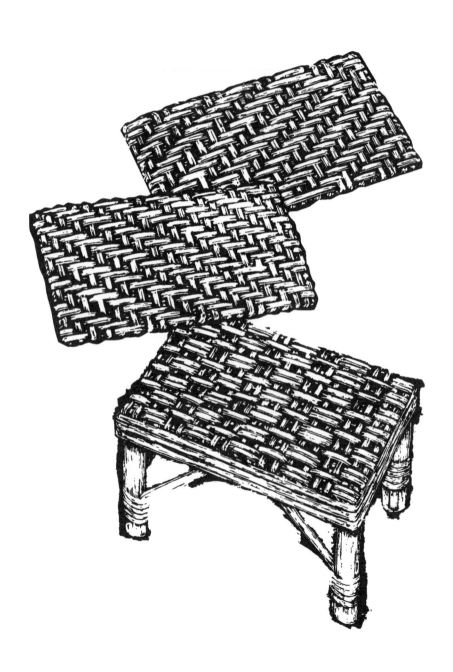

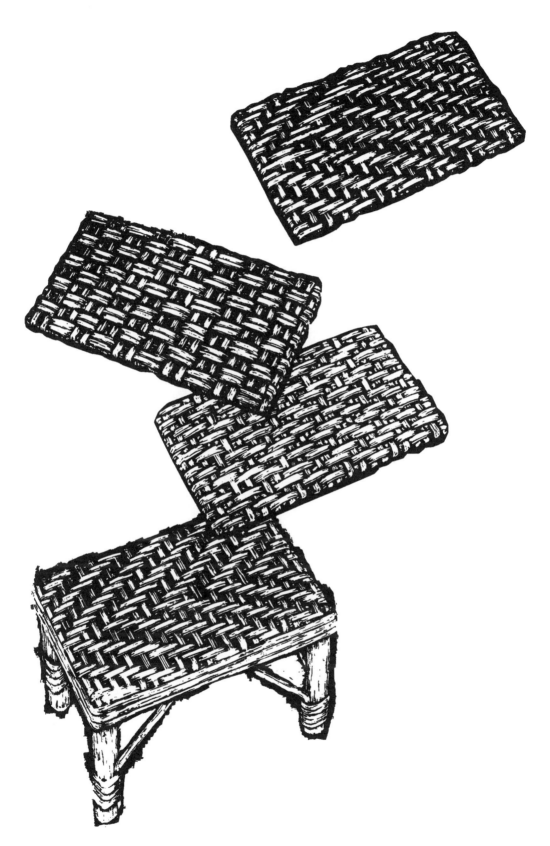

Treating and Caring for Finished Baskets

Bleaching

White willow rods are sometimes bleached, but more often the finished baskets are. Bleaching gives the material a fresh, clean appearance, although a misshapen basket won't look any better for it. Bleached baskets are also more resistant to mildew.

Bleached rods can be effectively combined with buff, black, or other colored rods. Basketry that will be used by children (for example, toys, beds, baskets for playthings) or used for foods (cheese platters, and bread, fruit, or harvest baskets) should not be bleached.

For your information, we've summarized here the general procedures for bleaching rods and baskets, but we believe you should avoid bleaching altogether, or do it only rarely. The chemicals are often toxic and harmful to the environment, and the results are by no means permanent. Bleached willow darkens in time and must be bleached again.

Sulfurizing When flowers of sulfur (sublimed sulfur), which are nontoxic, are burnt in the presence of steam, they yield vapors of sulfuric acid (a 5% solution has a toxic grade of 4). These vapors bleach the willow material. The baskets to be bleached are soaked for half an hour. They must contain absolutely nothing made of metal. Pins, nails, and hinges will rust immediately if exposed to the vapors.

The pieces are packed closely together and covered with plastic wrap that is free of perforations to create an airtight hood. Two to three tablespoons of flowers-of-sulfur powder (or one yellow flowers-of-sulfur paper) are put in a non metal container and set on fire. (This quantity is enough to bleach 10 to 15 baskets.) The tiny blue flame emits a dry, acrid, caustic smoke. The container and its burning powder should be placed immediately under the plastic hood, which should be made airtight right away. The baskets are left to bathe in the sulfur fumes for two to three hours. This method must be used only outdoors. The vapors should not be inhaled, or they can induce coughing and difficulty in breathing, as well as cause the eyes and skin to burn.

Hydrogen peroxide   Hydrogen peroxide can be bought as 20% to 30% solution (in this strength, it has a toxic grade of 3). The solution is usually brushed onto the surface of the weaving.

Potassium oxalate   Bleaching can also be accomplished with a 5% to 10% solution of potassium oxalate and water. The toxicity is reduced somewhat because of the dilution with water. The salt itself burns on contact, so it must be kept away from the skin and eyes. The rods or finished baskets are immersed in the solution for at least two hours, then rinsed.

Cleaning

Willow baskets without any surface finishes or varnishes are very easy to care for. A well-constructed shopping basket, for example, will remain attractive and useful for many years of normal use, although continuous exposure to the sun or to moisture is damaging.

The best way to maintain your baskets is by giving them a spring cleaning once a year. This cleaning not only makes them look fresh and new again, it also tightens up the weave structure.

Washing   Prepare a quantity of warm water and washing soda (hydrated sodium carbonate). Dip a somewhat soft brush in the solution and give the basket a good brushing. More delicately woven baskets must be brushed gingerly. If a basket is very dirty, soak it in the solution. If you have an old, forgotten, family basket to wash, simply soak it in water for some time. Cleaning gives older baskets in particular an unsuspected freshness and rich color. You can use a mild laundry soap for stubborn stains. Rinse washed baskets well under running water. The spring sunshine will dry them off and help to bleach the dark spots. In summer, it's best to let them dry in the shade. Don't wash varnished baskets in warm water or the finish will take on an unattractive, whitish appearance.

Cleaning without water   Baskets made with fabric, decorations, water-soluble colors, and leather should be given an energetic, dry brushing, and then rubbed down with a damp cloth. The woven surfaces can also be cleaned easily with a toothbrush, cotton swabs, or a vacuum cleaner.

Varnishing and Waxing

Willow baskets can be varnished or coated with synthetic resin. You often find commercially made baskets that are varnished. In order to keep down manufacturing costs and prices, large-scale producers keep the number of stakes in a basket to a minimum; this way the number of weaving strokes is sometimes reduced by as much as one half. The resulting basket, however, is shaky and weak. The varnish is then used to hold the weave structure together. One can only hope that consumers will change their buying habits and pay closer attention to the quality of the work than to the price tag.

Varnish and weatherproofing

Willow fences, wind screens, benches, garden houses, and toys intended for use outdoors all require a coat of weatherproofing. It's best to use an inconspicuous outdoor varnish, in matte or semigloss. The objects must be resurfaced every year.

In general, you can use any coating intended for use on wood for willow as well, but soft, elastic varnishes are most suitable for woven surfaces. Hard varnishes break where the rods cross in such a way that the varnish-soaked wood breaks with it.

Unvarnished willow basketry is always more attractive than varnished work. The varnishes give the natural surface of the rod a synthetic look, filling the small dents and tinting the color in such a way that the structure loses some of its vitality.

Outdoor objects that are made from heavy willow materials or that will be stored for the winter can be left uncoated. But whenever you are making objects that will be exposed to harsh weather conditions, consider whether you might use another type of weaving material that won't need to be so carefully protected.

Paint

The comments about varnishes apply equally to synthetic, resin-based paints.

Often baskets were coated with a glossy paint made of a mixture of linseed oil and resin. A prime coat was applied first to the willow, and many coats of paint applied afterward.

Individual pieces should be painted with a broad brush on both sides of the surface of the weave. Large quantities of baskets, such as those produced in commercial shops, are usually dipped or painted with a spray gun. Initials can be painted on or sprayed on with the help of a stencil.

Wax

To protect willow against water damage, any wood wax, such as those with a beeswax base, can be used. They are absorbed by the wood and provide more than a mere surface coating. Apply waxes with a soft brush and then polish the basket.

Glossary

This glossary lists the English translation of the German basketry terms that have been used throughout this book. Where possible, American and British alternatives have been listed, with which some basketmakers may be more familiar. The vocabulary of the basketry trade is not standardized, and terms vary according to region and tradition.

1/1, 1/3, 2/2, etc.: Weave-pattern abbreviations. For example, 2/1 indicates that a rod is worked over two stakes and behind one stake.

Awl (bodkin): Tool with metal point used to open or maintain space in the weave structure. Also used to secure the basket to the work surface.

Band: Woven width of multiple rows or rounds.

Base cross (base spokes, bass sticks, slath): Structure of base sticks, marking the center of the framework, and around which the initial rows of weaving are tied in. Generally in the form of a cross.

Bass strips (cleats, feet, heels, rails, runners, shoes, skates, skids, slats, slides): Added base supports, usually of heavy splints or split rods.

Bistaking (bispoking or bye-spoking, staking up): Process of adding warp alongside existing warp to add strength, stability, or to increase diameter. Forms framework for sides or wall.

Border (lip): Woven, braided, or wrapped, finished edge of the basket, usually created by turning down stakes and weaving them in pattern.

Bow: Thick rod used as the core for the handle. Also refers to a crossover, or cross, handle.

Brown willow: Unpeeled rods, with a variety of bark colors.

Buff willow: Rods that have been boiled and peeled, resulting in a chestnut color.

Butt: Thick, bottom end of a willow rod.

Cane (chair cane, natural strand cane, wrapping cane): The shiny, machine-cut, inner bark of rattan, used for chair seating.

Cane (pith cane, centre cane, pulp cane, rattan core, round reed): British term for reed, referring specifically to round reed.

Chase weave (chase randing, chasing weave, chasing): Continuous pattern using two weaving elements, where there is an uneven number of stakes. The stroke is randing, in front of one, behind one (1/1). One weaver chases the other, and catches up to it, but does not overtake it.

Cleave: Tool with three or four fins, used to split the willow rod lengthwise, which is part of the skein-making process.

Cleft: Split portion produced when the willow rod is worked with a cleave.

Cranking (twisting): Method used to twist or ply willow rods.

Cross: See Base cross.

Crossover handle (bow handle, cross handle): Type of handle that crosses the basket from one side to the other, usually at center.

Dome (crown, crowning, doming): Upside-down saucerlike shape of base. Doming, or crowning, refers to the process of creating a dome.

Double weaving: See Slewing.

Fitching (reverse pairing): Reverse twist of the pairing or twining stroke, generally used with openwork, where two rods originate from the back of the work, and the slant, or slope, of the twist is in the shape of a Z-twist.

Foot (false foot, foot border, footing): Border added to outer edge of base to elevate and protect it, and upon which the basket rests. Generally consists of waling strokes.

Foundation: Core materials around which elements are stitched in coiled work.

French randing: Weave pattern in which there is one weaver for each stake or in each interval. The weavers are added to the left while the weaving proceeds to the right in a randed, in front of one, behind one (1/1) stroke, resulting in a diagonal pattern.

Green willow: Freshly cut rods.

Inserting (adding in, joining): Continuing the weft elements by adding on or overlapping new weft elements.

Joining: See Inserting.

Lashing (binding, sewing): Method used to fasten two or more parts of the basket frame. Also refers to the materials and the stitches used in the process.

Mellowing: Curing process where soaked weaving materials are wrapped in towels for a period of time to become more pliable.

Opening up: Process of separating or spreading out the base sticks after two or more rounds of weaving to open up the base.

Over-and-under weave: See Randing.

Packing: Technique of randing in a series of short turns (back and forth) to build up or fill in areas, altering the line or level of the weaving.

Pairing (twining): The reverse of fitching, where two rods cross between stakes, creating a slant, or slope, that is referred to as a S-twist, and come to rest in the front of the work.

Pegging: Use of a stick or dowel to secure the position of the crossover handle on the basket.

Picking knife: Small knife used to trim, or pick off, material ends protruding from the weave structure: also used to upsett stakes.

Picking off: Process of removing the ends protruding from the finished weave structure.

Pitting: Process in which cut willow rods are kept alive, standing in several inches of water, so that the sap rises and buds and roots form. This allows one to peel rods at a time other than when harvesting.

Plain weave: See Randing.

Plaiting: The simple, over-and-under weaving of like elements in one or more multiple elements to resemble braiding.

Plying: Method of combining elements by twisting them together, in order to increase their strength or length.

Pricking up: Process of using a knife or awl to split a rod so that it will bend without cracking.

Randing (over-and-under weave, plain plaiting, plain weave, simple weave, single weave): Weave pattern in which a single weft element is worked alternately in front of and behind a single warp element (1/1). (See also Chase weave.)

Rapping iron: Rectangular, iron tool with one thick edge, which is used to compress a weave structure to even or level the rounds or to eliminate gaps.

Reed: Various shapes and sizes of flexible strands cut from the rattan palm core.

Reverse pairing: See Fitching.

Rib: Supportive framework elements, usually curved, that are added as warp in ribbed baskets.

Rib randing (Chinese randing, Japanese weave): Weave pattern in which a single weft element is worked in front of two, behind one (2 /1) and the total number of stakes (or warp) is not divisible by three.

Ribbed baskets (frame baskets, melon baskets): Basket built on a rigid frame or ring. The ribs (warp) are added during weaving from the outer edge toward the center of the frame.

Rods: Straight lengths of harvested willow.

Round: One complete circuit, or pass, of weaving elements that is continuous around the basket.

Row: One complete pass of weaving elements that is not continuous around the basket.

Scallom: Long, tapered cut on the butt of a rod, creating a thin tail or tongue. Used to fasten rods (as stakes) to the base or frame.

Screw block: Wooden clamping device, with wing nuts and screws, used to secure the warp when making squarework.

Sewing: Refers to the stitching in coiled work. See also Lashing.

Shave (planer): Tool used to remove the pith of a willow cleft. Used to cut away the under-surface when making skeins.

Side (siding): The wall of the basket.

Simple weave: See Randing.

Skeins: Peeled willow rods that are split into three or more clefts with a cleave, and then processed into fine, flat, oval lengths with a shave and upright.

Slath: See Base cross.

Slewing (double Japanese weave, double weaving): Randing with two or more weavers used together as if they were one, in a pattern of in front of one, behind one (1/1).

Slype (slyping): Long, slanted diagonal cut.

Squarework: Baskets with right-angled corners, in square or rectangular shapes, and variations.

Stake (rib, spoke): Warp elements that create the framework around which one works the weft elements.

Stake and strand (wickering, wickerwork): Refers to a basket style as a construction technique typically used with willow or other rodlike materials. The technique employs round warp and weft elements in a rigid framework. The weft is woven perpendicular to the warp, which radiates from a central point.

Staking up: See Bistaking.

Sticks: Thick, heavy rods, used in the base and as corner posts.

Stroke: One full repeat of a weaving pattern (for example, 1/1, or 2/1, or 3/2, etc.).

Three-rod wale (Japanese weave, three-rod waling, three-strand twining, triple twist, triple weave): In front of two, behind one (2/ 1) weave pattern, that may be used in single rounds as a wale in a specific location, such as the foot or near the border, or in several rounds to weave a large area of a basket.

Tip: Top, thin end of the rod.

Transition (change of stroke, change over, changing the stroke, step-up): Change of stroke at the end of each round of waling to complete the pattern and finish the appearance of the round.

Triple weaves: See Three-rod wale.

Turning down: Method by which unwoven warp elements are integrated in the border strokes as weaving elements.

Twining: See Pairing.

Tying (tying in, tying the slath): Process of weaving a few rounds around the crossed base sticks or warp elements to secure the initial framework.

Upright: Skein-making took that sizes the cleft by width.

Upsett (upstaking): Process of pricking up and turning the warp elements from a horizontal to a vertical position to form the basket wall. Also refers to the lowest rows of weaving on the basket wall, which hold the upsett warp in position.

Wale: Three or more rods worked in sequence, in front of two, three, or more stakes and behind one, with variations. Also used for upsetting, as well as for strength.

Weave (weave structure): Series of strokes used to interlace elements and creating patterns that make up the woven surface of basket . Also refers to the entire interlaced structure.

Weaver: See Weft.

Warp (spokes, stakes, ribs): Framework elements around which one works the weft material.

Weft (weaver, weaving rod, weaving skein): The length of material worked around the warp to fill in the framework.

White willow: Rods that have been peeled at harvest time or after pitting.

Whole willow (full willow): Rods that have not been cleaved.

Wicker: Refers to any round, shootlike materials used for basketmaking, for example, willow, oak rods, osiers, or round reed. Also refers to baskets made from round elements in stake-and-strand construction.

Wickerwork: See Stake and strand.

Bibliography

Although there are many books on basketry, the following English-language bibliography lists those basketry books whose primary emphasis is on willow or information related to willow-basket construction. The list of foreign-language titles is reprinted from the German edition, with the intention of providing as extensive a resource as possible to those interested in the very specialized topic of willow basketry, which has a long European tradition.

English-Language Publications:

Bagshawe, Thomas Wyatt. *Basketmaking in Bedfordshire.* Luton, England: Luton Museum and Art Gallery, 1981.

Benson, Oscar H., and Tod, Osma Gallinger. *Weaving with Reed and Fibers.* New York: Dover, 1975.

Butcher, Mary. *Willow Work.* London: Dryad Press, 1986.

Carpentier, Didier, and Bachelet, Joel. *Basketry.* Wakefield, West Yorkshire, England: EP Publishing, 1982.

Collingwood, Peter. *The Maker's Hand: A Close Look at Textile Structures.* New York: Sterling Publishing Co., Lark Books, 1987.

Crampton, Charles. *Canework.* 24th ed. Leicester, England: Dryad Press, 1984.

Elton Barratt, Olivia. *Basket Making.* London: Charles Letts and Co., 1990.

Gabriel, Sue, and Goymer, Sally. *The Complete Book of Basketry Techniques.* Devon, England: David & Charles, 1991.

Gordon, Joleen. *With Baskets, Traps and Brooms.* Halifax, Nova Scotia: Nova Scotia Museum, 1984.

Harvey, Virginia. *The Techniques of Basketry.* Seattle, Wash.: University of Washington Press, 1986.

Heseltine, Alastair. *Baskets and Basketmaking.* Buckinghamshire, England: Shire Publications, 1986.

Hoppe, Flo. *Wicker Basketry.* Loveland, Colo.: Interweave Press, 1989.

Johnson, Kay. *Basketmaking.* London: Batsford, 1991.

————. *Canework.* London: Batsford, Dryad Press, 1988.

Johnson, K., Barratt, O., Butcher, M. *Chair Seating.* London: Batsford, Dryad Press, 1990.

Kirmeyer, Maxine. *A Materials Guide for the Basketmaker.* San Jose, Calif.: Kirmeyer Publications, 1987.

Knock, A.G. *Willow Basket Work.* 8th ed. Leicester, England: Dryad Press, 1979.

Lasansky, Jeanette. *Willow, Oak & Rye: Basket Traditions in Pennsylvania.* University Park, Penn.: The Pennsylvania State University Press, 1979.

Maynard, Barbara. *Modern Basketry from the Start.* New York: Charles Scribner's Sons, 1973.

Newsholme, Christopher. *Willows: The Genus Salix.* Portland, Oreg.: Timber Press, 1993.

Okey, Thomas. *An Introduction to the Art of Basketmaking.* Norfolk, England: The Basketmakers' Association, 1986.

Richardson, Helen, ed. *Fibre Basketry: Homegrown & Handmade.* Kenthurst, New South Wales, Australia: Kangaroo Press, 1989.

Rossbach, Ed. *Baskets as Textile Art.* London: Van Nostrand Reinhold, 1973.

————. *The Nature of Basketry.* Rev. ed. Exton, Penn.: Schiffer, 1986.

Schanz, Joanna E. *Willow Basketry of the Amana Colonies.* Iowa City, Iowa: Penfield Press, 1986.

Smith, Sue M. *Natural Fiber Basketry.* Fort Worth, Texas: Willow Bend Press, 1983.

Speiser, Noémi. *The Manual of Braiding.* Basel, Switzerland: Eigenverlag, 1983.

Tod, Osma Gallinger. *Earth Basketry.* West Chester, Penn.: Schiffer, 1986.

Walpole, Lois. *Creative Basketmaking.* London: William Collins Sons, 1989.

Will, Christoph. *International Basketry.* West Chester, Penn.: Schiffer, 1985.

Wright, Dorothy. *Baskets and Basketry.* Devon: David and Charles, 1974.

————. *Basketry.* London: Batsford, 1975.

————. *The Complete Book of Baskets and Basketry.* New York: Sterling Book Co., 1992.

Foreign-Language Publications:

Anquetil, Jacques. *La vannerie.* Dessain et Tolra, Paris, France, 1979.

Association Amicale des Anciens Elèves de l'École d'Osiericulture et de Vannerie Fayle-Billot (Bulletin semestriel) (E.N.O.V.), Haute-Marne, France.

Avanthay, Henri. *La fabrication du'une hotte dans le Val d'Illiez.* Schweizerische Gesellschaft für Volkskunde, Basel, Switzerland, 1975.

Brockmann, Andreas. *Hand-, Lehr- und Musterbuch für Korb- und Strohflechter.* Weimar, Germany, 1882; Neudruck, 1984.

Bühler-Oppenheim, Kristin. "Primäre Textile Techniken." *Ciba-Rundschau* Nr. 73, October 1947, Basel, Switzerland.

Chmelar, Indrich, und Mensel, Walter. *Die Weiden Europas.* Neue Brehm-Bücherei, A. Ziemsen Verlag, Wittenberg Lutherstadt, Germany, 1979.

Cuestionario de Cesteria. Trabajo colectivo de Museo Etnologico de Barcelona, Spain, 1956.

Donaz Meilach. *le livre de la vannerie.* Éditions de l'Étincelle, INC, Montreal, Canada, 1974.

Duschesne R. Ferrand H. *La Vannerie—l'Osier.* J.B. Baillière et Fils, Paris, France, 1981.

————. *La vannerie, Tome I.* J.B. Baillière et Fils, Paris, France, 1963.

————. *La vannerie, Tome II.* J.B. Baillière et Fils, Paris, France, 1963.

École Nationale d'Osierculture et de Vannerie 1905-1986. Fayle-Billot, France, 1986.

Élouard, Daniel. *L'osierculture et la vannerie en Haute-Marne.* Wolf, Rouen, France, 1932.

Flechtkunst. Ausstellungskatalog, Gewerbemuseum, Winterthur, Switzerland, 1982.

Flechtwerk, Fachblatt für Korbwaren. E. Pastzschke, Neustadt b. Coburg, Germany, 1948-1970.

Fondeux, Jean, und Gigot, A. *La vannerie d'osier blanc.* Le Prat, Paris, France, 1943.

Galtier, Charles. *Les Vanniers de Vallabrègues.* Centre Alpine Rhodanien d'Ethnologie, Grenoble, France, 1980.

Gandert, August. *Tragkörbe in Hessen.* Schriften zur Volkskunde, Röth, Kassel, Germany, 1963.

Geuter, Klaus. *Das Korbwarengewerbe am Obermain.* Sonderdruck aus: Mitteilungen der Fränkischen Geographischen Gesellschaft Band 23/24, Erlangen, Germany, 1978.

Godet, J.D. *1. Buch Knospen und Zweige der einheimischen Baum- und Straucharten.* Arboris Verlag, Bern, Switzerland, 1983.

————. *2. Buch Bäume und Sträucher, einheimische und eingeführte Baum- und Straucharten.* Arboris Verlag, Bern, Switzerland, 1983.

Gruner, Arno. *Der Korbweidenbau.* Siebeneicher, Berlin, Germany, 1947.

Guggenbühl, Paul. *Unsere einheimischen Nutzhölzer.* Stocker-Schmid, Dietikon/Zurich, Switzerland, 1980.

Hävernick, Walter. "Die Formen des Tragkorbes in Thüringen" in: *Beiträge zur deutschen Volks- und Altertumskunde.* Hamburg, Germany, 1954.

Helvetia Archäologica Nr. 41, Schwabe, Basel, Switzerland, 1977.

Hess, Hans Ernst; Landolt, Elias; und Hirzel, Rosmarie. *Flora der Schweiz Band I.* Birkhäuser Verlag, Basel, Switzerland, 1967.

Huber, Hannes. *Korbflechten.* Eigenverlag, Basel, Switzerland, 1977.

Hugger, Paul. *Der Korbflechter.* Schweizerische Gesellschaft für Volkskunde, Heft 17, Krebs, Basel, Switzerland.

Internationales Symposium, Flechtwerk der Zukunft. Staatliche Korbflectschule, Lichtenfels, Germany, 1989.

Jentsch, Thunar. *Flechten, Handwerk mit Tradition.* Kinderbuchverlag Luzern, Switzerland, 1989.

Johnson, K., Barratt O., Butcher M. *Flechtwerk für Stühle.* Augustus, Augsburg, Germany, 1991.

Kaiser, P., und Scholz, G.A. *Korbweidenbau.* Hackmeister, Leipzig, Germany, 1952.

Korb- und Strohflechter 1882. Schäfer, Hannover, Germany, 1984.

Korbmacherlehrling, Der. Jahrgänge 1950-1959 als Buch gebunden.

Korbweidenbau. Deutsche landwirtschaftliche Gesellschaft, Berlin, Germany, 1928.

Kunz, Heinrich. *Peddigrohrflechten.* Paul Haupt, Bern, Switzerland, and Stuttgart, Germany, 1980.

Kuoni, Bignia. *Cesteria tradicional ibérica.* Serbal, Barcelona, Spain, 1981.

Lautenschlager, Ernst. *Die Weiden in der Schweiz.* Birkhäuser, Basel, Switzerland, 1989.

Lehmann, Johannes. *Systematik der Geflechte.* Leipzig o.J., Germany.

Leroux, Eugène. *L'Osiericulture.* J.B. Baillière et Fils, Paris, France, 1921.

———. *Manuel de la Vannerie.* J.B. Baillière et Fils, Paris, France, 1921.

———. *La Culture de l'Osier.* Librarie de la Maison Rustique, Paris, France, 1926.

Lesourd, F. *La Culture de l'Osier.* Librarie de la Maison Rustique, Paris, France, 1943.

Lötschert, Wilhelm. *Palmen.* Ulmer Verlag, Stuttgart, Germany, 1985.

Maki, Masako. *Mit Peddigrohr flechten.* Frech-Verlag GmbH, Stuttgart, Germany, 1988.

Mooi, Hetty. *350 Knoten.* Otto Maier, Ravensburg, Germany, 1984.

Nilsson, Eva. *Av näver och rot.* LTs Förlag, Stockholm, Sweden, 1984.

Ottilinger, Eva B. *Korbmöbel.* Residenz Verlag, Salzburg and Vienna, Austria, 1990.

Peddigrohrflechten/Vannerie travail du rotin. Schweizerischer Verein für Handarbeit und Schulreform, Liestal, Switzerland, 1959.

Phillips, Roger. *Das Kosmosbuch der Gräser, Farne, Moose, Flechten.* Frank'sche Verlagshandlung, Stuttgart, Germany, 1981.

Rossbach, Ed. *Flechtkunst.* Otto Maier, Ravensburg, Germany, 1973.

Schenk, Gerd. *Peddigrohr.* ALS Verlag GmbH, Frankfurt, Germany, 1982 (Arbeitsmappe).

Schier, Bruno. *Das Flechten im Lichte der historischen Volkskunde.* Schöps, Frankfurt/Main, Germany, 1951.

Schrede, Otto. *Fachbuch für Korbflechter.* Fachbuch Verlag. Leipzig, Germany, 1955.

Seiler-Baldinger, Annemarie. *Systematik der Textilen Techniken.* Wepf, Basel, Switzerland, 1991.

Staniok, Rudolf. *Korbflechten.* Leopold Stocker Verlag, Graz, Austria, 1984.

Stöckle, Frieder. *Vom Korbmacher—wo flinke Hände flechten und formen.* Franck'sche Verlagshandlung, Stuttgart, Germany, 1989.

Ströse, Susanne. *Werken mit Palmblatt und Binsen.* Don Bosco, Munich, Germany, 1966.

Valonen, Niilo. *Geflechte und andere Arbeiten aus Birkenrindenstreifen.* Vammala, 1952.

Vannerie traditionelle d'Afrique et d'Asie. Ausstellungskatalog, Musée des Arts décoratifs, Lausanne, Switzerland, 1981.

Vogt, Emil. *Geflechte und Gewebe der Steinzeit.* Birkhäuser, Basel, Switzerland, 1937.

Volkskunst. Viertelijahresschrift Nr. 3/81, 2/85, 3/86. Callwey, Munich, Germany.

Vorlagen für Korbflechter. Bernhard Friedrich Voigt. Weimar, Germany, 1886.

Will, Christoph. *Die Korbflechterei.* Callwey, Munich, Germany, 1978.

———. *Peddigflechten.* Otto Maier, Ravensburg, Germany, 1970.

———. *Flechtwaren.* Körting & Co., Bamberg, Germany.

Zander, Robert (Ende, Buchheim, Seybold). *Handwörterbuch der Pflanzennamen.* Ulmer Verlag, Stuttgart, Germany, 1984.

"Zürcher Seeufersiedlungen." *Helvetia Archäologica* 12/1981-45/48. Schwabe, Basel, Switzerland.

Sources

Suppliers of willow, basketry materials, tools, and books:

Allen's Basketworks, 8624 SE 13th, PO Box 02648, Portland, OR 97202 (503-238-6384). Basketry materials and tools.

American Willow Growers Network, RFD 1, Box 124A, South New Berlin, NY 13843-9653 (607-847-8264). Members receive an annual newsletter and, in spring, cuttings of willow. Membership is $7 ($8 in Canada; $10 overseas).

BVBA De Vos Salix, Eksaardedorp 19, B-9108, Eksaarde, Nr. Lokeren, Belgium. Willows.

Caners Corner, 4413 John St., Niagara Falls, Ontario L2E 1A4 Canada (416-374-2632). Basketry materials and tools.

The Caning Shop, 926 Gilman Street, Berkeley, CA 94710 (800-544-3373; 415-527-5010). Basketry materials, tools, and books.

C.B. Hector & Son, The Willows, Stoke St. Gregory, Taunton, Somerset TA3 6JD England. Willows, "starter" bolts in mixed bundles of brown, buff, and white willow.

Connecticut Cane and Reed Co., PO Box 762, Manchester, CT 06040 (203-646-6586). Basketry materials and tools.

Crafter's Haven, 121 Ilsley Avenue, Dartmouth, Nova Scotia B3B 1S4 Canada (902-468-5849). Basketry materials and tools.

Crooked River Crafts, PO Box 917, LaFarge, WI 54639 (608-625-4460). Basketry materials and tools.

D.L. Reed and Company, 153 Colbeck Street, Toronto, Ontario M6S 1V8 Canada (416-763-1079). Basketry materials and tools.

Hans Ender, D-8621 Hochstadt-Thelitz 12, Postfach 20, Germany 09574-1268. Willows.

English Basketry Willows, RFD 1, Box 124A, South New Berlin, NY 13843-9653 (607-847-8264). Imported European willows and traditional willow basketry-tools, books, and specialty publications on the cultivation and uses of willow. For catalogue, send $1. Includes samples of brown, buff, and white willow.

Forest Farm, 990 Tetherow Road, Williams, OR 97544 (503-846-6963). Willows.

The H.H. Perkins Co., 10 South Bradley Road, Woodbridge, CT 06525 (800-462-6660; 203-389-9501). Basketry materials, tools, and books .

P.H. Coate & Son. Meare Green Court, Stoke St. Gregory, Taunton, Somerset, England. Willows.

Plymouth Reed and Cane Supply, 1200 W. Ann Arbor Road, Plymouth, MI 48170 (313-455-2150). Basketry materials and tools.

R.R. Hector, Willow Growers & Merchants, 18 Windmill Hill, North Curry, Taunton, Somerset TA3 6NA England (08-23-490236 or 08-23-490686). Willows.

Royalwood Ltd., 517 Woodville Road, Mansfield, OH 44907 (419-526-1630). Willows, basketry materials, and tools.

St. Lawrence Nurseries, RD 2, Route 345, Potsdam, NY 13676 (315-265-6739). Willows.

Walters Ltd., Mountain Road, Washington Island 54246. Willows.

W.H. Kilby & Co., 1840 Davenport Road, Toronto, Ontario M6N 1B7 Canada (416-656-1065). Basketry materials and tools.

Guilds:

There are numerous local basketmakers' guilds. Here are a few of the larger organizations:

Association of Michigan Basketmakers, PO Box 216, Lake Orion, MI 48361.

Basketmakers' Association, c/o Sally Goymer, 37 Mendip Road, Cheltenham, Gloucestershire GL52 3EB England.

Basketry Network, c/o Melinda Mayhall, 16 Moore Avenue, Toronto M4R 1V3 Canada.

High Country Basketry Guild, PO Box 1143, Fairfax, VA 22030-1143.

North Carolina Basketmakers Association, PO Box 181, Waynesville, NC 28786.

European schools, associations, and museums:

AUSTRIA Burgenländisches Landmuseum, volkskundliche Sammlung, Eisenstadt [Burgenland State Museum, Collection of popular arts and crafts]

Historisches Museum der Stadt Wien, Vienna [The Vienna Historical Museum]

Niederösterreichisches Landesmuseum, Vienna [Lower Austrian State Museum]

Tiroler Volkskunstmuseum, Innsbruck [Tirole Museum of Popular Arts and Crafts]

DENMARK Korbmuseum Den gamle By, Arhus [Museum of Basketry in The Old Village]

ENGLAND British Museum, London

Victoria and Albert Museum, London

FRANCE Bambourseraie, Generargues, F-30140 Anduze [The Generargue Bamboo Park]

École Nationale d'Osiericulture et de Vannerie, Fayl-Billot, F-52500 Fayl La-Forêt, Haute-Marne [National School of Willow Cultivation and Basketmaking]

La Maison des Compagnons du Tour, Villaine les Rochers [House of Travelling Journeymen]

Musée Camarguais, Arles [Camargue Regional Museum]

Musée de l'Homme, Paris [Museum of Humanity, Paris]

Musée National des Arts et Traditions Populaires, Paris [National Museum of Art and Popular Traditions]

Musée de la Vannerie, Cadenet, Vaucluse [Museum of Basketry]

Musée de la Vannerie, Vallabrègues, Gard [Museum of Basketry]

Syndicat professionnel des Vanniers de France, ENOV, F-52500 Fayl La-Forêt, Haute-Marne [French Union of Basketmakers]

GERMANY Bayerisches Nationalmuseum, Munich [Bavarian National Museum]

Deutsches Korbmuseum, Michelau, Oberfranken [German Basketry Museum]

Heimatmuseum, Bad Windsheim [Country Museum]

Innungsverband der Korbmacher, Kreishandwerkerschaft Lichtenfels, An der Mainau, D-8620 Lichtenfels am Main [Association of Basketmakers, Lichtenfels Regional Craft Association]

Korbmuseum Grimma, Leipzig [Grimma Museum of Basketry]

Korbmachermuseum Dahlhausen, Beverungen [Basketmakers' Museum]

Museum f. Kunstgewerbe, Dresden [Museum of Arts and Crafts]

Spielzeugmuseum, Nuremberg [Toy Museum]

Staatliche Berufsfachschule für Korbflechterei, Kronacher Strasse 32, D-8620 Lichtenfels am Main [Public Trade School of Basketry]

Ulmer Museum, Prähistorische Sammlung, Ulm [Ulmer Museum, Prehistorical Collection]

POLAND Przemyski Wikliniarsko-Trzćiniarskiego W Kwidzynie, P-82-500 Kwidzyn [Polish Technical School of Basketmaking]

SPAIN Museo de Artes y Tradiciones Populareṣ, Madrid [Museum of Art and Popular Traditions]

Museo Etnológico, Montjuic, Barcelona [Museum of Ethnology]

SWEDEN Freilichtmuseum, Skansen [Open Air Museum]

Nordiska Museet, Stockholm [The Nordic Museum]

Västerbottenmuseum, Umea [Västerbotten Museum]

SWITZERLAND Chasa Jaura, Valchava, Münstertal GR [Chasa Jaura Museum]

Freiämter Strohmuseum, Wohlen AG [The Freiamt Straw Museum]

Freilichtmuseum, Ballenberg ob Brienz BE [Open Air Museum]

IGK Schweiz, Interessengemeinschaft Korbflechterei Schweiz, Bernstrasse 9, CH-3117 Kiesen [Swiss Basketmakers' Association]

Indianermuseum, Zurich [Indian Museum]

Musée d'Ethnologie, Neuenburg [Museum of Ethnology]

Museo Chiäsa Granda, Stampa, Bergell GR [Museum of Greater Chasa]

Museo Onsernonese, Loco, Onsernonetal TI [Onsernone Museum]

Weiden-Versuchspflanzung H. Oberli, Frau G. Oberli-Debrunner, Höhenweg 9, CH-9630 Wattwil, Living Willow Collection

Museum für Volkskunde, Basel [Museum of Folklore]

Schweizerisches Landesmuseum, Zurich [Swiss National Museum]

Bernard and Regula Verdet-Fierz, Chanastraria e Tessanda Korbflechterei & Handweberei, CH 7545 Guarda

Index